EVERYBODY HAS ONE:

THE THOUGHTS, OPINIONS, & COMMENTS OF A MIDWESTERN BABY BOOMER

Mark Dunavan

Publishing Assistance by BookCrafters
Parker, Colorado.
www.bookcrafters.net

CONTENTS

Preface

In February of 2021, I published (self) and distributed copies of my first book – "*Almost An Eagle: The Roots and Escapades of a Midwestern Baby Boomer.*" It was my memoirs, a compilation of life experiences, stories, and memories to date preceded by details of many ascendants. "*Almost An Eagle*" was not a commercial success, but that was never the original intent. I've raised the bar as concerns economic expectations for the book you are about to read. The lofty goal for book number two is to avoid red ink. Breaking even with revenues equaling expenses would be considered a financial windfall.

Decades ago, I recall hearing the expression: "Opinions are like rectums, everybody has one!" That comment remained lodged in the reptile part of my brain for some unknown reason. In due time, part of that rather random comment would serve as the title of this book. While my previous book was void of opinions in general, "*Everybody Has One*" is the opposite. It is a book that provides opinions regarding numerous political, economic, social, and philosophical issues. While I would not consider myself an activist, as a responsible citizen residing in a free country, I feel a duty to express my thoughts in a civil manner on some of the more material issues of the day.

As will become evident, my mindset, and worldview are fundamentally conservative in nature. Politically, I would describe myself as a moderate Republican with some Libertarian leanings. Economically – I would describe myself as subscribing to theories advanced by both Friedrich Hayek and Milton Friedman. Insofar as social issues, I would probably be considered more liberal than most conservatives. While I can be convinced by a strong, logical argument to take a non-conservative position on a particular issue, my default mechanism normally leads to conservatism.

I'm sure the fact that I was born in 1955 and raised in a quaint river town in the Midwest by two middle-class parents with conservative values started me down the path of conservatism. My three-decade tenure working for a commercial bank in my hometown also played a role as most bankers lean right. I would describe the majority (80%) of my friends as conservative. I sense I am considered a political enigma by many of my friends. I am considered liberal by conservative friends but considered conservative by liberal friends. This tells me I may be well-positioned in the sweet spot.

As a teenager, my interest in national politics and current world affairs exceeded the majority of my peers. I recall being captivated by the drama televised at the quadrennial national political conventions back when those events meant something. That interest in politics and current affairs moved to the back burner when I graduated from college and entered the real world of marriage, children, and in particular, full-time employment. Now, with children grown and retiring from work, free time is increasingly available. Part of that free time has been absorbed in rekindling my interest in politics and current affairs. Besides reading national and local newspapers daily, I also cherry-pick various articles available via the Internet and always have a non-fiction book under perusal. Lastly, I normally listen to an informative podcast while pursuing a daily cross-country trek on foot. I like to think I keep up with the issues of the day.

Many readers will automatically relegate my prose to the ramblings of a Grumpy Old Man. I will not concur with that assessment. While acknowledging the accuracy of my age and gender, I would object to the "grumpy" classification. The dictionary defines grumpy as "bad-tempered and irritable." I certainly have my moments, but that is not my general mood and disposition. If anything, I am overly optimistic as concerns people and the future of mankind. The art of free and critical thinking are not traits that are missing in action when I evaluate an issue and formulate an opinion.

CHAPTER ONE

LIFE

The Universe is approximately 13 billion years old. Our sun alone is 333,000 times larger than the Earth. There are billions of solar systems in our galaxy, the Milky Way, and the Universe has billions of galaxies like the Milky Way. In the big picture, we humans are a mere speck of cosmic dust. It is estimated that 100 billion people have lived and died on our planet. Life is fleeting and extremely short. Yet from our biased point of view, we are the most important thing to have ever existed. Never underestimate the unbridled magnitude of the human ego.

Although our insignificance is detailed in this chapter's first paragraph, there is no question that life is an exceptional gift that provides an opportunity to realize a positive impact during our short stint of consciousness. A sappy, inspirational quote from a gentleman named Terry Goodkind follows: "To exist in this vast universe for a speck of time is the great gift of life. Our tiny sliver of time is our gift of life. It is our only life. The universe will go on, indifferent to our brief existence, but while we are here, we touch not just part of that vastness, but also the lives around us. Life is the gift each of us has been given. Each life is our own and no one else's. It is the greatest value we can have. Cherish it for what it truly is. Your life is yours alone. Rise up and live it."

I am not so presumptuous to think I have figured out and understand the many facets of life and what constitutes a "good" life. That said, I am not hesitant to tender some opinions, thoughts, ideas, and insights accrued over 68 years of experience concerning that broad subject. In an intentionally random fashion, the following are some of my thoughts about the phenomenon we commonly refer to as "Life."

PARTICIPATION AND CONTRIBUTION

The comedian and comedy writer, Woody Allen, is often credited with the quote, "Showing up is 80% of life." The famous American inventor, Thomas Edison, supposedly said, "90% of a man's success in business is perspiration." I agree with Mssrs. Allen and Edison's sentiments. Far too many people believe the path of their life is pre-ordained and their various efforts and level of effort are irrelevant in determining where their path leads them. These people are prone to sitting on the sidelines, assuming the mantle of victimhood,
and offering nothing more than criticism and negative comments. Participation in society comes with an assortment of risks to the participant. Risks are well worth taking in my opinion. Achievement, success, and satisfaction in life are impossible without making the effort to be involved and contribute to the betterment of other people and organizations that we value and prioritize.

Teddy Roosevelt was both a great American and an exceptional president. I am fond of "The Man in the Arena" excerpt of TR's "Citizenship in a Republic" speech delivered in Paris, France on April 23, 1910. That excerpt is printed below:

'It is not the critic who counts; not the man who points out how the strong man stumbles, or where the doer of deeds could have done them better. The credit belongs to the man who is actually in the arena, whose face is marred by dust and sweat and blood; who strives valiantly; who errs, who comes short again and again, because there is no effort without error and shortcoming; but who does actually strive to do the deeds; who knows great enthusiasms, the great devotions; who spends himself in a worthy cause; who at the best knows in the end the triumph of high achievement, and who at the worst, if he fails, at least fails while daring greatly, so that his place shall never be with those cold and timid souls who neither know victory nor defeat."

INTEGRITY

In my opinion, the most important component in living a positively impactful life is living a life of integrity. Very few of us can pull this off without a few blemishes, but it is a worthy goal to strive for. Integrity implies the state of being complete, undivided, intact, and unbroken. It is a man's most valuable possession. Although it may seem counterintuitive, living with integrity is easier than living a deceitful life. There is no real happiness to be found in remembering your lies, living in constant fear of getting caught, and not feeling like you truly earned your reward. Living with integrity brings wholeness and peace. Your conscience can rest easy, and you can look at yourself in the mirror with pride. A man of integrity is a man others can count on. They know he will do what he says he will do. A commitment to live a life of integrity allows you clarity when you have to make difficult choices. The means do not always justify the end. This is probably the most common rationalization for breaking with your integrity. Living a life of integrity is a daily process that doesn't end until your life does. In reality, the journey towards an accomplishment or decision is just as important as the destination itself.

People need to take personal responsibility for their life. At the very heart of integrity is the ability to own up to the fact that you are in control of your life. Whether it be at work, in your romantic relationships, or with your friendships, you are responsible for both your successes and your failures. Nobody else but you.

FRIENDS

When comes to attaining happiness in life, your friends are one of the primary keys. As the saying goes, "You can't choose your family." With family, the relationships are there whether you like them or not. But friendship is different. Your friends are people you select based on shared values, ideals, experiences, interests, and beliefs. Your friends are your chosen family. You need different types of friends in the same way that you need food from different food groups. The benefits of friendships are numerous. Friends can give you vital life skills.

Friends can help you define your priorities. Having friends can help you find more friends. You're less lonely when you have friends. Friends can give you a reality check. Being a friend helps your friends. A word of warning midway through this subject: Some "so-called friends" aren't really who they claim to be. Beware of conditional, fair-weather, negative, spiteful "friends." Friendships, especially with men, sometimes ebb and flow. I've always been amazed at how easily and naturally two guys can resume an active friendship after an extended break. Best memories are always created when you're around your most special friends. With your inner circle of buddies, you will create the best of times, the times you will look back on years later and still burst out laughing. The kind of times you will tell your kids about. One doesn't have to have a huge entourage of friends; in the end, you will be able to count your most genuine friends on one hand. This life is about the people you share it with, surround yourself with good people. At the end of this segment, I find it necessary to issue a "shout-out" to my eclectic network of friends. I cannot fathom having a better group of friends and consider myself fortunate to have them in my life.

FORGIVENESS

The absolute power of forgiveness is nothing short of astounding. To withhold forgiveness keeps alive emotions of hurt, anger, and blame. This in turn discolors our perception of life. By holding on to pain and resentment, you unduly suffer due to the fact sorrow is intensified to keep it alive. To forgive, avoid ruminating on thoughts of being wronged. In a nutshell, forgiveness liberates the soul. There is also a close link between negative emotions and illness. Forgiveness can lead to healthier relationships, improved mental health, less anxiety, less stress, less hostility, lower blood pressure, fewer symptoms of depression, a stronger immune system, and improved self-esteem. Forgiveness is associated with your emotional welfare, not merely granting the other person a pardon. Note that forgiveness is not for the other person's benefit at all – it's for the benefit of the person offering the forgiveness. I would be remiss if I didn't mention that it is also important to forgive yourself. Many people, including yours truly, are harder on themselves than others are on them. Confucious said, "The more you know yourself, the more you forgive yourself." Forgiveness is a process. Also, forgiveness doesn't mean forgetting or excusing harm done to you. Some people are naturally more forgiving than others that tend to be grudge-holders. As you let go of grudges, you'll no longer define your life by how you've been hurt. And one last comment concerning forgiveness: You can't force someone to forgive you.

THE POWER OF APOLOGIZING

Never underestimate the impact of an apology, an act that usually prompts forgiveness. It is important to note that real, sincere apologies differ from pseudo-apologies. The information conveyed, along with moral and status indicators, and the speaker's effect conveyed in an apology, will determine its validity and lead to acceptance or rejection. There appears to be a growing usage of apologies over the past 20 years – especially ones issued by men and powerful public figures. The reason for this trend? People are coming to the realization that in the majority of cases, apologies can be very effective and diffuse conflict. An apology serves a variety of purposes for the recipient of the apology. Some of those purposes are itemized below:

1. Restoration of self-respect and dignity.
2. Assurance that both parties have shared values.
3. Assurance that the offenses were not the offended party's fault.

4. Assurance of safety in the relationship between offender and victim.
5. Seeing the offender suffer.
6. Reparations for the harm caused by the offense.
7. Allowing for meaningful dialogue between offender and victim.

In short, apologies restore a moral balance between offender and victim and renew the relationship between the two. Look at apologies as emotional peace offerings. There is an art to apologizing, a roadmap out of the doghouse.

CONTRARIANISM

For most of my life, I was mildly ashamed to be a contrarian. That changed a little over a decade ago. I am now out of the closet and have embraced my contrarian nature with enthusiasm. Being contrarian means considering a position that is opposed to that of the majority, regardless of how unpopular it may be. Evolutionary psychology tells us that humans' most essential desire is to survive and reproduce. Knowing the truth is simply not required in order to survive and reproduce. Knowing and expounding on the truth is not always beneficial for the expounder. Humans have an innate desire to conform. Conformity, even when it involves a falsehood, gives us a tribe that can protect us from danger. We are living in an era when so much of what we have assumed to be true is false. I feel it is acceptable, even recommendable, to question conventional wisdom and consider the opposite of conventional wisdom. However, the opposite of what most people think is not always true. It's O.K. to be wrong.

LUCK

The role of luck in life success is far greater than most realize. For example, genetic differences are of huge relevance. So is where you are born. About 50% of income differences worldwide can be explained by the country of residence. Studies have shown that those with last names earlier in the alphabet are more likely to receive tenure at top departments of higher education. People with easy-to-pronounce names are judged more positively than those with difficult-to-pronounce names. Females with masculine-sounding names are more successful in legal careers. The examples of the benefits of good luck are extensive. Luck is not everything. Traits such as talent, hard work, persistence, and openness to experience matter greatly as well. Certain personal characteristics allow a person to exploit luck.

Research indicates that the most talented individuals were rarely the most successful. In general, mediocre-but-lucky people were much more successful than more talented-but-unlucky individuals. A relatively high percentage (62%) of U.S. billionaires are self-made. Some might say business success is 10% luck and 90% hard work. Others will say the opposite. According to a 2018 study, luck accounts for up to 30% of business success. By adjusting your mindset, taking action, being a perpetual learner, and evolving, you can increase your chances of opportunity. It also should be pointed out that successful business- people have already learned from previous mistakes.

MEN AND MASCULINITY

I am biased, but I confess to being an advocate of masculinity, perhaps even at the toxic masculinity level. I must not be a total troglodyte, however, since I do like the poem "If" by Rudyard Kipling which appears below:

If

If you can keep your head when all about you
Are losing theirs and blaming it on you,
If you can trust yourself when all men doubt you,
But make allowance for their doubting too;
If you can wait and not be tired by waiting,

Or being lied about, don't deal in lies,
Or being hated, don't give way to hating,
And yet don't look too good, nor talk too wise:
If you can dream – and not makes dreams your master;
If you can think – and not make thoughts your aim;
If you can meet with Triumph and Disaster
And treat those two imposters just the same;
If you can bear to hear the truth you've spoken
Twisted by knaves to make a trap for fools,
Or watch the things you gave your life to, broken,
And stoop and build'em up with worn-out tools:
If you can make one heap of all your winnings
And risk it on one turn of pitch-and-toss,
And lose, and start again at your beginnings
And never breathe a word about your loss:
If you can force your heart and nerve and sinew
To serve your turn long after they are gone,
And so hold on when there is nothing in you
Except the Will which says to them: "Hold on!"
If you can talk with crowds and keep your virtue,
Or walk with Kings – nor lose the common touch,
If neither foes nor loving friends can hurt you,
If all men count with you, but none too much;
if you can fill the unforgiving minute
With sixty seconds' worth of distance run,
Yours is the Earth and everything that's in it,
And – which is more – you'll be a Man, my son!

—Rudyard Kipling

WORDS OF WISDOM

There is no shortage of cliches and proclamations concerning the subject of "Life." Following are some of my favorites written by Regina Brett, 90 years old, of the *Plain Dealer*, Cleveland, Ohio:

1. Life isn't fair, but it's still good.

2. When in doubt, just take the next small step.
3. Life is too short to waste time hating anyone.
4. Your job won't take care of you when you are sick. Your friends and parents will. Stay in touch.
5. You don't have to win every argument. Agree to disagree.
6. Make peace with your past so it won't screw up the present.
7. Don't compare your life to others. You have no idea what their journey is all about.
8. If a relationship has to be a secret, you shouldn't be in it.
9. Over-prepare, then go with the flow.
10. Be eccentric now. Don't wait for old age to wear purple.
11. No one is in charge of your happiness but you.
12. Always choose life.
13. However good or bad a situation is, it will change.
14. Don't take yourself so seriously.
15. Envy is a waste of time.
16. Yield.

LAUNDROMAT ARTICLE

It was Easter Day in 2005. Two months prior I had been legally divorced after 26 years of marriage. I was walking home after joining my parents for Easter dinner at their residence. About halfway home, near the intersection of State and Center Streets in South Ottawa, the heavens opened up and it started raining about as much as physically possible. I quickly took sanctuary in a laundromat on State St. and settled in for a respite from the downpour. Perusing an AARP magazine, an interesting article garnered my attention. It was interesting and good, so I stole the magazine and subsequently copied the article.

Following are some of the parts that hit home with me: "The first half of life is essentially a mistake," says James Hollis, a Jungian analyst, and author. "Once we reach middle age, our life's mission changes. The first 50 years were well-intentioned, maybe even productive. But psychologically and spiritually, they missed the boat. We may believe choices made in our early years were made freely, but we were just learning to fit in, to find a place for ourselves in the world. Our roles defined us. Often our true selves got lost in the process. At mid-life, we face an important crossroads. We can continue along pathways established for us by others, or we can finally grow up, breaking free of the past, and become true individuals. Such questions were pointless 100 years ago when the average life span for Americans was 47.

Most of us don't have permission to live our own lives. This can't be given; it has to be taken. Ask some hard questions – reset your inner compass. Listen to your dreams. Get down to basics – downsize or simplify one's life. We may also want to winnow down the number of people in our lives, investing our emotional energy in a few, close, important relationships in lieu of doing a lot of socializing. It's common to look within via meditation or prayer after age 50. Circle up – many, especially women, may find it helpful to meet regularly with a group of like-minded friends. Become a true character – as in, "He's quite a character." The essential, unique, even eccentric qualities that are etched in our souls from birth need to see the light of day. In conclusion, the key to making good use of the second half of life is realizing that it's going to pass quickly. You don't have all the time in the world."

THE MEANING OF LIFE

In July of 1931, author and philosopher, Will Durant, wrote to several notable figures and asked, essentially, "What is the meaning of life?"

His letter concluded:

"Spare me a moment to tell me what meaning life has for you, what keeps you going, what help - if any – religion gives you, what are the sources of your inspiration and your energy, what is the goal or motive force of your toil, where you find your consolations and your happiness, where, in the last resort, your treasure lies. Write briefly if you must, write at length and at leisure if you possibly can; for every word from you will be precious to me." Durant received many replies, a selection of which were compiled in the book, "On the Meaning of Life."

In the opinion of many, the greatest response came from H.L. Mencken. Mencken's classic response was two pages long and totaled eight paragraphs. I urge all readers to reference the Internet and read the letter in its entirety. My favorite excerpts are the first and last paragraphs and they follow below:

Paragraph #1 - "Dear Durant: You ask me, in brief, what satisfaction I get out of life, and why go on working. I go on working for the same reason that a hen goes on laying eggs. There is in every living creature an obscure but powerful impulse to active functioning. Life demands to be lived. Inaction, save as a measure of recuperation between bursts of activity, is painful and dangerous to the healthy organism. In fact, it is almost impossible. Only the dying can be really idle."

Paragraph #8 – "I do not believe in immortality, and have no desire for it. The belief in it issues from the puerile egos of inferior men. In Christian form, it is little more than a device for getting revenge upon those who are having a better time on this earth. What the meaning of human life may be I don't know. I incline to suspect that it has none. All I know about it is that, to me at least, it is very amusing while it lasts. Even its troubles, indeed, can be amusing. Moreover, they tend to foster the human qualities that I admire most – courage and its analogues. The noblest man, I think, is that one who fights God and triumphs over Him. I have had little of this to do. When I die I shall be content to vanish into nothingness. No show, however good, could conceivably be good forever."

Sincerely yours,
H.L. Mencken

PET PEEVES

I'm not sure if this is the proper place in the book for me to rattle off my most irritating "Pet Peeves", but it has to go somewhere. Anyway, itemized below, in no particular order of severity and irritation, would be my Top Lifetime Pet Peeves:

1. More than three pillows on a bed. Why in God's name do some people feel the need to cover every square inch on a bed with a pillow of some indeterminate size and shape?
2. United States flags constantly kept at half-mast. There are strict guidelines for this, and they should be abided by.
3. The audio recording at airports warns people on moving walkways that the walkway is coming to an end. Some personal injury attorney got rich on a mishap involving a blind client and the rest of us suffer the consequences.
4. Shrinkflation – a chicken-shit way for businesses to raise prices on their products.
5. Bad or confusing signage. This is especially maddening on roadways and in hospitals.
6. The Blame Game. This is just grating, and it appears to be getting worse in our overly-whining culture.
7. Drivers who drive at the speed limit or lower in the fast lane.
8. Politicians who leverage tragedies for their benefit or the benefit of their political party.
9. Shoppers who produce a boatload of coupons when checking out at the grocery store.
10. The jerk in the airplane aisle trying to jam an oversized piece of luggage in the overhead bin.
11. People that say they gave 110% effort. That is physically impossible.
12. People who say, "change is good". Oh, really? Some folks with health issues or other misfortunes would be happy to debate that ridiculous comment.

NARCISSISTS

Originally, I was going to include narcissism in my list of "Pet Peeves." After consideration, however, I decided to give this personality disorder a specific entry of its own. This is because, fundamentally, I can't stand narcissists. They are simply the worst. Narcissists have no sense of humor. Narcissists have no tolerance for being ignored, disrespected, rejected, or abandoned. They are self-serving, know-it-alls and relish belittling and humiliating friends, family, and total strangers. Narcissists are cowards and incapable of accepting even an iota of responsibility when their actions cause something to go south. As narcissists age, they often grow even more abusive. Narcissists live in mortal terror of death. This is because death the means complete annihilation of the ego. There's nothing more horrifying to a narcissist than that because their ego is essentially all they are.

CODE OF LIFE AND CONDUCT

In 1991, Louise R. Sims, my maternal great-grandmother and known by her family as "Gannie," died at the age of 101 after an exceptionally unique, interesting, and colorful life. During the administration of her estate, a document surfaced that I found pertinent. It was a typed spiel attributed to the journalist, H.L. Mencken. Above the typed print in Gannie's hand-written print was the single sentence; My code of life and conduct is simply this: "To work hard, play to the allowable limit, disregard equally the good or bad opinion of others, never do a friend a dirty trick, eat and drink what you feel like, never grow indignant over anything, never contradict anyone or seek to prove anything to anyone unless one gets paid for it in cold, hard cash, live the moment to the utmost of its possibilities, treat one's enemies with polite inconsideration, avoid persons who are chronically in need and be satisfied with life always, but never with one's self."

For myself personally, I would amend Gannie's code by adding the following policies: "Sometimes it's better to be peaceful and happy than right. It's O.K. to disregard utterly ridiculous regulations and rules. Besides taking a gun to a gunfight, make sure you take plenty of ammunition. Don't be a shell counter. Insofar as family and friends, be a net positive. Give more than take."

CHAPTER TWO

RELIGION

BLAISE PASCAL (1623 – 1662) was a French mathematician, physicist, inventor, philosopher, writer, and Catholic theologian. He is famous for laying the foundation for the modern theory of probabilities. Pascal also is well-known for positing that humans wager with their lives that God either exists or does not. Naturally, this proposition is known as "Pascal's Wager." Pascal's Wager argues that if we do not know whether God exists, then we should play it safe rather than risk being sorry. As Pascal says, "I should be much more afraid of being mistaken and then finding out that Christianity is true than of being mistaken in believing it to be true." If you believe that God exists, you win eternal salvation if he does exist; and lose nothing if he doesn't exist. If you do not believe in God and he does exist, then you lost the wager and lose everything. Thus, the advice is to believe in God.

It is difficult, if not impossible, to argue with the logic inherent in Pascal's Wager. Although it may appear one has a shallow, immature, and barely adequate level of faith to simply believe in God only as a bet, it does make eminent sense. The Wager appeals not to a high ideal, like blind faith, hope, love, or proof, but to a low one: the instinct for self-preservation, the desire to be happy and not unhappy. The Wager promotes a belief in God not because your reason can prove with certainty that it is true that God exists, but because your will seeks happiness, and God is your only chance of attaining happiness eternally. Either God is, or he is not. Reason cannot decide this question. If you win, you win everything; if you lose, you lose nothing. Since atheism gives you no chance of winning entry into the afterlife, Pascal deems atheism a terrible bet.

For the author, the subjects of God, religion, and faith have always been an enigma riddled with uncertainties, questions, and puzzlement. Of the three, organized religion is the one where I am least confused and uncertain. One of my favorite authors is Jon Krakauer. Some of his books include, *"Into the Wild," "Into Thin Air,"* and *"Under the Banner of Heaven."* In 2003, Jon Krakauer summarized his opinion of organized religion: "There are some ten thousand extant religious sects – each with its own cosmology and each with its answer for the meaning of life and death. Most assert that the other 9,999 not only have it completely wrong but are instruments of evil. None of the ten thousand has yet persuaded me to make the requisite leap of faith. In the absence of conviction, I've come to terms with the fact that uncertainty is an inescapable corollary of life. An abundance of mystery is simply part of the bargain – which doesn't strike me as something to lament. Accepting the essential inscrutability of existence, in any case, is surely preferable to the opposite: capitulating to the tyranny of intransigent belief." Those are exactly my sentiments as concerns organized religion.

Several years ago, I took a deep intellectual dive into religion. As I am prone to do, I compiled written lists that summarized my thoughts on the subject. Following is the itemization that details "Reasons (10) for my Reservations Regarding Religion:"

1. The concept of religion and divine powers has been around as long as humans have established social structures and communities. Thus, mankind did not exactly embrace organized religion and spiritual inclinations during a period of intellectual and scientific enlightenment. It wasn't too long ago that it was generally accepted that our planet was both flat as a pancake and at the center of our solar system. One can make the argument that people simply had

to invent religion and God to explain events and acts that could not be explained then.

2. The Bible is considered the sacred book of Christianity. However, the Bible seems to struggle with history when carbon dating and other scientific advances are brought into the equation. Which is accurate, the laws of physics or the printed words of men written in a period of relative ignorance?

3. The Bible was not written by one person who sat in a room for 16 years and composed inarguably the most influential and powerful piece of literature in history. The Bible was written by several different people over several hundred years, sometimes decades after the reported events. It is no secret that stories assume a life of their own over time and distortion and magnification become the rule and not the exception.

4. In my lifetime, or for that matter, over the past twenty centuries, an unexplained supernatural event (miracle) has not been proven or documented.

5. Darwin's theory of evolution simply seems to make sense. Survival of the fittest and genetic mutations offer a logical explanation for life. To a logical person, Darwin's theory seems logical.

6. Historically, there have been hundreds, if not thousands, of different religions. Each religion sincerely believes that they have it right and that everybody else is faced with perpetual damnation. The sheer diversity and lack of agreement in the religious arena lends itself to doubting the entire concept.

7. Historically, there has been a close association between religion and violence. How many lives have been extinguished in the name of religion? The Spanish Inquisition, the Crusades, the Witchcraft "cleansing", and the Holocaust are some of the more notable examples of religious zealotry breeding genocide. Should not violence and religion be contradictory terms and not associative terms?

8. Most organized religions are highly structured and explicitly definitive insofar as "acceptable" behavior and conduct. Those characteristics sometimes rob individuals of a diversity of thought and freedom. Some people believe, and I am one of them, that freedom is as important as the gift of life.

9. Some of the more prominent religions share the philosophy that there is little or no relationship between lifetime behavior and the possibility of perpetual rewards after death. I find it troublesome that there is no correlation between performing good deeds and being rewarded accordingly. Likewise, heinous, terrible behavior can be ignored at the end of life if the evil person ultimately does certain acts. Also, I may be blind, but I have a difficult time differentiating the prevalence of positive values between strong Christians, weak Christians and non-Christians. Often, weak Christians or non-Christians act in a Christ-like manner whereas their strong Christian counterparts display extremely un-Christ-like behavior.

10. It is common for some passionate believers of all different types of faith to harbor a profound arrogance for those parties they deem to be weak believers or non-believers. Those poor folks not considered to be in the "inner circle" or not part of this sacred fraternity are commonly treated with less respect, compassion, dignity, and reverence than like-minded individuals who share similar beliefs and passions. I guess that is human nature.

I came up with fewer reasons for embracing religion when the flip side was analyzed. Below is the itemization that details "Reasons (5) for Faith/Religion:"

1. There is no question that mega-institutions such as schools, churches, and government add stability to the various cultures in the world. This is even true in certain economically advanced countries where the traditional family unit is under siege. What was once stable and

constant (family), is now dynamic and inconsistent. The Church thus fills the important role of being one of the life jackets in ever-churning seas.

2. Religion is another source of help for economically disadvantaged parties in the world. Monies and volunteer work are routed to areas of great need. This aid assists in making a difficult life somewhat more tolerable. Helping people in need is always a positive element.

3. Man is a sociable animal. Religion provides an atmosphere of "community" for countless individuals. Especially in times of strife, people need other people. Ministers, priests, and other religious leaders are instrumental in assisting people who are dealing with problems.

4. Faith and religion provide a source of strength when the nasty elements of life "crash your party." It is impossible to put a price tag on the value of "peace of mind." Fellow human beings, whether individually or in a group setting can also help, but the inner strength provided by faith is all-powerful.

5. Pascal was a French philosopher from the 1600s. Pascal explained that either you believed in God or did not believe in God. If you bet against the existence of God, you run the risk of eternal damnation. The winner of the bet that God exists has the possibility of salvation. As salvation is preferable to eternal damnation, Pascal asserted the correct decision is to act on the basis that God is.

It is no secret that the importance and relevance of religion are declining on a global basis. That would in particular be the case in the developed, wealthy countries of Western Europe and North America. Secularism is defined as the indifference or rejection or exclusion of religion and religious considerations. We are gradually becoming a more secular society in America. The number of people going to church and considering themselves religious has been in free fall for 20 years. U.S. church membership stood at 70% of the population in 1999. Now (the early 2020s,) that percentage stands at 50% of the population, a significant decrease. Many Americans, especially younger citizens, have replaced religion with the worship of money and materialism or have embraced social causes such as environmentalism, antiracism, or the Pro-Choice movement. The activists in the vanguard of those causes often display fanaticism and zealotry once only expressed by certain religious followers. On a personal basis, I offer a confession at this time. In theory, there is still time, but in my 68 years of existence, religion has never "grabbed me" or even influenced me in any way. This is partly attributable to my parent's church-going habits – which is to say they simply never attended a church service unless it was a wedding, funeral, or baptism. My paternal grandmother, Hope Dunavan, was an active member of the First United Methodist Church of Ottawa, Illinois. She made an effort to save me from eternal damnation. I was baptized in this church as an infant and remember taking communion as a child. Through grade school and junior high I attended services with my grandmother about once every three Sundays. I was never "moved" by any of the sermons and adopted the attitude that occasionally attending services was a duty, an act that would please my grandmother.

Right or wrong, I have always associated spirituality and reverence with nature and the great outdoors. The following excerpt is from Jack London's classic short novel, "*The Call of the Wild.*"

"Unlike man, whose gods are of the unseen and the over-guessed, vapors and mists of fancy eluding the garmenture of reality, wandering wraiths of desired goodness and power, intangible outcroppings of self into the realm of spirit – unlike man, the wolf and the wild dog that have come into the fire find their gods in the living flesh, solid to the touch, occupying earth-space and requiring time for the accomplishment of their ends and their existence."

During the hunting season, say from Labor Day through New Year's Eve, I would hunt something on the majority of Sunday mornings during those 4 months. For a while, I had myself convinced that I was pursuing a religious experience when sitting in a duck blind and watching the sun rise or pheasant hunting the morning after a new snowfall. Eventually, I determined I was simply kidding myself and preferred hunting to spending time in church.

A first cousin to religion, if not incorporated into most major religions, is the belief that "everything happens for a reason." How many times have you heard this inane statement blurted to nearby listeners? I would hazard to guess quite often. In my humble opinion, the popular meaning of this statement is false, if not outright superstitious. Everything happens for a reason, but that reason is essentially "no reason." The universe is not trying to guide you toward eternal goodness or reward you for your behaviors. To interpret Karma as some sort of religious brownie points system whereby the Good People are rewarded and the Bad People punished goes against just about anyone's actual life experiences.

Some folks desperately want to believe that our actions will benefit us and that those who act badly will be punished, but there is no way of truly knowing how the complex workings of the world will respond to a given action. Every action has a reaction, just not the one we might expect. Trying to control those reactions causes nothing but stress. It is comforting to respond to events with the judgment that they happened for a reason, but this holds us back from honest spirituality. It prevents us from making peace with the fact that very often things happen spontaneously, or that the "reason" we think is behind events is vastly more complex than we might want to believe. We should acknowledge that we cannot control events and that sometimes things just happen. Also, you must recognize yourself as both significant and insignificant. The point is that there is no point. Just being aware and alive is the point.

It is interesting to note that many atheists also believe events happen for a reason. They often believe in fate-defined as the view that life events happen for a reason and that an underlying order to life determines how events turn out. Humans have a powerful drive to reason in psychological terms, and to make sense of events and situations by appealing to goals, desires, and intentions. Some people are more prone to find meaning than others. Highly paranoid people and highly empathetic people are particularly likely to believe in fate and believe there are hidden messages and signs embedded in their life events.

Religion has no place in politics. It's hard enough for voters and policymakers to hash through the real-world claims that fly around in politics. Trying to figure out what some silent, mythical god wants us to do is a fool's errand. That's probably one reason why politicians love to talk about religion. They can avoid substance and don't have to prove anything. A mystery to me has always been why so many Christians behave in an un-Christian manner. Some right-wing Christians vilify the poor, in direct contradiction to the teachings of Jesus. Some Christians vehemently object to the sexual preferences espoused by the Gay Community, despite the principles of general acceptance and tolerance stressed by the Bible. Why are so many devout followers of religion blinded by reality and steeped in hypocrisy? These people need to look in a mirror on a more frequent basis.

One of my numerous pet peeves is professional athletes who thank God for their success on the playing field. I find this extremely annoying. Baseball players point to the heavens after hitting home runs; NFL players pray in the end zone after scoring a touchdown. Competitors routinely thank Christ in post-game interviews. When did God become a sports fan? Does God care who wins on game day? And, if so, do the losers somehow have less faith? A cynical person would say these athletes are more interested in selling their goodness and their brand of faith to a captive audience. The argument can also be made that they harbor the illusion that the deity is watching over and favoring them. Excuse me while I roll my eyes and try not to vomit. Most everyone with an iota of common sense knows that it's training, hard work, and dedication that leads to athletic success in the long run.

The famous Scottish poet, Robert Burns, ends one of his death-related poems with the following stanza: "If there's another world, he lives in bliss; If there is none, he made the best of this." I've always found those words to be apropos for a funeral farewell. Another quote I like from the great American author, Mark Twain, "Go to Heaven for the climate. Hell for the company." Well, if the fire-and-brimstone advocates are accurate with their vivid predictions of judgment and eternal damnation, I am in big trouble. It is a risk I am willing to accept.

My belief level in the existence of God has remained amazingly consistent over the course of a lifetime. From an early age until now (age 68), I have never ruled out the possibility that God exists. That said, as a direct indictment of my weak faith, the probability level I affix to this possibility has never reached double digits and currently hovers in the 3% - 5% range. I have no empirical evidence to support that meager level of faith (3-5%). It is more of a function of how my brain processes information and experiences. I am rarely black or white on particular issues, almost always somewhere in the various shades of gray. In some respects, I am a bit envious of people of strong divine faith who just "know" and never question the viability of God. It would make life easier in many respects and no doubt reduce levels of uncertainty in terms of what happens after death. Alas, that is simply not me. I need to see miracles and have historical information and scientific data confirm the supernatural before blindly accepting a deity. Although Pascal refutes agnosticism as impossible, I would classify myself as an agnostic – not knowing, maintaining a skeptical, uncommitted attitude.

I distinctly recall a moment years ago when my lack of faith became profoundly self-evident. It was in the early 2000s, either 2001 or 2002. As was often the case back then, I was working late at the bank trying to catch up on some project that needed attention. My boss and I were the only two employees still in the building that particular evening. We were taking a short break and just shooting the breeze for a few minutes, idly chatting about some random subjects. Somehow, we landed on the topic of religion and God. We started proposing certain scenarios, immediately followed by an inquiry on our respective responses to the just-detailed scenario. My colleague tendered the following scenario to me: "You are in a room with two other people. One person is your young daughter. The other person is an infamous terrorist (picture Osama bin Laden or somebody equally evil). The terrorist is standing next to your daughter and has a 9mm Glock 17 trained two inches from her right temple. The bad guy says to me, there is one question for you to answer. If you answer the question accurately, you and your daughter both freely walk away. However, if you answer the question incorrectly, I (the bad guy) will pull the trigger." At this time, I should insert that the actual beliefs of any of the three people in the room are irrelevant. Either God is or God isn't. Without hesitation, I respond that God isn't.

The Roman philosopher, Cicero, receives credit for the following quote, "For there is assuredly nothing dearer to a man than wisdom, and though age takes away all else, it undoubtedly brings us that." At least in terms of my treatment of religion and its devout followers, I believe I have arrived at a state of mind that would be considered "respectful." Unfortunately, that was not always the case in my younger years. In my formative adult years, to be perfectly honest, I spent little time contemplating the concept we refer to as religion. It simply wasn't a topic that held any interest for this kid. As mentioned earlier, I attended church services occasionally but did so to appease other parties. Apathy reigned.

After getting married and getting my first real job, I developed an attitude toward religion that was less than stellar. As a young know-it-all, I was overtly critical of religion, especially Catholicism. Needless to say, those snide, negative comments were probably not beneficial to my marriage. I thought I was being funny and clever, but in retrospect, many of my religious comments demonstrated immaturity and behavior that was condescending. It was wrong of me to lack respect for those individuals who had total belief in the existence of God and were faithful to their religion of choice.

At some point in the past 15 years, I settled into a more mature, tolerant, and respectful outlook as concerns religion and its advocates. I decided to embrace the words in the First Amendment of the U.S. Constitution that stipulates, "Congress shall make no law respecting an establishment of religion, or prohibiting the free exercise thereof;" In other words, even though fundamentalists of a particular major world religion have a history of flying commercial airliners into skyscrapers in Manhattan, I would respect all individual's constitutional right to worship under a religion of their choice. The same would apply to the various sects that fall under the umbrella of Christianity. Freedom rules. I have no right to think less of people simply because of their religious beliefs. The bottom line, I don't have all the answers, especially in the spiritual realm of religion. In conclusion, I guess it is possible to "teach an old dog new tricks."

CHAPTER THREE

WOMEN, LOVE, SEX, AND GENDER

IT IS GENERALLY ACCEPTED by the majority of heterosexual men that women could control and dominate the world if they so desired. This concept flies in the face of the age-old cliché, "It's a man's world." A book authored by a young lady named Kara King and published in 2014 provides the theoretical basis for how women are in a position to exert raw power and run the affairs of the world. The name of Kara King's controversial book is "*The Power of Pussy*." The book, not read by me, "shares 12 powerful secrets that will transform any woman into the type of strong, desirable woman who can effortlessly obtain what she wants from men; including the love, respect, and relationship she desires." Weaponized sex should scare the wits out of any red-blooded American male, both on the micro and macro scale.

Desiderius Erasmus was a Dutch philosopher and Christian scholar who lived between 1467 and 1536. He receives credit for the well-known quote, "Women, can't live with them, can't live without them." The majority of contemporary men would agree with that rather bold statement. Besides the obvious factor of representing 50% (the more important half) of the reproductive process and thus perpetuating the species, women more than carry their weight when it comes to enriching life and advancing the case of human flourishment. A world without women would be an excruciatingly dull, boring world. It would be akin to watching ice freeze, paint dry or grass grow. Also, it would be a dramatically more violent world without women. Destruction would most likely be the end game. For the most part, men and women possess different strengths and weaknesses. For a couple, or in a group setting involving both men and women, this natural offsetting can be considered advantageous to the accomplishment of mutual goals.

I would be remiss if I didn't mention that for most of history, women were treated as second-class citizens in the majority of cultures. After a lengthy and difficult struggle, in 1920 the 19th Amendment to the U.S. Constitution granted women the right to vote. Progress has continued since then, particularly in the past 50 years. Advancements have been achieved across the board. All will not agree, but I believe that today in America, women have opportunities equal to those of men. There are more women now attending college than men. In 2019, the majority of U.S. medical students were women (50.5%) for the first time. In 2020, women outnumbered men in law school classrooms – 54% to 46%. There has been increasing representation of women in C-suites and on the Boards of various major corporations. Women have embraced the entrepreneurial spirit with vigor. Data collected from multiple sources and studies indicate that women are now more likely to start businesses than men.

VENUS AND MARS

There is another book, and unlike the aforementioned "*The Power of Pussy*," very well-known and one I have actually read. The name of the book is "*Men Are from Mars, Women Are from Venus*." The author of this best-selling book is John Gray and it was first published in 1992. This book confirms what the majority of individuals with a "Y" chromosome already knew. In general terms, there is a significant difference between men and women. Following is an itemization of two dozen differences between the two biological sexes. The order of appearance in the listing is entirely random and does not in any way indicate a prioritization of the severity of the behavioral contrasts between men and women.

1. Female babies like faces, and male babies like moving objects. During a research study, boys were twice as likely to prefer gazing at a dangling mobile and girls were more likely to look at a human face.
2. Most girls prefer drawing people, animals, and plants, whereas boys mostly draw action scenes with dynamic movement.
3. Females hear better than males. They not only hear better but can discern between a broader range of emotional tones in the human voice. Males will automatically block out certain sounds.
4. Females can verbally express their emotions better than males. Both positive and negative emotions are processed differently in post-puberty males and females. Men are wired to avoid contact with others when they are going through a rough time and even assume women would want to do the same.
5. Groups of boys play differently than groups of girls. Boys play in larger groups and are more physical, competitive, confrontational, and are more likely to use threats. Girls focus on relationship building, take turns 20 times more often than boys do and their pretend play is usually about caregiving.
6. Boys are more likely to take risks. Boys report feeling excited during a simulated collision, while girls report feeling fearful. Males are more likely to die from an accident than females.
7. Females are easier to startle and exhibit a stronger emotional response to the anticipation of pain.
8. Males are more likely to overestimate their ability.
9. Girls are more likely to perceive a neutral face as friendly, whereas boys are more likely to rate a neutral face as unfriendly.
10. Males are more likely to exhibit aggression physically. Females are more likely to exhibit aggression verbally.
11. Women read subtle emotions better than men.

12. Men thrive in conflict, while women avoid conflict. Females are more concerned with social approval and preserving relationships than males.
13. Men are more motivated by sex than women. Males have double the brain space and processing power devoted to sex.
14. Men are attracted to youth and beauty. Women are attracted to status.
15. Men want high-pitched voices for a partner. Women want deep voices for a partner.
16. Men pursue, women are pursued. The coyness of females and the sexual boldness of males is universal.
17. Contrary to popular belief, it's men that fall in love at first sight.
18. Men are more comfortable lying to the opposite sex. When measuring the vocal strains of men and women telling lies to each other, the men showed significantly less strain.
19. A man is more likely to sleep with a stranger than a woman. In an experiment on college campuses, three-quarters of men approached by an unknown woman agreed to have sex with her. When the reverse was done, zero women agreed to casual sex.
20. Females are slower at spatial tasks than males. When mentally rotating abstract three-dimensional shapes, females will get the right answer as often as males, but it will take them much longer.
21. Men are more consistent than women. Women are constantly under the influence of their hormonal shifts, and they are more severe than we would like to believe.
22. Mothers and fathers don't interact with their children in the same way. They truly do complement each other.
23. Women have many friendships which together act like an extensive emotional support network. Men's friendships revolve around common interests, activities, competition, and work.
24. Men's and women's brains age differently. Men lose more of the cortex and lose it faster than women.

The myriad differences detailed above represent the tip of the iceberg. To list all of the differences between men and women would require an additional 100 pages, single-spaced. Another major difference, implied but not specifically addressed previously, is the concept of masculinity. Historical social constructions of masculinity demand that men constantly prove and re-prove the fact they are men. Likewise, parents have leaned toward being more punitive with boys and expect more out of them. Society in general used to follow a similar pattern. Starting within the last two or three decades the tables have seemingly been turned and men and their behavior are treated with trepidation and contempt. The ideology of patriarchy is considered evil by some of the more vociferous activists of the Utopian cause. Traditional masculinity now is called "toxic masculinity" – a descriptive term that has negative overtones for anything masculine. Implicitly, young boys are being told they are the source of all of the world's problems. Until this attack on masculinity stops, there will be continued damage and risk to a vital element of our society.

LOVE

Love. In the history of mankind, no other subject has received more attention. It has been written about and talked about during literally all eras and in all civilizations. Love is arguably the dominant human emotion. Historically, this intangible emotion has been associated with the human heart, with no consideration given to the head playing a role. Sorry. The idea of love residing in the heart as opposed to the head is ludicrous. Like all emotions, love originates in the brain. We feel the passion of love because our brains contain specific neurochemical systems that create those feelings. The biological capacity for love is one way the brain prepares us for offspring who are born young and helpless and need tending to have the slightest hope of survival.

Romantic attraction activates portions of the brain with high concentrations of receptors for dopamine which is the chemical messenger associated with feelings of euphoria, cravings, and even addictions. When people are falling in love, they often exhibit signs of elevated dopamine levels including increased energy, less need for sleep and food, as well as highly focused attention. Mentally we can often confuse love with lust. It is not uncommon for someone to confuse lust for something greater and deeper. There is societal pressure to hurry to jump into a relationship… to almost "force" love to occur, which is rarely the outcome.

Love evolves from the early honeymoon, passionate stage to more mature, companionate love. We can't expect to feel the same heightened positive emotions later on as we do in the early phases of a relationship. Following is a brief description of what is generally considered the five phases, or stages of love:

Stage #1 – The beginning is dominated by romantic feelings and chemistry. Romantic love is driven by testosterone and estrogen. Mating is the evolutionary purpose of this stage of love. You feel exhilarated and even "high."

Stage #2 – This is when two people become a couple. If the honeymoon wears off, and you and your partner both decide that you still want to be together despite the acknowledgment of each other's flaws.

Stage #3 – Now comes the disillusionment phase of love. During this stage, you and your partner still have a strong connection to one another and are still in love, but you may start to feel trapped in your life.

Stage #4 – At this stage, a couple can create a real, lasting love. Love is an act of endless forgiveness, a tender look that becomes a habit.

Stage #5 – In the final stage, a couple finds their calling. You and your partner start to focus your energy outside of your relationship, rather than inward.

DATING

Normally a prerequisite stage for the kindling of love is the activity we refer to as dating. This is the evaluation period. Each party considers the other's suitability as a partner in a future intimate relationship. One also learns what they value and what they want and don't want. Additionally, a person has the simple opportunity to get to know another human being.

Needless to say, dating has changed in the past 200 years or so. A few centuries ago, dating was sometimes described as a "courtship ritual." Young women entertained gentleman callers, usually in the home, under the watchful eye of a chaperone. That system steadily eroded and eventually evolved into a self-initiated activity with two young people going out as a couple in public.

In the first quarter of the 21st Century, the Internet or online dating has come to play a prominent role in the dating world. In the United States alone there were approximately 45 million users of online dating services in 2020. It was a logical extension of the power of the Internet. The potential pool of interested daters is greatly expanded when this format is utilized. Potential dates are no longer restricted to meeting people through work, school, friends, and social gatherings. All is not rosy with Internet dating, however. A study conducted by the University of Wisconsin – Madison determined that 80% of online daters lie. Men lie about money and fidelity. Women lie about age and weight.

Dating in general can be challenging. It is particularly the case for daters over the age of 40. For those folks, it is harder to deal with change and they typically have more responsibility than their younger peers. There is often the divorce factor and the kid factor. On top of those complexities, older daters tend to be out of practice and are more prone to judge others harshly, or some may say more realistically. There are also unique disadvantages when dating somebody older or younger by 10 years or more. Those age-gap hardships include different goals, interests, and expectations. At times a social stigma can be affixed to the relationship. This is especially the case when the difference in age and net worth differential is a yawning chasm.

As mentioned earlier, dating is not easy for the vast majority of individuals. To make matters worse, some daters commit acts that either hinder their chances or blow the deal out of the water. Appearing below are some of the current dating dealbreakers:

1. Not having a photo (Internet profile).
2. Taking too long to reply to texts.
3. Running late without notice.
4. Being rude to others.
5. Excessive smoking and drinking.
6. Being needy.
7. Talking only about yourself.
8. Sloppy appearance.
9. Sexual incompatibility.
10. Poor communication.

IT'S OK TO BE SINGLE

Unfairly and inaccurately, a perception lingers in modern society that if you're single, you're unhappy to some extent, and if you're in a relationship, you're automatically happy. This viewpoint is especially prevalent with the World War II generation of women. Given how many people live fulfilling single lives and how many people settle into the wrong relationship, this is not always actually true. It's OK to be single, for multiple reasons. You have time to discover your passions. When you're single you can do whatever you want, whenever you want. There are no potential limitations. In the process, you can develop a deep understanding of yourself. The most important relationship you'll ever have is with yourself. There will be time to improve yourself and focus on what will be best for you. You will have the freedom to fully commit to your goals.

Other benefits of being single include having the time and the flexibility to date other people. You can prepare a mental checklist of what you do and don't want in a partner. You have less ex-drama and less likelihood of carrying emotional baggage into your next relationship from the bad experiences you had. There could be increased travel opportunities. Learning more about the world helps us learn more about ourselves. Plus, you might just find your match during your journey. You will never feel trapped. You don't "find" love. Love finds you when you go out into the world and begin chasing after your passions. It's smarter to wait for the right person to come along than it is to settle for all of the wrong ones.

SOULMATES

While the concept of a soulmate has existed for thousands of years, the actual term was probably only introduced in the 19th Century. Its first recorded use was in 1822, in a letter written by the poet, Samuel Taylor Coleridge. "To be happy in Married Life... you must have a Soul-Mate," he wrote. The idea persisted and then thrived. It rocketed in popularity, especially starting in the 1970s with the advent of the "me decade". A culture of individualism shifted our approach to relationships. There was a shift from a pragmatic approach to marriage to a more expressive, soulmate model of marriage where people's expectations are more psychological and less material. Too bad it's (soulmate) nothing more than a myth.

The perception there is one perfect person out there for each of us, a magical someone who fits our every whim, is nothing more than juvenile nonsense bordering on delusional, and a sure route to dissatisfaction. No one is perfect for you or anyone else. Mathematical estimates indicate that your chances of finding your soulmate are only 1 in 10,000. And yet, nearly three out of four people believe they are destined to find "the one" person out there for them. Most people don't stray far when finding their partner. The majority of Americans marry someone from the same state as them, and 43% marry someone whom they went to high school or college with. On a planet of nearly 8 billion people, it's quite a coincidence that so many people's soulmates are just in the next classroom.

Not only is the soulmate myth off-base, but it is also potentially damaging. Research into hundreds of relationships has shown expectations of finding a soulmate facilitate dysfunctional patterns of behavior and even make you more likely to break up with your partner. People who hold out for the perfect partner (impossible) are more likely to doubt their relationship or view a speed bump in the road as a dealbreaker. For some, believing in a soulmate is a way of constructing a cohesive narrative from the often chaotic and unpredictable experience of looking for love.

It's easy to see how people who believe in destiny or fate fall victim to the soulmate trap. They develop an image, a fantasy of their ideal type, their soulmate. The tendency to cherry-pick information that confirms our existing beliefs or ideas, formally known as confirmation bias, plays a role in leading some people down the wrong path. Initially the relationship with a "soulmate" can be absolutely wonderful, even seemingly perfect. However, once the infatuation phase is over, the idealized person becomes just another normal, flawed human being. The couples caught up in the fantasy bond typically focus on form over substance. That is, they place more value on symbols of their union than on maintaining genuine intimacy in real-time. Both people begin operating more from habit and a sense of obligation than from choice. We all know how that usually ends.

MARRIAGE

I've always been amused by the humorous adage, "Marriage is not a word, it is a sentence." Although in general decline over the past 30 years, the majority of Americans have voluntarily entered this time-honored tradition known as marriage. It is a defining experience in the lives of many individuals and underlines the importance of the institution of marriage. Human beings are a social species. We need to connect with others. Marriage would be the highest form of connecting. It is also one of the most demanding and difficult challenges in life. Few are prepared for what it takes to make a marriage work and last. Earlier in this chapter some of the major differences between men and women were detailed. Those differences were just a portion of the major hurdles encumbering a successful marriage.

Marriage is important for many reasons. Foremost would be the fact that marriage is the cornerstone for a stable society. Can you imagine the amount of chaos, craziness, and adultery if the institution of marriage suddenly vanished? Secondly, and of equal importance, would be that marriage provides the best environment in which to raise children. It's not the only option, but it consistently has demonstrated superior results in terms of raising children that will be productive, valuable citizens. Marriage creates a powerful synergy – the cooperation of two or more elements to produce a combined effect greater than the sum of their separate effects. Besides stability and children, there are myriad other reasons why people get married. Those other reasons include love, legal benefits, societal expectations, and financial benefits (including health insurance).

Some enter marriage with their eyes fully closed. They assume they will have a nice house, children, and lots of money, as well as many travel opportunities, awesome sex, and unconditional love. They will have everything they ever wanted, brimming with optimism and anticipation. In reality, marriage is more mundane and difficult. It's tough work, often messy and plodding. Perfect compatibility is neither possible nor necessary for a healthy and successful relationship. I believe compromise and putting yourself in your partner's shoes are vital components of an enduring marriage. Also, both parties should be motivated to find solutions to problems. Personal development and growth at a similar pace are important. Ideally, a couple will meld their lives together, each facilitating the other's wins and cushioning their losses.

Significantly increased life expectancies accrued over the past century have changed the concept of marriage. In the 19th Century and early part of the 20th Century, the average age at marriage was about 20 years old for women and 26 years old for men. People are now marrying later in life – an average of 28 years old for women and 30 for men. Another trend is the increasing use of Prenuptial Agreements (premarital contracts). They are commonly used in second or third marriages when there are children from previous marriages or a major discrepancy between the asset values of the involved parties. There are some "experts" who believe 10-year relationship contracts could replace conventional marriages. They believe that it is more realistic to commit for a decade than a lifetime. This concept retains some viability, but I don't see how it would work in practical terms if a married couple shares children.

DIVORCE

It appears the 7-year itch is in the process of being displaced by the 10-year itch. The new expiration date for many relationships is now considered to be one decade. According to a study at Brigham and Women's University, where over 2,000 women were surveyed, the highest level of marital dissatisfaction occurs around the 10th year of marriage. After 10 years of marriage, people tend to realize the fantasy they had envisioned will not come to fruition. Some turn bitter and focus on what they don't have. This is when they – "look outside the marriage for the few things they're missing."

Marriage fantasies are now replaced by divorce fantasies. The mindset becomes, "If we were single, everything would be fun and great. We can set new goals. We would find someone who filled every need before we ever settle down again." When people search for someone new, they find him or her. We hold on to this person, this transition person, while we go through the emotional trauma of divorce. After the divorce is final, we'll be ready to find the right person forever. We're afraid to be alone and don't want to give up what we have for the ultimate right person. Then we settle for less than we were looking for. As it turns out, this just-described transition relationship is more difficult to break than marriage.

Divorce is always painful, especially if children are in the mix. It is often compared to death. In my personal experience, that is an excellent analogy. There is an overwhelming sense of failure and feelings that you have been a major disappointment to the people you care the most about. It can put children at risk and irrevocably alter long-standing friendships. The dissolution of a marriage is no longer a rare event. About 40% of all first marriages end in divorce. About 60% of all second marriages end in divorce. About 73% of all third marriages end in divorce. I don't have a clue as to how many fourth marriages end in divorce.

SEXUAL ASSAULT

For much of history, sexual abuse, namely rape, was considered to be a defilement of a man's property (the father or the husband), rather than a crime against women. There was a disregard for the victim's feelings and trauma, and most of the punishments meted out reflect that environment. In ancient Babylonia under the Code of Hammurabi, the rape of a virgin was punished by death, and the virgin was held blameless. The rape of a married woman was considered adultery, and the woman was held equally responsible. The deaths of the rapist and victim were by drowning. The victim's husband had the option of rescuing his wife by pulling her out of the river. Ancient Assyrians adopted the "an eye for an eye" approach. The father of a raped virgin could rape the rapist's wife as punishment. The Hebrews of Yore abided by a complicated penalty system. They punished rape by stoning. If a virgin was raped within the city walls, she was stoned along with the rapist. If outside the city, she had to marry her rapist and he was forced to pay the bride price to her father. On the other hand, if the virgin was already betrothed, the rapist was stoned, and the girl was sold into marriage for a low price. Any married woman who was raped was stoned with her rapist for adultery, and the husband was not permitted to rescue her. Ancient Greeks considered rape of males as well as females. Punishment for rape consisted primarily of fines.

Over time the consideration and punishment for rape began to change, and we're to the point where rape is now justifiably treated as a serious, violent crime against women. Unfortunately, rape is not a rare crime against women, and on top of that, it is probably one of the most under-reported crimes. It is estimated that one in five women and one in 71 men will be raped at some point in their lives. Around 90% of rapes are committed by men known to the women they rape. Only 5.7% of reported rapes result in a conviction. College campuses, due to the age of students and the prevalence of alcohol, are especially risky environments in terms of sexual assault. There has been a movement toward intimacy requiring various stages of mutual consent. This approach sounds reasonable on paper, but in real life, it is both awkward and impractical. In other words – it doesn't work. I feel that when a young man on a college campus is accused of sexual assault and he is before the school's disciplinary body; it is vitally important that the legal principle of "due process" be honored. I agree that too much in our society celebrates coercing a woman into sex, unwanted groping, or raping women clearly too incapacitated to give meaningful consent. There is room for improvement. That said, we have to be careful with blindly accepting every accusation of bad or improper sexual behavior. Estimates of the frequency of false reporting on sexual assault run from 2% to 10%. I don't know if it's right or not, but my attitude on this matter is quite simplistic – innocent until proven guilty. If it's a "she said – he said" proposition, my default is the man's version of events unless there is solid evidence to the contrary. I will also say that most men are probably unable to fully understand the adverse impact of rape on a woman. Lastly, a woman fully owns her own body and men need to respect a woman's unilateral power to determine what she does with her body when it comes to sex and other activities.

HOMOSEXUALITY

Societal attitudes toward same-sex relationships have varied over time and place. In some societies, homosexuality is accepted, in others, it is frowned upon but tolerated, in others, it is a serious crime, possibly punishable by death. Ancient Greek and Roman civilizations were somewhat tolerant and were not known for the persecution of non-heterosexuals. Among Indigenous peoples of the Americas before European colonization, several Nations had respected ceremonial and social roles for homosexual individuals. On the other hand, Spanish conquerors of the New World were horrified to discover sodomy openly practiced among native peoples. They attempted to crush it by subjecting the natives to severe penalties. These penalties included public execution by burning and being torn to pieces by dogs. Among modern Middle Eastern countries, same-sex intercourse officially carries the death penalty in multiple nations.

Sexuality cannot be pinned down by biology, psychology, or life experiences, because human sexual attraction is decided by all of those factors. There is no single gene responsible for a person being gay or lesbian. Furthermore, all of the information stored in our genes and passed between generations can only explain 8% - 25% of why people have same-sex relations. Also, sexuality is polygenic – meaning hundreds or even thousands of genes make tiny contributions to the trait. Fraternal birth order has been correlated with male sexual orientation. A large volume of research indicates the more older brothers a male has from the same mother, the greater the probability he will have a homosexual orientation. There is a preponderance of clinical evidence that gayness is not simply a "personal choice." Ill-conceived practices such as conversion therapy and "praying the gay away" can be very harmful. At first glance, gayness seems to run contrary to the theory of evolution. I and others have struggled with what is known as the "Darwinian Paradox." In rudimentary terms, Darwin stipulated that all species of organisms arise and develop through the natural selection of small, inherited variations that increase the individual's ability to compete, survive and reproduce. Well, being gay does not present any obvious reproductive or survival benefits. Yet at a rate somewhere between 3% - 7% of the population, same-sex sexual behavior would not be placed in the rare category, thus the paradox. A couple of theories exist to explain this matter. One is genes that code for homosexuality do other things as well. The other theory is that gay people were "helpers" in the nest in tribal settings.

According to contemporary surveys, 11% of Americans experience same-sex attraction, 8.2% have engaged in same-sex behavior, and 3.5% identify as lesbian, gay, or bisexual. Pockets of homophobia, particularly within the fundamental religious far-right, still exist in the United States. These fundamentalists believe that equality is not the goal of gay activists. They believe that gays want total domination in some cases – not just "accept them," but to bow to them and their wants. Some far-right Christians say they are not just opposed to homosexuality but to all sins such as adultery. They go on to point out that adulterers aren't having parades in the streets.

Until about 50 years ago, homosexuality was widely considered a sin in America. Besides being considered morally deficient, it was also treated as a mental illness. Fortunately, that all started to change after the Stonehenge riots in New York City in 1969. At about the same time a gay rights movement started in San Francisco and soon spread to other large, urban centers across the country. For such a major transformative social change, the pace of change was relatively expeditious. A small minority of Americans (27%) supported the legal recognition of gay and lesbian marriages in 1996. Fast forward now to June of 2022 – 71% of Americans say they support legal same-sex marriage. My views on this issue are not complex or nuanced. No one deserves more human rights than anyone else. No one is better than anyone else. The gay issue should be moot and not be an issue in any quarters.

TRANSGENDERISM

There was once a time, actually not that long ago, when someone's biological sex at birth lined up and was in sync with that person's gender. For various reasons, some rather dubious, that is no longer necessarily the case. Where once there were boys and girls, men and women; now like the ice cream section at your local grocery store, there are many flavors to choose from. Each human being normally has one pair of chromosomes in each cell. The "Y" chromosome is present in males, who have one 'X" and one "Y" chromosome, while females have two 'X" chromosomes. This determines the biological sex of an individual. Another tell-tale sign of an individual's sex is said individual's ability to birth children. Can a man give birth? No. Human males do not possess a uterus to gestate offspring.

Sticking with the ice cream analogy, there is no longer just vanilla and chocolate. The cultural menu now offers these flavors: Cisgender, Transgender, Non-Binary, Intersex, Genderqueer, Gender Fluid, Gender Non-Conforming, Gender Non-Expansive, Agender, Gendervoid, Bi-gender, Omnigender, Pangender, Two-Spirit. It is all rather confusing for an old curmudgeon like me. For those not on the cultural cutting edge, please note the determination of gender now is defined as a socially constructed vast range of identities that no longer correspond just to established ideas of male and female. Also of note, the term "Transgender" is defined as denoting or relating to a person whose sense of personal identity and gender does not correspond with their biological birth sex.

In the world's general population, it is estimated that the rate of transgender occurrence falls between .1% and .6% (less than 1%). Starting not long after the introduction of smartphones in 2007, there was a significant surge (skyrocketing) in the number of children experiencing gender dysphoria. Gender dysphoria is a term that describes a sense of unease that a person may have because of a mismatch between their biological sex and their gender identity. Besides the pronounced increase in children and young people wanting to transition to a gender different than their biological sex, there is a marked change in the nature of the "from" to "to". Traditionally, about two-thirds of the individuals transitioning were boys. Male to female was more common. Recently, that status quo has reversed, and female-to-male transitions have become overwhelmingly the majority.

Theories abound as to why the relatively sudden increase in adolescents wanting to make this dramatic change. Advocates believe that the removal of social condemnation and repression of transgenderism is the primary reason. I don't fully sign on to this reasoning and believe the corrupting influence of social media and pop culture plays a part. I also opine that the persistent social battering of males in general, and the patriarchy in particular, has taken a toll. It's simply not considered cool and "with it" to be an evil oppressor as represented by a heterosexual, white male. God forbid. In today's upside-down world, the incentive is to be on the receiving end of "oppression" and thus anything else but a heterosexual male lacking melanin. It pays to be a victim.

Frankly, I could care less what an adult (legally emancipated at 18) does with his or her body and chosen identity. My issue is only with the medical transition of minors, in particular pre-puberty children. Except for exceptional and rare cases, this is fundamentally wrong and dangerous. First, children are notorious for lacking a good grasp on reality, being mercurial with the decision-making process, and deficient in the ability to assess risk. Medical transitioning may not make things better and have the potential to backfire and make things worse. Once puberty blockers, hormones, and even surgeries enter the equation, the possibility of irrevocable physical damage and significant mental impairment often increases. I tender the opinion that a lengthy and extensive psychoanalysis of the patient should be required before any transitioning program is initiated.

The United States is an outlier with its aggressive approach to gender-affirming medical interventions. Now is an opportune time to call a time-out in the culture war over trans kids and study this matter in more depth. Earlier in 2022, Sweden's National Board of Health and Welfare (NBHW) released new guidelines for treating young people with gender dysphoria. A summary of this report follows: "The NBHW deems that the risks of puberty-suppressing treatment with GnRH-analogues and gender-affirming hormonal treatment currently outweigh the possible benefits and that treatments should be offered only in exceptional cases." Finland's Council for Choices in Health Care (COHERE) came to almost the same conclusion a year earlier, saying: "The first-line intervention for gender variance during childhood and adolescent years is psychosocial support and, as necessary, gender-explorative therapy and comorbid psychiatric disorders. In light of available evidence, gender reassignment of minors is an experimental practice. Gender reassignment medical interventions must be done with a great deal of caution, and no irreversible treatment should be initiated," COHERE wrote.

Transgender women athletically competing against biological women is an absolute joke, although it is hardly a laughing matter. A case in point would be Lia Thomas, formerly known as William Thomas. William Thomas was an exceptionally average Men's Division I swimmer for most of his tenure representing the University of Pennsylvania. After one year of hormone-suppressant therapy, William Thomas became Lia Thomas and as a transgender female athlete was eligible to compete in women's sports. As a "woman", Lia kicked ass, winning the 500-yard freestyle event at the NCAA Women's Swimming and Diving Championships in March of 2022. Her victory was an insult to the biological women who raced against her. It was also an insult to those who fought for Title IX and equal opportunities for female athletes. Regardless of hormone therapy, there are unmistakable physiological differences between the male and female sexes. The hormone therapy requirement of 12 months didn't account for the earlier advantages of Thomas undergoing male puberty and significant previous testosterone production. Those natural advantages included a 6-3 frame, greater natural strength, larger hands and feet, and enhanced lung capacity. A transgender female competing against biological females is not a fair fight.

PRONOUNS

According to some, a person doesn't have the right to invalidate someone's chosen identity and pronouns. Continually using the wrong pronouns to address or refer to someone is supposedly a form of hostility, also known as microaggression. If it ever gets to the point where this is considered a crime, yours truly may someday be paying a fine or spending a period behind bars. I detest this pronoun declaration movement and will not participate in this ludicrous practice of narcissistic validation. I am told that addressing a person the way they have requested is a sign of respect. The operative word in that last sentence is "respect." It has consistently been my position that respect is earned. If my respect is earned, I'll oblige and comply with the pronoun-centric person's request. Otherwise, forget it. In addition, I was under the impression that we still lived in a free country protected by the First

Amendment. I acknowledge the possible inherent risk (a punch in the nose or worse), but do I not still retain the freedom to address or refer to a fellow human being as I so desire? Also, for what it's worth, language and words are not violent. Violence is physical in nature, not semantical.

CHAPTER FOUR

EDUCATION

I AM NOT COGNIZANT of any Americans with an excess of one ounce of awareness that believes our educational system is not one of the half-dozen primary pillars that support a prosperous society. Similarly, a surplus of people believes our educational system has a lot of room for improvement. That is a nice way of saying it has either stagnated, or even regressed, and if we fail to get our act together regarding education, there will be grave consequences down the pike. Besides pointing out glaring problems with education in the United States, I will offer some suggestions for improvement in this important area. I further promise to do my utmost to avoid digressing into old coot syndrome. Such as stating, "When I was a kid, I would walk three miles to and from school. In the snow and uphill."

TEACHERS' UNIONS

I might as well get this out of the way right off the bat – I detest public school teachers' unions. This is not a recent phenomenon brought on by teachers' unions promoting remote learning over the past few years and using the pandemic to extort more money and benefits for its members. There is a huge problem with public sector unions in comparison to unions in the private sector. In the private sector, there is a healthy, adversarial give-and-take between management and labor during the collective bargaining process.

The same cannot be said for public sector negotiations. In this case, there is an unhealthy, almost incestuous, relationship between labor and the taxpayers' elected representatives. All too frequently, elected officials fail to act in a fiduciary capacity for the electorate. Besides obvious political campaign contributions, a mutual power exists to determine government employees' wages, benefits, and work conditions. All at the expense of taxpayers. In addition, the very nature of many public services grants the government a monopoly or near monopoly. Striking public employees could in effect hold the public hostage.

Randi Weingarten, head of the 1.7- million-member American Federation of Teachers, wakes up every morning in search of ways to keep children confined to traditional public schools, regardless of their quality. She and her thousands of state and local affiliate unions do this because it is good for their dues-paying members, and those interests come before the students and their families. Unions' ironclad control over public education does serious harm to children. A failing school may be a disaster for students, but it still means a lot of middle-class jobs for union members. Union-controlled schools have an abysmal record when it comes to educating minorities. If there's anything more systemically racist than white, liberal elites sentencing black and brown children to educational oblivion, I don't know what is. Liberals like to complain about persistent racial inequality, but a decent education is the first step in addressing it. Teachers' unions are firmly standing in the way of educational progress in the inner cities.

The Biden administration didn't "follow the science" during the pandemic, it followed orders from the Teachers' unions. The negative effects of remote learning won't be fully understood for some time. Reasonable people understand that the damage – scholastically and emotionally – will be profound. During the pandemic, the political ruling classes sent their children to private schools that were open for in-person learning. Meanwhile, they condemned children without financial means to rot in front of a video screen. Americans learned during the school lockdowns the degree to which unions control not only the public school systems but by extension the everyday lives of tens of millions of parents with school-age children.

Without a doubt, the poster child for ineptitude, avarice, and inflicting harm on students would be the Chicago Teachers' Union (CTU). With over 340,000 students and 21,000 teachers, the City of Chicago School District #299 is the third largest school district in the United States. Over the past decade, due to labor strikes, the CTU has shut students out of the classroom on five different occasions for varying periods. This is deplorable. Illinois unions are empowered by some of the most union-friendly collective bargaining laws in the country. Illinois is an outlier when it comes to giving public-sector unions power over ordinary residents. The state gives public-safety workers the power to force arbitration and allow teachers to strike – one of only 13 states to do so. States like North Carolina, Texas, and Georgia, by contrast, put the needs of taxpayers before those of their public-sector unions. Those states ban collective bargaining with teachers' unions altogether.

Although the CTU should be called out and criticized for its consistent militancy, Illinois lawmakers are equally culpable for creating the train wreck otherwise known as inner-city public schools. For decades, big-city Democrats who oversee Chicago and other large school systems have enabled the teachers' unions in return for generous political support. Union members' dues are spent on lobbying, legal issues, and political campaigns for the candidates they support. It is an unhealthy and never-ending cycle of quasi-corruption. In return for maximum support for getting elected or re-elected, the lawmakers "take care" of the public employee union members. The average career Chicago educator retires at 62 with a starting pension of $74,000 and a compounding COLA of 3%. The losers in this arrangement? Only the students and the taxpayers.

With the COVID-19 pandemic, many parents have a new appreciation of how mediocre a job the public schools were doing. The uptick in students attending private schools will continue. The same can be said for homeschooling. This is what happens when teachers refuse to do their jobs. It turns out home-schoolers are better at it anyway. During the pandemic, many parents formed "learning pods." Small groups of families joined together to hire a teacher or a tutor to teach their kids. As schools sat empty and homebound teachers drew their regular salaries for less effective work, both resentment and opposition to additional funding for public schools accelerated.

Hopefully, despite vehement opposition from the unions, the restrictions on the formation of charter schools will end and there will be a significant increase in the number of charter schools. A charter school is a school that receives government funding but operates independently of the established state school system in which it is located. They also tend to be more responsive to parents and can more easily fire poor teachers. Public schools are dominant because they don't need to compete for funds. Taxpayers are forced to finance them. Charter schools would offer strong competition and give parents and their children a viable, affordable option in areas where public schools are failing. This would primarily be in urban centers that are dominated by minority students.

CHARTER SCHOOLS

We are told constantly by defenders of the education status quo that the learning gap between whites and non-whites is rooted in poverty, segregation, and "systemic" racism." It is not quite that cut and dry. The best schools in New York State are public charter schools. In 2019, 23 of the top 30 schools in the state were charter schools.

Those schools sported student bodies that were more than 80% Black and Hispanic, and some two-thirds of the kids qualified for free or discounted lunches. Opponents of charter schools claim charters "cherry-pick" the smartest and most motivated minority students. This is not the case. Numerous empirical studies have shown that charter schools outperform similarly motivated peers in traditional public schools who applied to a charter but weren't admitted. As the well-known author, Thomas Sowell, writes, "When charter schools take a fraction of the children from motivated families, why does that prevent the traditional public schools from comparably educating the remaining majority of children from motivated families?"

SPECIAL EDUCATION

Next, I will attack an education "sacred cow" – Special Education. Like so many other government programs and mandates based on good intentions, Special Ed has evolved into a costly failure and a scandalous waste of money. Originally passed by Congress in 1975, the Education of Handicapped Children Act guaranteed a public school education for children with disabilities. It guarantees access to free appropriate education in the least restrictive environment for every child with a disability. In 1990, and again in 1997 and 2004, additional amendments were passed to include the following:

a.) Greater access to the general education curriculum.
b.) Provide early intervention services for children from birth to age 5.
c.) Offer transition planning for teens as they age out of programs.

Originally, the program cost roughly $1 billion per year – a reasonable price -tag for bringing millions of children into the mainstream. Today, Special Education is costing taxpayers about $60 billion a year - $3 billion from the federal government, and $57 billion from states and local districts. Of every dollar spent on education in the United States, 20 cents is allocated to these programs. Per pupil, about twice as much is spent on the 5 million Special Ed students than on the 52 million regular students. Furthermore, once a child is labeled as needing special education, regardless of the specific reason(s), he or she can't be expelled by the public school system. The level of disruptive behavior is considered irrelevant. A sharper line should be drawn between disability and disciplinary problems. Public schools should have the right to expel disruptive students regardless of whether or not they're disabled.

We have experienced over 40 years of a special education system that is largely procedural, highly regulated, places parents in adversarial positions with schools, and is much more expensive than it needs to be – all without achieving the positive outcomes that we desire for these students. Many smart, affluent parents use special education laws to demand special privileges for their kids. Abuses include parents who demanded karate lessons for a kindergartner, school-paid trips to Disneyland, and horseback lessons. Many school districts have "gone overboard" in directing an inordinate amount of resources for a limited number of students. When will we figure out that we are unable to do everything for everybody?

Disruptive Special Education students were mentioned in a previous paragraph. There is no shortage of non-special ed students who are exceedingly disruptive in the classroom and other locations on the school property. I have little tolerance for this type of behavior and recommend permanent expulsion when actions are frequent and egregious enough to justify this severe approach on disciplinary matters. It appears relatively few numbers of bad actors cause most of the problems. I would hazard estimating that 10% of the students are responsible for 90% of the negative incidents. It perturbs me that one or two rogue students in a classroom can make it practically impossible for a teacher to effectively teach and for the other students to effectively learn in a safe environment. The student's race and gender are irrelevant in terms of discipline. If they consistently are disrupting and destroying the ability of other students to learn – then these troublesome students should be removed.

SCHOOL BOARDS

In watching and reading various media sources over the past few years, one gets the impression that serving on local school boards at the elementary or secondary levels offers much in the way of headaches and little or nothing in terms of satisfaction or financial compensation. According to the National School Boards Association, school board members are typically volunteers who receive no annual compensation for their services. Approximately 75 percent of small district school board members receive no salary. Some large district school board members in California and Florida do receive healthy amounts of financial benefits.

I opine that all school districts would be better off if they paid compensation to school board members. It would increase the pool of qualified and capable citizens running for school board positions. It would also translate into school board members spending more time reviewing various issues. Most people take things more seriously when they are being paid for their hard work and services.

YEAR-ROUND SCHOOL AND OTHER TWEAKS

Several countries have academic years that go year-round. It would be in the best interest of the United States to follow suit. The traditional schooling calendar was created to allow children to help plant and harvest crops with their families when we were primarily an agrarian society. That is no longer the case. In the year-round scheduling approach, the summer break is replaced by shorter "intersessions" throughout the year. In year-round schools, kids attend classes for six to nine weeks at a time, with two- to-four- week breaks. Multiple studies have shown that students lose a portion of their literacy development during the three months of summer. This is especially pronounced for low-income students. When teachers are required to be on campus year-round, struggling students have access to regular tutoring and support they otherwise would not have in the summer months. Shorter breaks between school terms mean that students can avoid gaps in learning.

Proponents of year-round schooling mention other benefits, including:

1. Saving money on school facilities and staff resources.

2. Reducing class sizes and overcrowding in classrooms.
3. Decreasing teacher and student absences.
4. Preventing student and teacher burnout.
5. Increase respect and compensation for teachers.
6. Easier to schedule vacations.

It is also the case that the world is becoming increasingly competitive. The two largest countries in the world, China and India, have their children spend 25% to 30% more time in school compared to the U.S.There are a couple of additional tweaks to school schedules that I would also advocate. The first concerns the daily school start times for middle and high schools. The vast majority of American adolescents start school too early and are chronically sleep deprived. The American Academy of Pediatrics has recommended that middle and high schools start at 8:30 a.m. or later to allow students to get the amount of sleep they need. The other matter relates to the proclivity of schools to cancel classes due to snow, cold, heat, or some other natural occurrence. I can understand cancellations attributable to multiple feet of snowfall combined with 50 mph winds. It just seems like school administrators push the panic button and shut things down whenever they see a snowflake or there is a forecast of inclement weather. I'm no doubt exaggerating, but the point I'm attempting to make is that sometimes it seems we are teaching our children to be fearful of, well, everything. Circumstances can be challenging at times. Surmounting adverse conditions can build strong-minded, resilient young people.

PHYSICAL EDUCATION

Whether it be daily physical education classes or extracurricular athletic involvement, it cannot be emphasized enough how important physical activity is in our various educational systems. Physically active students tend to have better grades, cognitive performance, and classroom behaviors. A daily regimen of physical education can provide students with the ability and confidence to be physically active for a lifetime. This is noteworthy and relevant as the epidemic of obesity spreads across the country and more children take on sedentary lifestyles. P.E. improves motor skills and increases muscle strength and bone density. Besides the obvious physical benefits, activity and exertion provides multiple benefits for the brain and mental health.

Physical education that begins in early childhood demonstrates the value of cooperation while being part of a team and gives young people a sense of identity. It enhances essential communication skills and social skills, as well as learning the ability to work alongside a diverse range of teammates and be able to support others. Learning the fundamentals of team sports provide a constructive way for students to fit in with their peers. Playing team sports in a structured environment reinforces discipline, leadership, and good sportsmanship. All in all, schools need to offer opportunities for their charges to build and maintain strong, healthy bodies.

STATISTICAL GAMES

It has been perceived for some time now that many school systems play games with statistics and data to obfuscate the measurements of learning and educational achievement. The most common play is the aggressive application of grade inflation. What does grade inflation mean? It is the tendency to award progressively higher academic grades for work that would have received lower grades in the past. It is awarding higher grades than students deserve. Systemic grade inflation has been deemed insufficient in elevating and coddling marginal students. During the 2020 school year,, the Madison (Wisconsin) School District proposed reducing the traditional 100-point grading scale by 50%. In other words, a student who answers 20% of questions correctly on a test would receive the same grade as a student who answers 50% of the questions correctly. Ridiculous.

An equally ridiculous trend in education is advocating far less or no testing, particularly in the realm of standardized testing. This is a mistake and still another sign of the abdication of responsible policy in the education system. Standardized tests offer an objective measurement of education and a good metric to gauge areas for improvement. Teachers' grading practices are inherently uneven and subjective. Standardized tests offer students across the country a unified measure of their knowledge. The data from these tests offer meaningful information to help students in marginalized groups. Testing is a tool to hold the system accountable and to make sure the students have what they need to succeed. Besides students, standardized tests are useful metrics for teacher evaluations. These tests provide a consistent measure across classrooms and schools. Lastly, standardized test scores are good indicators of college and employment success. They are accurate predictors of aptitude and correlate with IQ results. The tests can offer evidence of and promote academic rigor. There is a strong argument that tests create a "gravitational pull" toward higher achievement.

AMERICAN HISTORY AND CIVICS

It is abundantly clear that American History and Civics have been sorely neglected in our schools over the past half-century. There is a general lack of knowledge about how our system of government works. More than 80% of college seniors at 55 top-rated schools would have earned a "D" or "F" on historical knowledge. The same survey determined that half of the respondents were unable to state the length of the terms for the United States Senate and House of Representatives. Compared to the not-too-recent past, students in general are increasingly less prepared to become informed citizens. Americans' understanding and participation in civic life are essential to sustaining our democratic form of government.

Our various school systems must reinvigorate the teaching and learning of American History and Civics. This should be done in a manner that pursues an honest accounting of our U.S. constitutional democracy and history that shows the uniqueness and significant accomplishments of our Republic. It should also not ignore the wrongs of the past without falling into the trap of overt cynicism. Furthermore, the tone of the American founding and the treatment of the Founders should be appreciative without tipping into adulation. That would require curriculums that achieve a more plural and complete rendering of U.S. history, while simultaneously forging a common story, the shared inheritance of all Americans.

GIFTED STUDENTS

Handicapped students in Special Education programs will in all likelihood not be in the pool from which society's leaders, Nobel Prize recipients, and intellectual heavyweights are selected. A brilliant innovator that develops a product or service that changes the direction of mankind will most likely come from the pool of students who are categorized as gifted. The U.S. Department of Education estimates that 6% of public school students are enrolled in gifted and talented programs. For the reasons just listed, these are the students who should be given special attention and resources for continued intellectual development. Unlike Special Education, the federal government does not provide funding directly to local school districts for programs and services for gifted and talented students. In addition, not all states spend money on gifted and talented education. This needs to change.

The benefits offered by programs for gifted students are numerous. Being labeled as gifted certainly is a boost to one's self-esteem. Knowing that you are one of the "smart kids" can't help but make you feel good about yourself. Being in a gifted education program side-steps the issue of talented students thinking the coursework is too easy and not academically challenging. Kids are more likely to reach their potential when challenged. Exceptional students often find general education boring and thus easily lose interest. By increasing the difficulty of the work, and focusing more on specific interests, students stay engaged in their education. Another ancillary benefit is that teachers are forced to raise their level of instruction when educating gifted students. This in turn will benefit non-gifted children in their other classrooms. Lastly, gifted students appear to be more comfortable socializing and making new friends when in an environment with students sharing similar intellectual aptitudes.

CRITICAL RACE THEORY

A relatively comprehensive review of the current status of our educational system would not be complete without spending some time on Critical Race Theory (CRT). CRT dates its origins back to the 1970s when law professors including Harvard Law School's Derrick Bell began exploring how race and racism have shaped American law and society. Until the last couple of years, CRT was considered nothing more than an obscure academic concept. Now it has become a fixture in the fierce debate over how to teach children about the country's history and race relations.

The basic theory underlying CRT rests on the premise that racial bias - intentional or not – is baked into U.S. laws and institutions. For what it's worth, I personally fundamentally and vehemently disagree with the arguments set forth by proponents of Critical Race Theory. That said, for academic freedom and discussion, I believe it is within acceptable parameters to be a subject at post-secondary levels of education. College level, in particular graduate level, is the proper venue for this controversial theory. CRT should not be in the curriculum at the elementary and high school levels. This should be the case both formally and informally. All too frequently instructors with an activist bent introduce the "spirit" of CRT to the classroom. This would only serve to widen the wedge between societal groups that are already exceedingly polarized.

Since the subject is somewhat related, this would be an opportune time for me to compliment the State of Florida legislature and Governor Ron DeSantis for recently codifying into law the "Parental Rights in Education" bill. This bill was vigorously opposed by most Democrats and all LGBTQ advocates. Criticism of the bill was also forthcoming from Florida's largest employer, the Walt Disney Company. The most contentious element of the bill prohibits teachers from leading classroom lessons on gender identity or sexual orientation for kindergarten through third-grade students. It further prohibits those lessons for older students unless they are "age-appropriate or developmentally appropriate." I'm sorry, but does anybody in their right mind think it's a good idea for a First Grader (age 6) to learn about gender identity and sex in a classroom environment? Obviously not. This matter is best left to the discretion of the children's parents.

TEACHERS

No single factor is more important in determining the success, or lack thereof, of our educational systems than the quality of the teachers that staff schools at the various rungs of the education ladder. Absolutely nothing in education should be more relevant than limiting the number of bad teachers that pollute the teaching profession. What are the traits of a bad teacher? First and foremost, is a lack of classroom management skills. This issue can be the demise of any teacher regardless of their intentions. If a teacher cannot control their students, they cannot teach them effectively. Another major downfall of a bad teacher is that he or she does not know the course content well enough to teach it. Teachers will lose credibility with their students quickly if they do not know what they are teaching, thus making them ineffective.

Teachers who are deficient in organizational skills will be overwhelmed and thus exposed to failure. A general lack of professionalism and poor judgment can quickly result in a lack of respect from students and administrators. Ineffective teachers are often tardy or absent or use inappropriate language in their classrooms. Good communication is essential in the teaching profession. A sub-par teacher communicates poorly or not at all. Lastly, some teachers simply lack motivation. They spend the minimum amount of time on their job, never arriving early or staying late. These teachers lack creativity in their teaching, never challenge their students, are often behind on grading, and frequently show videos. On top of those dismal traits, they display no commitment to improving.

Fortunately, the majority of teachers are not bad teachers. A significant number, probably actually a super-majority, would be considered a good teacher. What are the traits of a good teacher? To a certain extent, the opposite of what would be considered a bad teacher. Communication and dedication would be at the top of a list of qualities requisite for a good teacher. Connecting with students is vitally important. Part of that process is understanding student psychology and then expressing concepts fluidly and in relatively simple terms. Listening skills also help a teacher better understand their students and tailor lessons to teach them how they learn best. Good teachers often work effectively in a group. They maintain an open mind and learn from other educators. Effective teachers need to be able to work in a constantly evolving environment and adjust their teaching methods based on the ages of their students and available resources. They also must be able to adapt to changes in curriculum, practices, and requirements.

Being able to engage students with humor, creative lessons, and a strong classroom presence is an important part of what makes someone a good teacher. Another key to engaging students is to treat each student as an individual. Everyone learns differently, whether it be faster or slower than normal, or learns better by writing, reading, or hands-on instruction. Patience is another important skill incorporated by a good teacher. For that reason, I would have failed miserably in the teaching profession.

An obvious conclusion after a bad teacher/good teacher comparison is that our educational system would improve, perhaps drastically, if there were a decrease in the number of bad teachers and a corresponding increase in the number of good teachers. The eternal question is how to accomplish this challenging feat. It will not be easy. A good start would be the eradication of tenure from the teaching profession. Education is somewhat of an outlier in the modern economy in terms of prioritizing seniority and providing certain job protections that elevate job security. In the business world, and the vast majority of other occupations, an employee not doing their job at an acceptable level of competency is either demoted or fired. The same treatment should apply to teachers.

Enticing talented people who desire to be teachers is also challenging, but essential. There is no question that we need an increase in good teachers if the goal of dramatically improving our education systems is to be realized. Working conditions, school leadership, and resources for teaching and learning are determining factors in recruiting and retaining top-notch teachers, but nothing will carry more weight than salaries and other forms of compensation. If we as a society want educated students able to function and contribute as productive citizens, then we need to prioritize the importance of teaching and pay accordingly. Effective teachers should be paid more than average or marginal instructors. Great teachers should be financially rewarded even more than good, effective teachers. Unleash capitalism on the education system. For way too long, seniority and egalitarian attitudes concerning compensation have dominated in this area.

PARENTS

A deep dive into education would not be complete without touching on the participation of parents in their children's education. Research shows that parental involvement leads to greater student success and increased confidence. This is consistently the case regardless of race, class, or parent's level of education. There's no question that parents who take an interest and actively support their children's learning giving their kids the best opportunity for school success. Ways to show support include attending parent nights, conferences, and open houses. Showing that you care about what they're learning helps reinforce the importance of education. Lastly, parents who keep a positive attitude about education are more likely to pass that sunny outlook on to their children. It doesn't happen all of the time, but to experience an environment where your children like school and are excited about going to school is priceless.

POST-SECONDARY EDUCATION

After spending time on elementary and high school education in the United States, it is time to focus on college and university levels of education. If anything, there are more issues and problems with colleges these days than the lower levels on the educational ladder. Without a doubt, the 800-pound gorilla in the college arena would be the cost, the sheer unjustified expense of attending college. With the possible exception of medical costs, nothing has escalated more in financial costs than college. The cost has risen at a consistently rapid pace, much more than general inflation. It might not be a reach to bluntly state that attending college is the ultimate financial rip-off. Over the past 35 years, the cost of a college education at public universities has nearly quadrupled. Once, baby boomers paid for a major portion of college with the monies they made from their summer jobs. That is no longer even remotely within the realm of possibility.

EXCESSIVE COST AND THE REASONS WHY

It seems at times that money gets sucked into colleges like they are a black hole. Public investment in higher education in America is significantly larger today in inflation-adjusted dollars compared to the 1960s. Proportionately, and again adjusted for inflation, our nation's military budget is about the same today as it was in 1960, whereas legislative appropriations to higher education are more than ten times higher. Part of the reason for this unbelievable money flow to colleges can be explained by the fact that overall enrollment has increased by 50% over the past three decades. However, other more disturbing reasons also explain skyrocketing costs involved with securing a college degree.

The astonishing rise in college costs correlates closely with a huge increase in taxpayer-funded programs for higher education. Federal student loans and grants stand at the forefront as the primary culprits. It is simple economics. Colleges were able to charge more and more for the "products" they were offering. This was due to the never-ending flow of government funds to students or other individuals who at least temporarily considered themselves students.

Interestingly, the increased spending at various colleges across the land has not gone into the pockets of the typical college professor. Salaries (inflation-adjusted) of full-time faculty members are on average the same as 50 years ago. Back then (1970), 78% of college and university professors were full-time. Today, half of the faculty members are lower-paid, part-time employees. So where is the money going? In simple terms, it is going to the constant expansion of university administrators. Admin positions have increased more than ten times the rate of growth of tenured faculty positions over the past couple of decades. In a dated study from 2010, a professor at California Polytechnic University, Pomona, found that, while the total number of full-time faculty in the CSU system grew from 11,614 to 12,019 between 1975 and 2008, the total number of administrators grew from 3,800 to 12,183 – a 221% increase.

The administrative bureaucrats that haunt just about all venues of higher education are parasitic in the extreme. They are woke crusaders who devour academia's scholarly mission by terrorizing professors and students of a particular political bent. These bureaucrats serve no worthwhile purpose. They are nothing more than threat discerners, diversity planners, bias detectors, sensitivity – promoters, and sustainability guarantors. They are direct beneficiaries of today's multi-billion-dollar social justice industry. I feel they are counterproductive to the true purpose of what has made universities a special environment for both faculty and students. I'll return to the Diversity/Equity/Inclusion (DEI) Gestapo later in this section, but it is appalling that these cretins do everything possible to stifle intellectual diversity, undermine equal opportunities, and exclude dissenting voices.

There is another factor contributing to runaway college costs, in particular at elite, private schools. These schools have adopted a "high-tuition, high-aid" model. This allows them to attract wealthy and high-achieving students. It is related to the "you get what you pay for" belief. Incredibly, some people think that the quality of education is directly correlated to the tuition paid for an education. Wealthy parents believe if their children attend an expensive private school, it facilitates opening certain doors for their children's future financial prospects. These parents frequently and pretentiously use their children's school of attendance in the social status game they play.

Mark Twain once said, "History never repeats itself, but it does often rhyme." In May 1991, facing Justice Department charges that they violated Federal anti-trust laws, the eight colleges and universities in the Ivy League agreed to stop sharing information on student financial aid and to avoid collaborating on tuition increases. This had been transpiring for 40 years. In the world of business, this practice would be considered "price fixing" and is also highly illegal. In the hallowed halls of Ivy League institutions, it was known as "business as usual."

Fast forward to mid-January,2022, when a lawsuit filed in federal court in Chicago accused 16 of the nation's leading private universities of conspiring to reduce the financial assistance they award to admitted students through a price-fixing cartel. There's that word again. The lawsuit targets a decades-old anti-trust exemption granted to the universities for financial aid decisions and claims that the colleges have overcharged an estimated 170,000 students who were eligible for financial aid over nearly two decades. The schools accused of wrongdoing are Brown, the California Institute of Technology, the University of Chicago, Columbia, Cornell, Dartmouth, Duke, Emory, Georgetown, MIT, Northwestern, Notre Dame, the University of Pennsylvania, Rice, Vanderbilt, and Yale. The group is referred to as the 568 cartel – after Section 568 of the Improving America's Schools Act of 1994. It will be interesting to see the ultimate disposition of the case.

STUDENT LOANS

Over the years, actually, over many decades, student loans have been ubiquitous in the process of students securing the funding to pursue their higher education goals. The first federal student loan program was created in 1958. Up until 2010, commercial banks made these loans with the borrowing guaranteed by the federal government. The Democrats used the 2007 – 2009 Recession to justify the federal take-over of student loans. These loans were problematic before then, but the loans spiraled into a national catastrophe shortly thereafter. Currently, some 43.2 million Americans (26 million over $100,000) owe a total of $1.75 trillion in student loan debt. This translates into an average of $39,351 per borrower. One in six Americans is obligated to the government under the student loan programs. It's no longer a question if U.S. taxpayers will incur a massive loss on these loans, it is simply the degree and magnitude of the losses that are in question.

A moratorium on student loan repayment began in March 2020 at the beginning of the pandemic. It will now last at least two and a half years after being extended again in April 2022 – an unprecedented respite. This is beyond comprehension and utterly reprehensible. Though the unemployment rate among bachelor's degree recipients has fallen to 2.3%, the Biden administration continues to kick this can down the road for nakedly political reasons. The ultimate goal for progressives on the farthest left segment of the spectrum is to have student loan debt disappear with the wave of the government wand. Senate Majority Leader, Chuck Schumer, D-N.Y., and U.S. Senator, Elizabeth Warren, D-Mass., proposed that the Biden administration discharge $50,000 of student loan debt per borrower. If enacted at that level it would cost taxpayers approximately $1 trillion, not exactly pocket change. Most sane and reasonable people would consider that a boatload of money. But for those on the left who believe a proverbial money tree should grow in every backyard, it is a mere pittance.

On principle, the unconditional abatement of federal student loan debt is dead wrong. It sends entirely the wrong message. Nobody twisted the arms of student loan debtors and forced them to assume these legal financial obligations. It is not fair to the millions of previous borrowers who diligently paid back every single penny of their educational loans. It is not fair to the millions of parents of students who worked hard and saved money to help fund their children's college expenses. It is patently unfair to the individuals who never attended college. Lastly, it is unfair to the taxpayers of America who would be saddled with paying a rather sizable tab. Another aspect of proposed student loan forgiveness to keep in mind is the creation of moral hazard. Future students will seek credit with the understanding that Uncle Sam will bail them out if they don't feel the need to satisfy their student loan borrowing.

Aside from being wrong on principle, the case for writing off student loans across the board is logically lame and highly regressive in nature. Many people carrying large student loan debts have the sort of degrees and jobs that make repayment quite feasible. A University of Chicago study in December 2020, estimated that the top 10% of households by income would receive seven times as many benefits from a $50,000 loan write-down as the bottom 10%. The proposed income limits for write-down eligibility are generous - $150,000 for an individual and $300,000 for a married couple. Is this not a transfer of wealth from the struggling to the well-off? A reverse "Robinhood" effect? There is a better option: let borrowers discharge excessive education-related debts through the process of bankruptcy.

Federal student loans are not currently dischargeable via bankruptcy laws. Consideration should be given to legislation that would include debt of that nature in bankruptcy proceedings. In a society based on property rights and free markets, traditionally the stench of disgrace was attached to those who fail to repay what they owe. But these days, bankruptcy carries about as much stigma as skipping church on Sunday. Allowing the orderly discharge of unpayable debts would introduce a desperately needed element of mercy without showering benefits on the undeserving. It can be argued this solution is unfair to those who took out loans and paid them back. Although the same can be said of bankruptcy laws in general, which are an accepted part of our economic system. In the words of Henry David Thoreau, "Bankruptcy and repudiation are springboards from which much of our civilization vaults."

ALTERNATIVES TO COLLEGE

Both of my parents attended college. My mother graduated from

Illinois Wesleyan University and my father attended Knox College and the University of Illinois. From an early age, they both made it abundantly clear to me that I was expected to go to college. Whenever I questioned this assumption and direction in life, their typical response was something like, "Do you want to get a decent job, or do you want to dig ditches for the rest of your life?" Since my enthusiasm for ditch digging was low, and I appeared to have the relevant attributes for doing well in college, I was a good candidate for college. The same can't be said for a growing number of young people, who for a variety of reasons, have decided to give college a shot, an expensive one at that. The push for broader college education has steered too many students who aren't either qualified or motivated enough to tackle the requirements of a college education.

Unfortunately, many students don't seem to be getting much out of college. For these individuals, higher education can be a considerable waste of time and money. Trying to spread success with education spreads education but not necessarily success. There is no question that college is beneficial, if not requisite, for certain students and occupations. The key issue isn't whether college pays, but why it pays for some and not all. There is a disconnect between college curricula and the job market. Educators teach what they know, or what they think they know. Most have little firsthand knowledge of the modern workplace. For this reason, among others, even graduates are coming out of college unprepared for their job and the world. Critical thinking skills are explicitly lacking.

Employers have discovered that college graduates are far from a finished product. These businesses often find it necessary to spend time and money to prepare their charges for the real world. Education does confer some marketable skills, namely literacy, and numeracy. And academic success is a strong signal of future worker productivity. Employers have traditionally rewarded educational success because of what it shows (signals) about the student. It is estimated that signaling accounts for at least half of a college's financial reward, and probably more. Most of the salary payoff from college comes from crossing the graduation finish line.

About one-half of college students graduate from a 4-year college. As a society, we continue to push the ever-larger number of students into ever higher levels of education. The main effect is not better jobs or greater skill levels, but a credentials arms race. For most students, college is not overly demanding. Fifty years ago, the typical student spent 40 hours a week in class or studying. That number now stands at 27 hours per week. What are students doing with their extra free time? Having fun.

The college-for-all mentality has fostered neglect of a realistic substitute: vocational education. Vocational education teaches specific job skills, and all vocational education revolves around learning by doing, not learning by listening. There is a plethora of opportunities in the building trades. Not everybody is capable or motivated to be a computer coder or mechanical engineer. For the indefinite future, however, our society will also need carpenters, plumbers, electricians, steelworkers, roofers, and drywallers, just to name a few of the trades. Besides a rewarding and fulfilling job, the financial compensation for many of those occupations is very good. Consideration should be given to emulating the Apprenticeship Programs common in Germany. There, some 60% of high school graduates undertake an apprenticeship through the Dual System, that is, part-time at a workplace and part-time at a vocational school.

DOMINANT VIEWS ON CAMPUS

Wokeness and illiberalism are running rampant and are totally out of control on many college campuses. Conservatives are rapidly becoming an endangered species in contemporary academic life. College campuses have always been a hotbed of radical ideologies and the various movements of activism that spring to life from said ideologies. What has changed is the pure level of progressive views and the fervent embracement of these views. Simultaneously there has been a pronounced decrease in tolerance and openness to non-liberal viewpoints. The argument can be made that the First Amendment in general and free speech in particular is under assault on college campuses. Unlike the turbulent 1960s, the assault is not coming from the political right. It is coming from the political left.

Here's the current pecking order at American universities: A fairly liberal student body is being taught by a very liberal professoriate that is overseen by an ultra-liberal cadre of administrators. It varies by school, but numerous surveys and studies indicate that liberal students outnumber conservative students by a minimum of 2:1. The same studies indicated that conservative students are hesitant to express their thoughts on political issues and often feel intimidated and silenced by their peers on campus. Diversity of thought has seriously eroded at the faculty level of most major universities. The ratio of liberal professors to conservative professors now stands at 12:1. In other words, for every conservative professor, there are a dozen liberal professors. Even more egregious and disconcerting is that only 6% of campus administrators identify as conservative to some degree.

A case in point of the blatant inconsistency, dual standards, and intolerance for conservative speech and opinions in the academic world involves Ilya Shapiro. After a distinguished career with the Cato Institute, Mr. Shapiro was set to begin his role as a senior lecturer and executive director of the Georgetown Center for the Constitution on February 1, 2022. Less than a week before Shapiro arrived on campus, he tweeted a comment on President Biden's promise to nominate a Black woman to the U.S. Supreme Court. His tweet read as follows, "Objectively best pick for Biden is Sri Srinivasan, who is solid progressive and very smart. Even has the identity politics benefit of being the first Asian (Indian) American. But also doesn't fit into the latest intersectionality hierarchy so we'll get a lesser Black woman." Granted, Mr. Shapiro's words could have been selected on a more judicious basis considering the times.

The term "a lesser Black woman" promptly infuriated the Woke Mob. Predictably, the applicable spineless dean at Georgetown deferred Mr. Shapiro's employment tenure and unleashed his school's Office of Institutional Diversity, Equity, and Affirmative Action (IDEAA) to investigate this supposed transgression. The

IDEAA determined that the tweet criticizing President Biden for limiting his Supreme Court pool by race and sex required; "appropriate corrective measures" to address Shapiro's "objectively offensive comments and prevent the recurrence of offensive conduct based on race, gender, and sex." After a four-month investigation, the Georgetown University Law Center reinstated Shapiro to his position and effectively put him on probation under the threat of discharge if he made a future comment that someone could find offensive. Under these untenable circumstances, Shapiro resigned. I am hopeful that Ilya Shapiro subsequently files a lawsuit against Georgetown and wins a substantial monetary judgment.

There are numerous examples of Georgetown inconsistently applying its "principles" depending on the ideology of the accused. The following is classically representative: In 2018, Prof. Carol Christine Fair of the School of Foreign Service tweeted during Justice Brett Kavanaugh's Senate confirmation process – "Look at this chorus of entitled white men justifying a serial rapist's arrogated entitlement. All of them deserve miserable deaths while feminists laugh as they take their last gasps. Bonus: we castrate their corpses and feed them to swine? Yes." Georgetown held this to be protected speech. One has to be ideologically blinded not to grasp the dual standards openly being weaponized at our country's most prestigious bastions of higher education.

ENROLLMENT BIASES

One hundred years ago, in the 1920s, getting into Harvard and other elite schools wasn't so difficult, at least by modern standards. These colleges accepted almost all applicants who passed a required entrance exam, which according to various sources wasn't very demanding. At the time, applicants to these institutions largely were affluent white students from prominent boarding schools. But then something interesting began to unfold. Due to an influx of immigrants in the early 20th Century, the nation's Jewish population ballooned. Smart, ambitious Jewish students sought enrollment at elite colleges. In 1900, 7% of students at Ivy League schools were Jewish. By 1922, that figure had jumped to 21.5%. A couple of years later, Harvard's Jewish population was 25%.

Lawrence Lowell, Harvard's president, suddenly had a "Jewish problem." He feared the presence of too many Jewish students would cause wealthy Protestant families to choose other colleges over Harvard. Thus, Lowell sought to cap Jewish enrollment at 15%. Beginning in 1922, applicants to Harvard had to answer questions about race, color, and religious preference. A new Harvard committee began classifying students by different categories – J1, J2, and J3 – based on the likelihood a student was Jewish, with J1 being conclusive. Applicants were then interviewed and judged based on character and fitness. At the same time, the university instituted legacy preferences to provide advantages to children of alumni. This blatant process of raw discrimination worked. The percentage of Jewish students entering Harvard dropped from 27% in 1925 to 15% the following year and remained unchanged for two decades.

As so often happens, history is in the process of repeating itself 100 years later in 2022. Harvard is now dealing with their "Asian-American problem." Like with Jews a century past, Harvard and other elite schools stand accused of discrimination against Asian Americans. For a few years now, it appears these schools have gerrymandered their freshmen classes with the intent to achieve prescribed racial quotas. The big winners in this rigged and unfair process would be underqualified Blacks and the big losers would be academically qualified Asian American students. Asian Americans are not innately born with superior cognitive abilities. They outperform whites and other minorities due to a greater effort facilitated by a culture and parents who prioritize academic achievement. High School study habits are a major component in determining this difference. On average, Asian Americans study 13 hours per week, whereas whites average 5.5 hours. Black and Hispanic high schoolers average less than 5.5 hours per week.

On behalf of Asian-American students, an entity known as Students For Fair Admissions, Inc. filed a lawsuit against Harvard. The suit accuses Harvard of discriminating against Asian American students by disregarding test scores and other objective measures and favoring subjective standards to gauge certain character traits. Those traits would include such wishy-washy items as likeability, courage, and kindness. The lawsuit has made its way through the legal system and now is in the hands of the U.S. Supreme Court. A ruling is expected in early 2023. The future of affirmative action in education may be determined by the Court's ruling.

BACK TO THE FUTURE

Regardless of the Court's decision, the time has come for universities to abandon their efforts to achieve superficial, artificial diversity based on race. The right approach is to implement a program based on meritocracy. The adoption of merit as the guiding principle for college admission may not result in the kind of racial and ethnic representation that universities now desire, but its result would be more authentic diversity. The use of merit-based standards would also end the need for bloated bureaucracies that enforce diversity, inclusion, and equity mandates throughout universities – mandates that sacrifice academic goals for social, ideological, and political agendas. Real equality does not require massive bureaucracies. The current system of university admissions does not encourage hard work, diligence, and achievement. Instead, it rewards identity politics. This must change, with meritocracy leading the way.

It is high time we get our educational system back on the rails. The world is getting more competitive on an economic basis. Our young people must be adequately educated and trained to be productive citizens and contributors to the continued prosperity of America. Our educational system would not receive a "D" or "F" on its report card, but there is obvious slippage and stagnation in our overall academic system. Again, this must change. Sooner rather than later.

CHAPTER FIVE

MONEY, THE AMERICAN ECONOMY, AND INVESTMENTS

World's First Shared Religion

MONEY IS A TERM difficult to define. It is a concept subject to deep individual interpretation. For some, money means power, to others, a way of living; some say it begets stability, and some believe it is the center of everything. I see money as something that can become anything due to its existence as a medium of exchange. It is something universal, in the sense that the entire world accepts its existence and value, and it represents a common want, and to a degree, a common need among all people. This universal importance makes it in some ways similar to a religion. The world has evolved into a place where people are driven to consume and spend, and money has become as natural to all of us as it possibly could. If money is scarce in our lives, we tend to value a certain amount of it more than someone who has plenty, and therefore behave differently towards it.

The origin of money can also affect our behavior. The way we value money is affected by how much we have worked to attain it. The different interpretations and ways in which people value money all have one thing in common: it is something inherent in all their lives. This is very similar to the way Medieval Europe saw Catholicism. During the Middle Ages, the Catholic Church controlled almost every part of society. In Western Europe,

Catholicism was something everyone took for granted because that is what people were taught since the beginning of their lives. Money plays a similar role in today's society. The value of money is something no one questions, and everyone believes in it or is forced to believe. If we look at a person's belief in religion in general, our belief in money is very similar. In a religion, its followers share a belief that no one is supposed to question. We all believe in money as a medium of exchange. Therefore, it has a similar purpose to religion – uniting people in having faith in it. This, in turn, provides stability.

Another thing the value of money and religious faith have in common is that they are both intangible and subjective. It is not possible to determine how much faith someone has. Furthermore, if a person claims to be religious, we cannot determine the validity of those claims because he or she may be lying. Conversely, while the amount of money someone has is a hard number, no one can say whether it is valid. If the value of money were taken away from our world, we would end up in chaos. It has become something so natural and central in our lives, we cannot imagine ourselves without it. Eliminating money would be taking a huge step backward in history. While it is up to each person to define money the way he or she wants and needs it, the definition can and does change throughout our lives, and history as a whole.

The fact that money has become something so important to us makes it our universal religion – the one we all believe in, and the one that shapes the majority of lives.

THE ROOT OF ALL EVIL

So, is money the root of all evil? No. Is it the root of some evil? Sure. Money greases the wheels of evil opportunities, from terrorist groups and violent dictatorships to human traffickers – just to name a few. It can provide a path to greed, excessiveness, and cruelty. There is no question that the unlimited pursuit of material wealth can drive us to do despicable things. People often do terrible things to one another for the sake of money. There again, they also do terrible things to one another for the sake of any number of other things. How you use money is a reflection of who you are and what you value. In my opinion, when you see other people as mere objects that can be exploited to improve your wealth accumulation, that qualifies as evil. As an example, companies selling known carcinogens for consumption and not labeling them accordingly are evil. There are many other examples of the corruptive influence of of legal tender. The bottom line, however, if the concept of money were suddenly abolished, the concept of evil wouldn't just disappear. In summary, money is the root of some evil, but not all.

SOURCE OF STRESS AND ARGUMENTS

Couples disagree and argue over many subjects, but there's a particular subject that tends to be more damaging to relationships than others - money. A study published in 2013 in the journal, "Family Relations," examined more than 4,500 couples. The study found that about one-third of couples bicker about money, and also determined that fights about money were a top predictor of divorce regardless of income, net worth, or debt levels. Even in cases when decreased relationship satisfaction attributable to financial issues doesn't lead to divorce, it can increase stress and hurt the health and happiness of other members of the family, including children. A difference in spending habits is the number one culprit. Resentment and frustration can grow if one of you feels helpless in the face of the other person's habits – or if one feels that the other is spending all their money with no thought for the future. Couples don't only fight about the spending habits of one another – they often disagree about how (and how much) to save. For example, some people might be so focused on saving that they're willing to pass up many life experiences, from travel to eating out at a restaurant, while others appreciate a little splurge now and then. One-half of a couple might be nervous about investing in stocks and prefer only to invest in bank Certificates of Deposit or savings accounts, while the other half is amenable to more risk.

It's fairly common for one partner to earn more than the other, and income disparity can lead to fights and feelings of resentment or insecurity. Additionally, one partner may feel inclined to have more of a say over what happens to the money if there is a big difference in income. Having one person handle the budgeting and bill paying can make sense. However, issues can crop up when one person oversteps the boundaries or tries to take full control of a couple's financial situation. Although the exact cost of raising children varies based on where you live, it is estimated that a middle-income, two-parent family can expect to spend between $12,000 and $15,00 per child, per year. No wonder couples often fight over whether to have kids and what to do about them once they arrive. How much debt each of you brings into a relationship, as well as your attributes toward tackling it, can be a source of strife. As with other financial matters, a couple may have different mindsets when it comes to debt, from whether it's acceptable to carry a credit card balance, to whether you should be in a hurry to pay off your student loan debts. In conclusion, many people would rather talk about death, politics, and religion than what they earn, spend, or owe. This common aversion to talking about money needs to be overcome if there is going to be a long and happy relationship between partners. Letting financial concerns simmer beneath the surface leads to fights – and in many cases, these fights potentially lead to break-ups or divorce.

WHAT TO CHOOSE: TIME OR MONEY?

Which would lead to greater happiness – more money or additional time? In a paper written for the journal, "Social Psychological and Personality Science," it stated that most people value money more than time. Sixty-four percent (64%) of the 4,415 people surveyed chose money.

The same survey asked respondents to report their level of happiness and life satisfaction. In this case, it was determined that the people who chose time were on average statistically happier and more satisfied with life than the people who chose money. The individuals who elected time focused more on how they would spend it. They focused on needs rather than wants and on other people rather than themselves – two expenditures that have previously been linked to elevated levels of happiness. Other research indicates that more income is positively related to happiness up to a certain point ($75,000 annually, in the U.S.), and then the correlation tends to plateau. Circumstances might oblige you to favor money over time. This is especially true when there are dependents and there is not enough to make ends meet. But if someone has a decent income and is financially "comfortable," time can be a viable option vs. more and more money. When is enough considered enough? Going back to the previously mentioned study... Older people in general were more likely to value time, which makes sense since older people have less time left above the dirt. Also, older people who are retired value free time due to the fact they have the luxury of time after slogging in the trenches for several decades. Married people and parents also tended to place more value on time. In these cases, those with spouses and children presumably either cherish time with them or feel they steal all their time. One crucial finding was that it's not "having" more time that makes you happier, but "valuing" it more.

WHAT IS "RICH" THESE DAYS?

Strictly confined to financial features, according to the 2022 Schwab Modern Wealth Survey, the magic number is $2.2 million. This is up from $1.9 million, which is the average net worth Americans indicated would make someone wealthy in 2021. The average net worth of all U.S. households was $748,800 in 2019. The median net worth for U.S. households was $121,780. The 2022 survey varied greatly by geographic location. The average net worth for millionaires in Denver was $2.3 million, while San Francisco was much higher at $5.1 million. Continuing the statistical avalanche ... People with the top 1% of net worth in the U.S. in 2022 had $10,815,000 in average net worth. The top 2% had a net worth of $2,472,000, the top 5% - $1,030,000, the top 10% - $854,900, top 50% - $522,210.

Some may consider it splitting hairs, but there is a difference between "rich" and "wealthy." The rich may have a significant income, but many also tend to make it quite obvious that they are driven to spend lavishly on material possessions and "stuff." Their lifestyle requires that they have to have the best of everything. Living paycheck to paycheck is not unheard of for these super-spenders. Earning a lot of money is not the same as being wealthy. The wealthy buy income-producing assets instead of depreciating assets. They don't blow their money. For the most part, the wealthy live modest lives, saving and investing diligently in the course of their lives. It should also be noted that incomes considered "poor" in the U.S. could put you in the "rich" or "wealthy" categories in several developing countries. The wealthy may have a soft spot for certain indulgences, but they invest in memorable experiences rather than in an abundance of material objects, including those that fly and float. Experiences tend to make us happier compared to material things. A non-financial definition of "rich" is that you are rich if you think you have enough. In other words, "rich" is a relative term and also highly subjective. Perceptions of receiving a financial windfall like winning a state lottery can be influenced by the level of winnings and the age of the potential winner. In my case, I'll confess it would be nice to win something in the $5 - $10 million range. That said, I do not think it would be healthy for me to win a lottery in the "9" figure range. It would irrevocably alter relationships with family, friends, and all other acquaintances. And it wouldn't be for the better. Plus, I'm a firm believer that the "journey" is what is important, and not an undeserved pot of gold dropped in my lap. These thoughts are probably moot. Being a mathematical and probability guy, I purchase lottery tickets about as frequently as 17-year locusts appear on the scene.

THE MILLIONAIRE NEXT DOOR

The term "Big Hat, No Cattle" is used by wise and wealthy Texans when they encounter people who flash expensive cars, watches, clothes, and other status artifacts that are unsupported by real wealth. These pretentious spenders lacking real substance are typically full of big talk. They also typically have friendly bankers who are poor judges of character and credit risk. The fact of the matter is that it's practically impossible to discern the financial status of the vast majority of American millionaires. He or she is not the big shot at the country club buying a round for everybody at the bar. He commonly is the one driving a three-year-old American-made car and residing in a modest subdivision. Who is the prototypical American millionaire? He is a 57-year-old male, married with three children. About 70% of these fellows earn 80% or more of the household's income. About one in five are retired.

About two-thirds are self-employed. Interestingly, self-employed people make up less than 20% of the workers in America but account for two-thirds of millionaires. Three out of four of this group who are self-employed consider themselves to be entrepreneurs. Most of the others are self-employed professionals, such as doctors and accountants. Many of their businesses are far from glamourous -welding contractors, auctioneers, rice farmers, owners of mobile-home parks, pest controllers, coin and stamp dealers, and paving contractors. The typical American millionaire lives well below his means. He wears inexpensive suits and drives relatively modest cars. Only a minority drive a current-model-year automobile. Only a minority ever lease a motor vehicle. They have a "go-to-hell fund." In other words, they have accumulated enough wealth to live without working for ten or more years. As a group, they are fairly well educated. Only about one in five are not college graduates. They spend heavily on the education of their children. About two-thirds of these individuals work between 45 and 55 hours per week. They are fastidious investors – on average investing almost 20% of household income each year. As a group, they feel that their daughters are financially handicapped in comparison to their sons. Last, but not least, the typical American millionaire is a tightwad. His favorite charity is himself.

Most of America's millionaires are first-generation rich. These folks have confidence in their abilities and don't spend time worrying about whether or not their parents were wealthy. They do not believe that one must be born wealthy. Fewer than 20 percent inherited 10 percent or more of their wealth. More than half never received as much as $1 in inheritance. Certain ancestry groups historically have experienced higher concentrations of millionaire households in America than others. The Russian ancestry ranks first, the Scottish ranks second, and the Hungarians rank third. Although the Russian ancestry group accounts for only about 1.1% of all households in America, this grouping accounts for 6.4% of all millionaire households. The Scottish ancestry group makes up only 1.7% of all households. But it accounts for 9.3% of the millionaire households in America. In general, the longer the time an ancestry group is here in America, the less likely it will produce a disproportionately large percentage of millionaires. Primarily this is because the longer the average member of an ancestry group has been in America, the more likely he or she will become fully socialized to our high-consumption lifestyle. Also, first-generation Americans tend to be self-employed. As noted previously, self-employment is a major positive correlate of wealth.

THE MYTH OF AMERICAN INCOME INEQUALITY

I opine that the obsession with American income inequality is dominated by emotion, misinformation, incomplete knowledge, and a fundamental misunderstanding of statistics. Power-hungry, populist politicians from both sides of the aisle significantly contribute to the clamor and confusion surrounding this issue. America is the world's most prosperous large country, but critics often attempt to tarnish that title by claiming income is distributed less equally in the U.S. than in other developed countries. These critics point to data from the Organization for Economic Cooperation and Development (OECD), which ranks the U.S. as the least equal of the seven largest developed countries. American progressives frequently weaponize statistics like these to urge greater income redistribution. But the OECD income-distribution comparison is biased because the U.S. underreports its income transfers in comparison to other nations. When the data are adjusted to account for all government programs that transfer income, the U.S. is shown to have an income distribution that aligns closely with its peers.

There are variations in how each nation reports income. The U.S. deviates significantly from the norm by excluding several large government transfers to low-income households. Inexplicably, the Census Bureau excludes Medicare and Medicaid, which redistribute more than $760 billion a year to the bottom 40% of American households. The data also excludes 93 other federal redistribution programs that annually transfer some $520 billion to low-income households. These programs would include the likes of Obamacare, SNAP (food stamps), various welfare programs, and unemployment benefits. States and localities directly fund another $310 billion in redistribution programs also excluded from the Census Bureau's submission of information. This means current OECD comparisons omit about $1.6 trillion in annual redistributions to low-income Americans – close to 80% of their total redistribution receipts. The poorest fifth of U.S. households receive 84.2% of their disposable income from taxpayer-funded transfers, and the second quintile gets 57.8%. U.S. transfer payments constitute 28.5% of Americans' disposable income – almost double the 15% reported by the Census Bureau. That's a bigger share than in all large, developed countries other than France, which redistributes 33.1% of its disposable income. The progressive dream of an America with massive income redistribution and a highly progressive tax system has already come true. I urge readers to remember these facts the next time they hear elected leaders and the mainstream media describe America as a Dickens novel of haves and have-nots.

INHERITANCE – WHAT TO EXPECT FROM MOM AND DAD

The Federal Reserve Bank's 2019 Survey of Consumer Finances found that the average inheritance in the United States is $110,050. Studies looking at inheritances show that the range of money left behind ranges dramatically. If you compare the average to the median, you get a much different story. The median U.S. inheritance is much lower than the average inheritance numbers would suggest.

As indicated, a lot depends on circumstances. A 2021 University of Pennsylvania study found that households in the top 5 percent of the nation's income distribution receive inheritances between 4 to 12 times larger than households in the bottom 80 percent. And regardless of income, the median inheritance for someone aged 56 – 65 was about $19,800. The median inheritance for groups younger than 46 or older than 75 was consistentlyunder $10,000. If current trends continue, younger generations will have even less of a chance of getting a piece of their parents' nest egg.

Not only are retirees living longer and paying more for health care, they feel less pressure to leave money to the next generation. The national average cost of a private room in a nursing home was $108,405 per year based on a 2021 Cost of Care Survey conducted by Genworth Financial. Many retirees are living a more active lifestyle than their predecessors. Some retirees, not all, have adopted the attitude that their priority is to take care of themselves and if that means there is no money left, so be it.

ECONOMIC ILLITERACY

Political scientists have documented that rougly half of all U.S. citizens do not know that each state has two senators and that only a quarter realize that senators serve six-year terms. As valuable as studies of political illiteracy are, they hit only the tip of the iceberg of public ignorance. One of the primary roles of government is to determine economic policies. Sound and intelligent policies are unlikely to emerge if the voters are economically illiterate. The unfortunate reality is that more than half of the electorate suffers from economic illiteracy. It is fair to say that an ample majority do not understand the basics of how economics work. The problem is not that voters lack doctoral-level expertise in economics, or that they make an occasional error. Most voters lack even an elementary understanding of economics. They are especially confused about labor markets, international trade, and the profit motive; they tend to cluster around the same errors – like blaming foreigners and greedy corporations for all their woes, real and imagined.

Let's take the perception of corporate greed as an example of economic nescience. When the price at the pump rises appreciably for gasoline, a lop-sided fraction of the public – 74 percent – places the blame on oil companies for trying to increase profits. Most people believe that prices go up when businesses suddenly start to feel greedier. Economists, in contrast, expect businesses to be greedy, year in and year out, but only if supplies have gone down (or demand has gone up) can they greedily increase prices without losing business to competitors. Free markets give people choices. You can go elsewhere if a greedy corporation fails to satisfy you. Thus, the best way for the corporation to pursue self-interest is to be attentive to the consumers' needs. Sadly, the policies economists deplore often turn out to be immensely popular with voters. Why should we think that politicians fail to listen to the voice of the people when heeding the voice of the people is the usual path to political power in a democracy? Politicians listen all too well, and as a result, they heed a host of economically illiterate demands.

CAPITALISM VS. SOCIALISM

Ali vs. Frazier. Godzilla vs. King Ghidorah. God vs. Satan. Although all would be considered epic rivalries, none holds a candle to capitalism vs. socialism. In terms of economic systems, this would be the existential battle in the world over the past 170 years. To discuss these two competing economic systems, it's necessary to offer general, textbook definitions for each. In capitalism, the means of production are owned by private firms. Goods and services are distributed according to a pricing mechanism. This system is known for its lack of government intervention. Socialism, on the other hand, incorporates government ownership of the means of production. The pricing of goods and services is set by government price controls. The entire spectrum of the economy is planned by the government under the socialist model.

This will not be an unbiased comparison of capitalism and socialism. I am an unabashed supporter and admirer of capitalism and feel strongly that socialism is wrong in every way and an abject failure in every instance it has been implemented in the history of the world. I would be remiss not to mention that capitalism incorporates its fair share of abuses and injustices. It is imperfect because men created it. Humans are not perfect, nor are they capable of perfection. Capitalism may be the worst economic system, except for all the others. Following are my thoughts and comments regarding these dual economic systems. Comments on capitalism will be short and sweet. Conversely, comments on socialism will be lengthy and anything but sweet.

Capitalism has been the most dynamic force for economic progress in history. Over the past century, it has delivered billions of people out of miserable poverty, raised living standards to once unimaginable heights, and enabled an unprecedented flourishing of productive creativity. The positive attributes of capitalism are overwhelming. Nothing compares to it in terms of economic growth. With firms and individuals facing incentives to be innovative and work hard, this creates a climate of innovation and economic expansion. This helps to increase real GDP and leads to improved living standards. It also contributes to increased efficiency. Firms in a capitalist-based society face incentives to be efficient and produce goods that are in demand. These incentives create the compulsion to cut costs and avoid waste. Capitalism is also intertwined with political freedom. It is rare to have one without the other. Lastly, though capitalism is far from perfect, there are simply no better alternatives. At a recent shareholders' meeting, JP Morgan CEO, Jamie Dimon, warned that "socialism inevitably produces stagnation, corruption and often worse." He was echoing Winston Churchill's observation that socialism allows for "the equal sharing of misery."

Under socialism, politics rather than productivity drives employment. Technological innovation is suppressed. This is unilaterally disastrous since technological progress is the only way to raise living standards over the long run. Socialism is about maximizing power, not maximizing profits. The government doesn't make profits, has no motivation to show profits and wouldn't know a profit if it hit it in the head. Inside the government, there are no markets or price mechanisms to act as a divining rod for finding hidden productivity. Socialism handcuffs Adam Smith's invisible hand. Some polls find young American adults prefer socialism to capitalism. The University of Chicago's Gen Forward Survey of Americans ages 18 – 34 found that 62 percent think "we need a strong government to handle today's complex economic problems," with just 35 percent saying, "the free market can handle these problems without government being involved." Sixty-one percent of Democrats take a positive view of socialism - and so do 25 percent of Republicans. I offer the following comments regarding this disturbing trend: 1.) It's likely most of those who favor socialism have never lived in a country where pure socialism is practiced. Perhaps a lengthy stay in Cuba or Venezuela would offer an eye-opening revelation; 2.) People who claim to prefer socialism are probably reaping capitalism's benefits; 3.) Those who favor socialism over capitalism and socialist countries over America are spoiled rotten. They seem to take it for granted that the political and economic freedoms they enjoy dropped from the sky and were not achieved by the hard work, blood, sweat, and tears of others. Socialism stifles incentives and makes people dependent on the government, not themselves, which appears to be the liberal ideal. Some would rather get a check than earn one. Socialism is little more than mutually shared poverty, a version of "spreading the wealth around" with the government taking from the productive and giving to the nonproductive. Yet, socialism's appeal continues, despite historical and contemporary evidence that it delivers a bad deal for those who embrace it.

INFLATION

My career as a commercial banker started on May 15, 1978. I tell people I cut my teeth as a banker during the final 4-5 years of the worst stretch of inflation since World War II. In the early 1980s, the legendary central banker, Paul Volcker, slayed the inflation monster when he convinced his fellow FOMC members to raise interest rates to whatever level it took to kill inflation. The commercial "Prime Rate" charged by major banks topped out at 21.50% in December of 1980. At the same time, Thirty- year U.S. Treasury Bonds peaked at slightly over 16%. I was conditioned to think inflation would forever be a part of our economic landscape. Fortunately, it was not, as inflation retreated into deep hibernation.

Before unleashing hell on the ill-advised fiscal policies of the Biden administration, some blame for our current plight should also be pointed in the direction of the Trump administration. Unlike typical conservatives, Trump had no reservations about running large budget deficits and pushing for lower and lower interest rates. As I write this section in the second half of 2022, inflation's 40-year hiatus from history is over. Extraordinary excesses in monetary and fiscal policy caused the inflation dragon to resurface after 40 years of dormancy. The Biden administration, Congress, and the Federal Reserve Bank have been prolific and creative in pointing fingers for causes of inflation, not at themselves, but outward in a lame attempt of misdirection. Blame was incorrectly pointed at Covid supply chain issues, greedy price-gouging businesses, and the war in Ukraine.

By artificially maintaining ultra-low interest rates well past their shelf life, combined with an excessively expansive monetary policy facilitated via Quantitative Easing, the Federal Reserve Bank has managed to both bring inflation to life and create the 'Mother of All Asset Bubbles." The Fed increased the nation's money supply by 38% between 1/1/20 and 12/31/21. That level of increase in two years is unprecedented. To quote Milton Friedman: "Inflation is always and everywhere a monetary phenomenon." During the same period, the United States Congress spent enough money to cumulatively create deficits of $5.9 trillion. It would be a miracle if we weren't experiencing high inflation. Ideally, the Biden administration and the Fed would implement fiscal and monetary policy to bring inflation down. That would require political courage and policy conviction, so it is highly unlikely to transpire. Even if it did happen, there is a time lag between policy implementation and real economic effect.

To further complicate matters, President Biden has promised to add regulatory assaults on energy, finance, small businesses, labor, and health care. With an inflation rate of 8.25% and a Fed Funds Rate currently at 3.25%, "real" interest rates are currently (9/25/22) at negative 5.0%. In my opinion, inflation will not be cured until "real" interest rates are positive. If Fed Chair, Jerome Powell, has the will, courage, and perseverance to go down that road, it will be a bitter pill to swallow and undoubtedly throw the economy into recession. However, there is no choice in the matter. Either we have a nasty economic contraction now to stop inflation in its tracks, or we can continue kicking the can down the road and deal with a super-nasty recession in a couple of years. I vote for now.

FEDERAL DEBT

As of the end of the 3rd Quarter of 2022 (9/30/22), the United States owed its creditors approximately $31 trillion. By the end of 2022, federal debt held by the public is projected to equal 98 percent of GDP. By comparison, Russia's economy supports a debt- to- GDP ratio of only 19%; Germany's ratio is 66.4%, and China's ratio is 68%. France and the U.K.'s debt- to- GDP ratio is similar to that of the United States.

The United States has transformed from the world's largest creditor nation to the world's largest debtor nation. No president since Bill Clinton has made deficit reduction a priority. Messrs. Bush (W), Obama, Trump, and Biden enacted big, deficit-busting plans within two years of taking office. What's even scarier is that unfunded liabilities for Social Security and Medicare are four times the current public debt level. Unbelievably, it appears the vast majority of politicians, economists, journalists, and American citizens are not overly concerned with our federal debt levels. They should be.

How did we end up in this mess? Congress has displayed a voracious appetite for spending money over the course of several decades. Since the end of World War II, federal tax revenues have grown 15% faster than national income – while federal spending has grown 50% faster. The culprit is easy to identify – entitlement spending. Entitlement programs include Welfare Programs, Social Security, Medicare, Medicaid, and Unemployment. Entitlement spending now accounts for nearly two-thirds of federal spending. The share of GDP that is spent on national defense and nondefense discretionary programs combined is no higher today than it was seven decades ago. The contrast between the long-term increase in entitlement spending and the long-term decline in defense spending reflects the profound transformation of the federal government's priorities from providing for the nation's defense to redistributing income.

How does the debt story end? Badly, unless America gets its act together and cuts prolific spending while simultaneously increasing tax revenues. The current deficit and debt levels are simply unsustainable. We've had years of denial, delay, and neglect in confronting the national debt problem. Today's high rate of inflation is a foreshadowing of what could come if the U.S. is forced to monetize the bulk of its national debt. The Fed is currently increasing interest rates to combat inflation.

Servicing costs on the federal debt will soon reach $1 trillion a year, becoming the largest expenditure in the federal budget, exceeding both entitlements and defense spending. The idea that America can borrow forever, without ever having to pay any of the money, is absurd. What happens when America's creditors finally say, "no mas." Well, the game, as they say, will be over. The Fat Lady will sing. Don't look for spineless politicians to suddenly develop a case of fiscal responsibility. They will do as they always do and default to doing what is politically expedient. In other words, blame everything and everybody but themselves. I'm afraid it could get ugly.

U.S. DOLLAR

The dollar has been the world's reserve currency since the Bretton Woods Agreement in July 1944, with the dollar pegged to gold and other allied currencies pegged to the dollar. The dollar earned this elevated status with the United States being in a position of strength after funding the allied effort in World War II. America almost lost this privileged status in 1971 when deficits from the Vietnam War and new domestic social programs introduced during the Johnson administration led President Richard Nixon to drop the gold standard. Nearly 60% of the worldwide currency reserves are dollars, down from 70% at the turn of the century.

Some policymakers and economists maintain that sustained harmful inflation can never happen here due to the unique ability of the U.S. (due to reserve currency status) to export some inflation abroad. Those misguided souls argue that because the dollar is the world's reserve currency, investors will always want U.S. debt and the Treasury will always be able to roll that debt over as it matures. But "always" is a long time. What backs the dollar is the future tax-generating ability of America's growing productive economy and a defense structure to defend that economy's strength. Investors will continue to purchase U.S. Treasury debt as long as they believe they'll get their money back. But what happens if one day bondholders begin to see the Chinese yuan as a safer bet than the dollar? History shows that the outcome will be even higher inflation. The United States dollar must remain the world's reserve currency. As Ben Franklin might tell today's leaders, "You have the reserve currency status if you can keep it."

TAXES

It's time to dispel another economic myth perpetuated by the liberal left. That is the verifiably false claim that Americans with high incomes don't pay their "fair share" of taxes. In no other country do the rich bear a greater share of the income tax burden than they do in the United States. Organization for Economic Cooperation and Development data show that the top 10% of American households earn about 33.5% of all earned income but pay 45.1% of all income taxes, including Social Security and Medicare payroll taxes. That progressivity ratio of 1.35 is far higher than in any other country. The ratio in France is 1.10. In Germany, it's 1.07, and in Sweden, it's 1.00.

In terms of federal income taxes, the top 1% of taxpayers in the U.S. pay 40% of taxes paid, the bottom 20% have negative tax rates. According to the Tax Policy Center, 43% of households pay no federal income tax. When comparing total federal, state, and local taxes with total income including government transfer payments in 2019, the bottom quintile of income earners paid 7.5% of their total income in taxes. The second quintile paid 14.1%, the middle quintile paid 22.7%, the fourth quintile paid 28.4%, and the top quintile paid 35.2%. The left persistently portrays that large corporations are more than capable of paying a significantly larger percentage of their earnings in taxes. The Democrats can get away with pretending that raising corporate taxes represents a tax on the rich only because people don't understand that corporations don't essentially pay taxes. If there is anything economists agree on – and there isn't much – it's that all taxes imposed on corporations fall in part on the consumers of their products and in part on their stockholders and workers. Workers pay between 50% and 70% of the corporate tax that isn't passed on to consumers in the form of higher prices. Another factor with corporate tax rates is that rates must be competitive with other countries. It also should be noted that corporate earnings are taxed at the corporate level and then taxed again at the individual level when dividends are distributed to shareholders.

I would make a couple of tweaks to the tax code if I was suddenly anointed the "Tax Czar." First, I would not allow the interest paid on a mortgage for one's primary residence to be tax deductible. Secondly, I would lower the $10,000 cap for deductions for state and local taxes. This would force high-tax states to be more fiscally responsible. Conservative politicians frequently claim that lowering the top marginal tax rates automatically translates into increased tax revenues. This is not the case. Only about 40% of projected revenue benefits from the tax cut comes to fruition. A significant number of taxpayers of modest means support the concept of taxing the hell out of affluent taxpayers. It seems both unfair and illogical to demonize and target the taxpayers who tend to be the smartest, hardest working, most innovative risk-takers.

In conclusion, I will quote Louis XIV's finance minister: "The art of taxation consists in so plucking the goose as to obtain the largest possible amount of feathers with the smallest possible amount of hissing."

PRICE CONTROLS

Price controls should be relegated to the history books and used as a prime example of how well-intentioned economic policies invariably end in disaster. Price controls never have worked, and never will work. It is ludicrous to even consider their implementation. Not only do price controls fail to cure the problem, but they also accentuate the problem. Typically, price controls are introduced as a desperate measure to control inflation. They always fail in this quest. Miserably. A well-known example of nonsensical price controls would be rent controls. While rent control appears to help current tenants in the short run, in the long run, it decreases affordability and supply of new units. The same principle applies to a price limit on gasoline. If the price ceiling were fixed below the market price, supply would no longer meet demand.

Price controls do nothing to tackle the underlying reason for inflation – too many dollars chasing too few goods. Price controls can reduce the incentive for firms to increase supply. For example, if prices are rising due to supply issues, the rise in prices will create an incentive for firms to increase supply. However, if the government pursues price controls, then this incentive to increase supply is diminished. Therefore, far from solving the problem, price controls can make a shortage last longer. Price controls have an unpleasant habit of creating shortages. Prices allocate scarce resources. Price controls distort those signals, leading to the inefficient allocation of goods and services.

Price controls can lead to wasteful economic activity as people wait in line to get limited goods. With price controls, there is wasteful spending on government bureaucracy. Another problem with price controls is that it is likely to cause growth in the underground economy. When demand is artificially reduced, there will be a temptation for consumers to buy at an artificially low price and sell at a higher price on the black market. And, lastly, with price controls, firms will have less incentive to produce goods, leading to lower employment levels.

MINIMUM WAGE

What are the effects of legislatively increasing minimum wages? Any Econ 101 student can tell you the answer: Job losses. This reason and more are why nearly three-quarters of U.S.-based economists oppose a federal minimum wage of $15 per hour. It would primarily hurt low-skilled workers. Evidence shows minimum wage increases disproportionally harm the people they're supposed to help. Employers will hire entry-level positions with greater skills. A $15 per hour minimum wage would especially have negative effects on youth employment levels. Evidence suggests that minimum wage increases do nothing to reduce poverty. If minimum wages reduce employment of low-skilled workers, then minimum wages are not a "free lunch" with which to help poor and low-income families but instead pose a trade-off of benefits for some versus costs for others.

A $15 per hour minimum wage for small businesses would hurt these businesses. It would no doubt make it harder for them to survive and stay in business. Instead of looking for the government to elevate compensation, there are numerous fundamental mechanisms to raise one's wages: personal effort, elevating your performance, acquiring additional skills, adding to your education, becoming more productive, asking for additional responsibilities, seeking other employment that offers more avenues for growth, to name just a few.

UNIVERSAL BASIC INCOME

Universal Basic Income (UBI) is a policy in which citizens receive a regular stipend from the government, say, every month to be used at their discretion. The idea that every individual should receive a monthly cash transfer from the state is a radical departure from past and present public policy. UBI is unequivocally a terrible idea. First and foremost, the price tag is sky-high. Presidential candidate (2016), Andrew Yang, proposed a "Freedom Dividend" that would pay $1,000 per month to every adult citizen in the country -almost 260 million folks. That adds up to over $3 trillion per year, in excess of half of the federal budget for 2022. Inarguably, guaranteed income programs encourage laziness. If you give people money for doing nothing, they have no incentive to work. UBI gives money to the rich and poor alike. Even millionaires would receive monthly payments they don't need.

UBI doesn't address the root causes of poverty. It amounts to putting a band-aid on the problem. Of related concern is the decrease in the labor force participation rate. This rate was 63.7 percent in 2012 and stands at 61.6 percent in 2022, over a 2% decrease in one decade. The unemployment rate was 3.5% in July 2022, the same as in February 2020, but the U.S. has three million fewer workers. Where did everyone go? This is an economy with 11.2 million job openings. It's mostly men 25 to 54 who haven't come back to work. A McKinsey study suggests that 40% of workers are thinking of quitting their jobs. Does anyone want to work anymore? One theory is that during the Pandemic too many workers got a taste of not working and like it. A lot. Until recently, many people could make more money by not working and became glued to screens and living an easy life. The "nose to the grindstone" approach to work appears to be the exception now and not the rule. The workforce is dominated by "quiet quitting" and "ghosting coasting." It is hopefully not extinct, but it looks like the "American work ethic" has entered a period of dormancy.

MONOPOLIES

Monopolies in the second half of the 19th century made some men in America as rich as Midas. The era hearkens back to such famous names as Rockefeller, Carnegie, and Vanderbilt. Vast fortunes were accrued by those who controlled entire industries in railroading, steel production, oil, and others. Monopolies in the first quarter of the 21st Century are prone to be less obvious, and more subtle. They are primarily confined to Big Tech companies such as Facebook, Google, and Twitter. Facebook accounts for around 75% of all social media site visits in the U.S. Google's desktop search engine market share is 85%, while Google's mobile search engine market share is 95%. Those are staggering numbers. When you post on Facebook or search on Google, your data makes those platforms valuable to advertisers. Advertising is the primary source of revenue for these technology giants. Consumers have grown accustomed to "free" access and have sacrificed their privacy at the expense of Big Tech monetizing the consumers' data.

If the antitrust division of the DOJ ever goes after Facebook or Google, they may run into a brick wall. How exactly will the Justice Department be able to show that these types of monopolies are adversely affecting the pocketbooks of consumers when the service is free? Monopolies are not inherently evil. The more important component is the behavior of a business, not its size and dominance. It is severely simplistic and wrong to postulate that small = good and big = bad. Large companies dominating a market have a financial incentive to develop innovations to stay on top. Certain industries are more conducive to applying the economics of scale. History shows us that markets find a way for domestic and foreign competition to eventually surface. For that reason, monopolies tend to be short-lived. It is wrong to punish a business for being smarter, more efficient, and more productive than its competitors.

TICKING TIME BOMB

State and municipal governments are facing a harrowing financial future. Politicians have put taxpayers into a bottomless fiscal pit by committing taxpayers to significant future unfunded spending. This mostly takes the form of pension and postretirement health care obligations for public employees. Many states protect public pensions in their constitutions, meaning they cannot be renegotiated. Future pension obligations simply must be paid, either through higher taxes or cuts to public services. Illinois is the poster child for terrible policy decisions leading to excessively generous pension benefits. Local school districts are negligent when they spike salaries near the end of a teacher's career to raise guaranteed pension payments. Over 20,000 Illinois teachers/administrators have pensions exceeding $100,000 annually. Approximately $1 of every $4 collected by the Illinois income tax goes toward these retirement annuities for teachers. People are departing states like Illinois in droves and will continue to leave as state debt gets bigger, the taxes get higher, and the spiral continues.

Property values must ultimately support the obligations that politicians have promised because real estate is the only source of state and local revenue that can't pick up and move elsewhere. When property owners choose to sell and become tax refugees, they pass along the burden to the next owners. Buyers of properties in troubled states will demand lower prices if they expect property taxes to increase. In time, unfunded pension obligations will reflect in real estate prices, if they aren't already. A state's unfunded liabilities are effectively a stealth mortgage on private property. On average nationwide, unfunded state and local pension burdens represent 20% of real estate values. What is the end game for this ever-increasing financial debacle? Several serious people are suggesting the "B" word – bankruptcy for some states. I firmly believe that idea is worth considering.

GETTING THINGS DONE

America built a transcontinental railroad in the 19th Century in six years. The Hoover Dam and adjoining power plant were built in five years during the Great Depression. The country's Interstate Highway System was primarily built in the 1960s. Those were all amazing engineering and construction feats. They were also apparently relics of the past in terms of getting things done expeditiously and competently. Because that is not the current modus operandi in the United States. California tried to build a high-speed rail line. But after more than a decade of government incompetence, lawsuits, cost overruns, and constant bureaucratic squabbling, they have all but given up. When California had to replace a quarter-section of the earthquake-damaged San Francisco Bay Bridge, it turned into a near-disaster, with 11 years of acrimony, fighting, and cost overruns. Yet 82 years ago, our ancestors built four times the length of the single replacement span in less than four years. Bottom-line, our ancestors were builders and pioneers and practically fearless. Sadly, we are regulators, auditors, bureaucrats, adjudicators, censors, critics, plaintiffs, defendants, social media junkies, and thin-skinned scolds. A distant generation created; we mostly delay, idle, and gripe.

FUTURE ECONOMY

It appears I have painted a bleak picture of the current status of the United States economy – especially as concerns national debt, inflation, the dollar, and our work ethic. I well could be unduly cynical, and the future will be coming up roses for our economy. Time will tell. One imperative component is for Congress to get its act together and rediscover fiscal responsibility. A combination of spending cuts and increased tax revenues is necessary. Our educational systems need to be enhanced to meet the challenges of international competition. There should be incentives to work and disincentives to exist on the dole.

Change, particularly technological change, will continue to be fast and often radical in nature. Certain industries and their jobs will evaporate and be replaced by entirely new industries and occupations. Workers will have to be mobile and embrace the strategy of lifelong learning. Robotics and Artificial Intelligence will increasingly be prevalent in the future economy. It will simultaneously be a scary and exciting time. Opportunities will be there for Americans willing to move forward and take advantage of an opportunity. As in the past, courage, learning, and effort will be the keys to success.

FINANCIAL/INVESTMENT ADVISORS

In a nutshell – beware. There has been a proliferation of salespeople masquerading as financial advisors. Salespeople are not inherently bad, evil, or ne'er-do-wells. They simply have a job that creates conflicts of interest that are detrimental to the financial planning process. The top salespeople out there should be serious experts in the products that they offer, but that isn't enough. A real financial advisor takes a wider view to improve your chances of accomplishing your objectives by offering solutions that are often outside the range available to sales-oriented representatives.

It is essential to select an investment advisor who will be acting as a fiduciary, not as a broker. An investment advisor acting as your fiduciary requires the advisor to act with prudence, loyalty, and care. The advisor should put the client's interest ahead of his own – all fees and any conflicts should be disclosed in a written contract before any investment is made on behalf of the client. When in the process of retaining a new financial advisor, you want to determine how they are paid, the extent of their licenses and credentials, and how many clients or customers to which they provide professional services. Top advisors will nearly always be fee or fee and commission based, have all of the minimum licenses as well as advanced licenses or other credentials, and have a higher number of hours available to dedicate to their clients.

Certain types of behavior are conducive to losing money, often 100% of the initial investment. Losing that much is difficult to offset with other investment gains. Thus, it is important to avoid certain approaches. Following is a short list:

SOME THINGS TO AVOID

1. Some people have made money with Initial Public Offerings (IPOs) when stock is first made available to retail investors, but those people are far and few between. The founders of the company and the investment bankers underwriting the public issuance of stock realize the most

profits at inception. I wouldn't touch an IPO, any IPO, with a 10-foot pole. My personal risk tolerance is not sufficiently high enough to weather the volatility storm that will be present for the first months after an IPO. I recommend sitting back and evaluating a minimum of two or three quarters of earnings before serious consideration is given to the purchase of shares.

2. Is day trading a profitable pursuit? Day trading is not worth it for the vast majority of investors who partake in this activity. Anecdotally, it is widely estimated that 95% of day traders ultimately lose money, and it's been empirically demonstrated that about the same percentage of unprofitable day traders continue despite losing money.

3. Stock tips do not work and never will. They are blind trades without justification for why a certain stock will go up or down to certain levels. We all want to become rich effortlessly and quickly. But the world's most successful investor, Warren Buffet, says: "Nothing sedates rationality like large doses of effortless money." The only way to make money successfully in the market over time is to find good companies and buy their stock at a bargain. This often involves holding the stock for the long term.

4. Meme stocks like GameStop and AMC took Wall Street by storm in 2021. Fueled by the insane actions of Reddit investors and WallStreetBets members, the valuations of these highly speculative stocks reached dizzying heights entirely unsupported by any underlying financial fundamentals. These young investors became heroes in the eyes of many by applying a "short squeeze" on some Hedge funds. They are the exact opposite of heroes. They are nothing more than basement-dwelling gamers playing games with financial markets that harm all investors to some extent. I find their collusion, manipulation, and borderline "pumping and dumping" repugnant. Stay away from meme and momentum stocks.

RISK – RETURN TRADE- OFF

The risk/return tradeoff could easily be called the "ability to sleep at night" test. While some people can handle the equivalent of financial skydiving without batting an eye, others are terrified to climb the financial ladder without a secure harness. Deciding what amount of risk is tolerable while remaining comfortable with the investment portfolio is vitally important. Risk essentially means you have the possibility of losing some, or even all, of your original investment.

Low levels of risk normally are associated with low potential returns. High levels of risk normally are associated with the possibility of high potential returns. It is a common misconception that higher risk equals greater return. Just as risk means higher potential returns, it also means higher potential losses. Determining the appropriate risk level for an investor can be demanding. Risk tolerance differs from person to person. Before participating in the investment world, an investor needs to conduct some serious introspection and determine where they land on the risk spectrum.

CRYPTOCURRENCIES

As of mid-July 2022, there were over 20,000 different cryptocurrencies in circulation. The only one that I would not immediately write off as worthless is Bitcoin. The primary problem with cryptocurrency is that it is void of intrinsic value. Those who opine that crypto replicates the financial attributes of gold are mistaken. Besides a six-thousand-year history of stored value, gold has myriad uses. Applications in jewelry, electronics, aerospace, dentistry, and mobile phones would rank high in the commercial uses of gold. Central banks across the world are becoming increasingly fearful of cryptocurrencies destabilizing their financial systems. They will act accordingly to defend their turf. Defenders of Bitcoin (60% of the market) proclaim the supply is limited to just 21 million bitcoins. While that is true, the other competing digital currencies (40% of the market) have no such limits. Owners of cryptocurrency have only one way to make money with this so-called asset – locate a willing buyer, sucker may be a better term, willing to pay more than they did. That said, I would be a buyer of Bitcoin at $6,000 per coin, and a serious buyer at $3,000 per coin.

VARIABLE ANNUITIES – NO THANK YOU

There are a few instances when variable annuities can make sense – but very few. More often than not, it's clear that variable annuities always benefit the seller, and only infrequently benefit the buyer. Fees typically are high, normally 2% per year or higher. Investment options often are limited. The insurance component is misleading. "Insurance" in variable annuities typically provide a guarantee you'll receive at least the amount of money you initially invested into an annuity if you die. Annuities are disadvantageous to inherit if they don't go to a spouse. Variable annuities typically lack liquidity and can tie consumer money down with prolonged surrender penalty periods. Variable annuities can pose some unfavorable tax treatment if the annuity is purchased with after-tax dollars. For these reasons and more, I dislike variable annuities. Some feel variable annuities were created for only one reason – to make money for the financial advisor selling you those products.

ESG

The acronym, ESG, represents Environmental, Social, and Governance criterion that establishes a set of standards that supposedly socially responsible investors use to evaluate a company. I consider ESG a massive heap of cow dung. Milton Friedman had it right when he said, " The social responsibility of business is to increase its profits." Fund managers are abdicating their fiduciary obligations if they base fund allocations on "social responsibility" and deviate from the maximum shareholder value approach. Shareholders elect a corporation's Board of Directors who in turn guide the company. Shareholders also have the right to bring important decisions, including social justice and morality issues, up for a vote among all of the shareholders. Some smart people believe it is possible to have both ESG and profit maximization coexist in the same company. I disagree with this contention.

I also struggle with the concept of corporate business leaders publicly opining on controversial political and social issues. The argument can be made that these actions are nothing more than glorified PR stunts. What is the purpose and logic of taking risks that potentially antagonize 50% of the company's customers and shareholders? Even the ongoing trend away from shareholder capitalism to stakeholder capitalism is latent with pitfalls. Good luck appeasing the various, and often conflicting, interests of employees, customers, suppliers, local communities, and shareholders. My preference would be for corporate management to focus on building the real business and legally and ethically making money for the shareholders.

MY INVESTMENT PREFERENCES

In my opinion, regardless of an investor's age, an investment portfolio should be constructed on a foundation of common stocks (equities) that will comprise between 50% and 70% of the portfolio. Unless the investor has the time, inclination, and intellectual ability, he or she should stick with low-fee mutual funds or ETFs that are indexed to the general equities market. A prime example would be a Vanguard fund indexed to the S&P 500 Index. For the relatively small percentage of investors that have the time, ability, and sufficiently sized ego: analyzing the financial fundamentals and selecting individual companies is in my mind an alternative strategy that holds much appeal. These investors would fall into the "stock pickers" category, and I consider myself one of them. Many people consider successful stock picking a myth. I disagree. The naysayers hang their hats on the efficient market hypothesis (EMH). That concept implies that market participants are sophisticated, informed, and rationally act only on available information. Since everyone has the same access to that information, all securities are appropriately priced at any given time under the EMH theory. In reality, markets are full of inefficiencies. How can there not be? It is human beings, after all, that are making investment decisions.

I would not recommend using debt or establishing a margin account from which to fund the acquisition of securities. Leverage can be a powerful tool when you hit paydirt with a stock purchase. It can also bury you when selections of certain companies go south. Stay away from debt for that reason.

Another suggestion is to strive to be emotionless when making a trade. This is easier said than done. Human emotion, positive or negative, is not beneficial to making money in the capital markets. Allowing emotion to guide your investments is a sure-fire way to lose money. Although for the last decade or so, growth stocks surpassed value stocks in annual returns, my preference remains with value stocks supported by strong fundamentals. In terms of dividends, in my mind, the propensity or not to pay dividends is irrelevant when determining the viability of investing in a company.

All matters being equal, a company with a "wide moat" (weak competition) should get the nod over a company with a "narrow moat" that is subject to intense competition. This sounds elementary - but buy low and sell high. Sometimes stocks are unreasonably discounted and for sale at bargain prices. It helps to have a contrarian mindset when the markets are in duress and the future appears dismal. Lastly, don't be afraid to sell a stock and realize a profit. There is no such thing as a "bad profit." The concept of diversification (of assets) is continually reinforced to all investors, both at the institutional and individual levels. I've always found it interesting that great wealth is typically always attained via concentration, not diversification. Diversification is in turn utilized to maintain or protect the accumulated wealth. Diversification is also applicable in the process of accumulating modest wealth over an extended period.

If an investor elects to purchase stocks on an individual company basis, I advocate a stock portfolio of six to twelve different companies. My emphasis would be on domestic companies, but I would not be averse to 25% - 35% of the amount invested in stocks placed with foreign companies. After equities, the next asset type preferences would be real estate and fixed-income instruments. For real estate, I would favor farmland and for bonds, I would recommend "laddering" U.S. Treasury securities. Besides cash, I would also allocate a modest percentage of funds to gold and foreign currencies. Gold would be held both in physical form and through a low-expense ratio Exchange Traded Fund (ETF). The foreign currencies would be held via an ETF for specific currencies. The precious metals and foreign currencies would compose approximately 10% of the investment portfolio and primarily serve in a hedging capacity.

OPTIONS

I probably should have included options in the previous section, because they should be included in many investor's playbooks. Options, whether they are call options or put options, appear to be more complicated than is the case. My advice would be to read a book or two about options and then do some trades of nominal value before taking higher dollar amount positions. Here is a succinct definition of this instrument: "Options are financial derivatives that give the buyer the right to buy or sell the underlying asset at a stated price within a specified period." Oftentimes, options are used to hedge existing and unrealized gains in stocks. When used strategically, options can limit investors' losses to a fixed amount. Buying a put option on a stock or index is a classic hedging instrument. Purchasing put options achieves the same purpose as "shorting" a stock. You are betting the value of the stock will drop. In other words, you can make money in the market even when valuations are in decline. In a relatively stable market, an investor can also make money by selling, not buying, call and put options. I don't think it's an entirely deplorable idea to take risk with a small percentage of one's investment portfolio. This might best be done by buying call or put option contracts on stocks where there are signs and indications that a sizeable price increase or price decrease may be forthcoming in the next year or less.

TIMING THE MARKET

According to conventional wisdom, any attempt to time the market is fundamentally flawed. The pundits say that stock markets follow a "random walk," and no one can predict the market's next move, so trying to do so will end up costing you money. These so-called "experts" go on to say that a lot of your long-time gains will come from a few big "up" days, and these are completely unpredictable – so if you are out of the market when they happen, you will miss out on a lot of profits. Money managers frequently promote this concept to their gullible clients. It has, from their point of view, a lucrative side benefit. It helps keep the clients fully invested at all times, which means their assets are generating more fees. But is the concept, the idea of not timing the market, sound? The simple answer: No. While it's true most people who try to time the market end up screwing it up – buying and selling at the wrong times. That, however, does not mean the idea is wrong or flawed. On the contrary, historically smart timing, based on market fundamentals, has been one of the soundest ways to beat the market and produce above-average investment returns over the long term. It is all about cutting your exposure to stocks when the market is expensive relative to the fundamentals, and keeping your exposure down – if need be, for years -until the market becomes much cheaper. It then involves increasing your exposure, and keeping it high, again for years, if necessary.

THE MYTH OF DOLLAR COST AVERAGING

Dollar cost averaging is an investment strategy that is credited with almost magical abilities by many investment advisers. The argument goes something like this: "You can't accurately predict the highs and lows of the market, so just invest a constant amount in regular intervals, and you will buy more shares when the market

103

is lower and fewer shares when the market is higher." There are some psychological benefits to dollar cost averaging as well as the imposition of a savings discipline that is ancillary to dollar cost averaging. But this notion of being economically better off by spreading out your investments over time just doesn't hold water. The idea of a mindless process producing better-than-average results over time doesn't sit well with me. One obvious fallacy with the claim is that the market tends to move up over time. It has a positive expected return. Therefore, the faster you put your money in the market the faster it's going to grow. So, if you are sitting on a pile of money, the smartest approach is to invest it all as soon as possible in one lump sum. If you have money to invest in a lump sum, dollar cost averaging is not the route to take. Two researchers (Williams and Bacon) have discounted dollar cost averaging by statistically showing that putting all the funds in at one time is superior two-thirds of the time. The lump sum approach displayed an annualized return of about 12.75%, while the dollar cost average was just 8.50%. Reducing the dollar cost average from once a month to three or four times per year also increased the return.

25 INVESTMENT RULES

1. Bulls and bears make money, and pigs get slaughtered.
2. It's O.K. to pay taxes.
3. Don't buy all at once, arrogance is a sin.
4. Look for broken stocks, not broken companies.
5. Diversification is the only free lunch.
6. Buy and homework, not buy and hold.
7. No one ever made a dime by panicking.
8. Own the best of breed, it is worth it.
9. He who defends everything defends nothing.
10. The fundamentals must be good in takeovers.
11. Don't own too many stocks.
12. Cash and sitting on the sidelines are fine alternatives.
13. No woulda- shoulda- coulda.
14. Expect corrections, don't be afraid of them.

15. Don't forget bonds.
16. Never subsidize losses with winners.
17. Hope is not part of the equation.
18. Be flexible.
19. When high-level people quit a company, something is wrong.
20. Patience is a virtue, giving up on value is a sin.
21. Just because someone says it on TV doesn't make it so.
22. Always wait 30 days after an earnings preannouncement before you buy.
23. Never underestimate the Wall Street promotion machine.
24. Be able to explain your stock picks to someone else.
25. There is always a bull market somewhere.

BOOK RECOMMENDATIONS

There are numerous good books concerning finance, economics, and investing. In the interest of focusing on what I consider "masterpieces," I will hereby mention and recommend four books:

1. *"The Armchair Economist,"* by Steven Landsburg. A very provocative and interesting book. It will appeal to any contrarian, as well as others.
2. *"Secrets of the Temple,"* by William Greider. Far and away the best book ever written about the Federal Reserve Bank.
3. *"The Big Short,"* by Michael Lewis. The most entertaining book concerning financial history that I have ever read. It reads like a novel.
4. *"Rule #1 Investing,"* by Phil Town. In my opinion, the bible for fundamental analysis and buying stocks at a discount. The author addresses what he calls the 4 "M's" – Meaning. Moat, Management, and Margin of Safety. There is also an emphasis on what he considers "The Big Five Numbers:"
    1.) Return of Capital (ROC), 2. Sales/Revenues 3.) Earnings per Share (EPS), 4.) Book Value, 5.) Free Cash Flow.

CHAPTER SIX

GUNS & GUN CONTROL

WITH THE POSSIBLE EXCEPTION of abortion, probably no other issue in America ignites polarizing viewpoints and controversy than guns and the political efforts to ban, limit and control them. Before taking a deep dive into the topic, I feel obligated to issue a brace of disclaimers. First, I have enjoyed a 60-year positive relationship with shotguns, rifles, and handguns. Although not considered an avid collector of these weapons of limited destruction, I own and use multiple guns frequently. This would be primarily for my favored avocation of hunting, but also skeet, trap, sporting clays, and target shooting. The second disclaimer would be that I have held a lifetime membership in the National Rifle Association (NRA) since 1973 courtesy of a gift from my father.

It's one of the cruel ironies of life that many fun and enjoyable activities are simultaneously potentially dangerous and even life-threatening. For instance, motorcycles. Fun, but certainly dangerous. Alcohol. The proverbial double-edged sword. Often fun and entertaining, but if used to excess, potentially a threat to the well-being of the imbiber and others. And then there are guns. An essential tool in the realization and enjoyment of myriad recreational activities, but also a prominent instrument in the snuffing out of innocent human lives. In my unprofessional opinion, for me in particular and even for society in general, the benefits and positives provided by guns outweigh the costs and the negatives.

The "Great Gun Debate" continues to ebb and flow in the

political dialogue of our country. As America evolves even more from rural to urban the debate will only intensify. To simplify matters, I'll categorize the opposing viewpoints into two distinct groups – anti-gun people (anti-guns) and pro-gun people (pro-guns). Acknowledging nothing is ever that cut and dry, to establish opposing sides of an argument will serve a generic purpose. Another generalization that I will employ is that the "anti-guns" desire either the banning of guns or strict control and oversight of private ownership of guns. While the "pro-guns" desire the complete freedom to own any type of gun with controls and limitations kept at a bare minimum, if any. A significant percentage of Americans fall somewhere in the vast middle – preferring some modest controls.

The Second Amendment of the United States Constitution reads: "A well-regulated Militia, being necessary to the security of a free State, the right of the people to keep and bear Arms, shall not be infringed." The Second Amendment is the second for a reason. It's not the Seventh. It's not the Twenty-Fifth. It's only behind the First Amendment in the Bill of Rights. The right to bear arms is almost as essential to the maintenance of a free republic as the freedom of speech, the freedom of the press, and the right to peaceably assemble. The primary purpose of the Second Amendment is not about protecting hunter's rights or even allowing a person to defend himself or herself. It's about keeping the citizens armed against tyranny. You are unable to keep a government in check if the government thinks its citizens are defenseless. I make no bones about this issue, I don't trust our government and fail to understand why any reasonable person would feel otherwise.

History provides multiple examples of what can happen when the population of a nation is disarmed via government mandate. The one-time leader of Cambodia, Pol Pot, disarmed the population through strict gun control edicts. He subsequently managed to kill 2 million souls -25% of the population. Mao Ze Tung proclaimed those loyal to him would have guns. Everyone else would need to just make due. Over the course of four decades, once defenseless, 20 million Chinese were exterminated. Stalin took guns away in 1929 and then murdered 20 million people. The reason most often given for disarming the populations by these "leaders" was naturally, "public safety." The life of a tyrant or an everyday thug is far more dangerous when the intended victims can shoot back.

I will fully acknowledge that the National Rifle Association (NRA) has power and influence that is disproportionate to the level of membership numbers. Also, the organization's executive director, Wayne LaPierre, is a certified wingnut. However, it is time to shatter the myth that the NRA is composed of a bunch of old white men that are forking over gobs of legal tender so crazy young men can slaughter innocent schoolchildren. Likewise, it is erroneous to believe that the NRA has a stranglehold on the legislative process that has precluded the introduction of many gun control measures. Between 1998 and 2017, the NRA expended approximately $48,000,000 in lobbying efforts. Whereas AARP has contributed a whopping $275,000,000 for lobbying in that 1998 – 2017 time period.

One of my favorite quotes is as follows, "God created man, and Sam Colt made them equal." No amount of Utopian wishfulness will ever change the fact that we are all responsible for our defense. For self-defense in a variety of situations, the gun is simply unsurpassed. In the face of a deadly-force attack, or when there is a great disparity of force between attacker and victim, the gun is the great equalizer. Nationally, there is a 15-minute response time for the police to come to the aid of someone being physically accosted by a criminal, thug, or punk. A lot can happen in 15 minutes, and most of it is bad. The hardcore element of the "anti-guns" tend to inhabit a world of rainbows and unicorns encased in a veil of goodwill and love. Sorry, but if in a serious pinch, I would prefer the company of cold steel to ward off evil intent.

The mindset between the "anti-guns" and the "pro-guns" is fundamentally different. Anti-gun supporters think the vast majority of gun owners are "nuts" and a collection of ignorant yahoos. While gun owners tend to believe that the anti-gun people are a bunch of coastal, elitist know-it-alls who think they always know what is best for all others. Many anti-gun people form their feelings on not much more than moral outrage. To them, even one death caused by a gun is too many. On the other hand, many pro-gun people form their feelings based on facts, so they tend to articulate numbers and statistics with hard definitions. Lastly, I would be remiss if I didn't mention a CDC 2013 study that determined defensive use of guns outweighed the offensive use of guns.

Mass shootings are incidents involving multiple victims of firearm-related violence. Every time there is a mass shooting an outcry is unleashed, "We must do something to keep this from ever happening again!" Subsequent inaction is then denounced as shameful. Unfortunately, no plausible options offer more than the faintest prospect of preventing a massacre in the next year or decade. Our constitutional framework was not designed to facilitate drastic government action based on emotion. It was designed to prevent it in the absence of a clear and durable public consensus. In this instance, there is none. Mass shootings are a horrific problem that is peculiarly resistant to solutions. To a great extent, public policy is impotent. Until the advocates of new, reasonable restrictions can make the case that they would make a difference, little is likely to happen.

The notion that more guns equate with more shootings is simplistic and false. The number of guns in America rose nearly 50% between 1993 and 2013. During that same period, gun homicides fell by nearly 50%. Taking guns from law-abiding citizens does nothing to take guns away from lawbreakers. Statistics prove that the vast majority of gun owners are responsible with their guns. There are about 10,000 murders involving guns each year in the United States. Most of those homicides occur in urban centers and both assailants and victims are disproportionately Black. A University of Chicago study found that only 3% of Chicago gun crimes were committed with legally purchased guns. By and large, the problem isn't guns, it's that people that shouldn't have them are getting them and using them. I reside in the proximity of Madison, Wisconsin. Madison's Black community represents 7% of the city's population. However, that particular ethnic group is responsible for 70% of the illegal shootings for the span between 2015 – 2020. Any reasonably intelligent person would find that statistic disturbing.

The one type of gun that seems to receive the most vilification and scorn would be the AR-15 rifle. The amount of negativity surrounding this gun is undeserved. There are multiple misunderstandings if not outright myths concerning the AR-15 style rifles. One falsehood would be the acronym "AR" stands for "Assault Rifle." In fact, "AR" stands for Armalite Rifle. If someone refers to the AR-15 as a "weapon of war", kindly inform him or her that it has never been used in a war. The basic act of referring to certain guns as "assault weapons" is an erroneous, misleading description. Any gun can be used for offensive or defensive purposes. Many people believe that AR-15s are responsible for a significant number of gun-related homicides. They are wrong. Rifles of all kinds account for just 3 percent of the murder rate. Handguns are the instrument of choice for murder.

For gun advocates, the proverbial line is crossed in the sand when the word "ban" is uttered. The majority of gun owners do not have significant reservations concerning multiple gun control laws. They simply do not trust the anti-gun fraternity and firmly believe the anti-gunners end game with gun control is a complete ban on guns. In my opinion, those concerns are entirely justified. Fundamentally, the legal and responsible use of guns need not be justified. The most vocal advocates of gun control often get basic facts wrong and have a history of praising countries that have all but banned guns outright for normal citizens. What would America look like if the gun controllers started to rack up policy victories, confiscating guns from law-abiding gun owners? Millions of Americans would have their darkest suspicions confirmed. Anger and resentment would intensify. It would degrade into ugliness with civil war conceivable. Thankfully, a supermajority of Americans (76% to 23% per Gallup) do not support a ban on private gun ownership.

I believe our fellow citizens are gullible to a certain extent if they think increased gun control measures will materially affect the number of deaths in our country attributable to firearms. They may help marginally, but not in a significant or dramatic way. There are a few gun control measures that make sense and would be endorsed by the majority of gun owners. First and foremost, would be universal background checks for the acquisition of guns. That would include closing the gun show loophole for background checks. I also would require a license to possess firearms. The license would be issued through the gun owner's state of domicile. Similar to driving privileges, periodic testing would be mandatory, and a license could be revoked for various reasons.

Mental health issues typically are involved in shootings, particularly mass shootings. This is an exceptionally sensitive issue concerning drafting the optimum policy positions. Too broad an exclusion (of gun ownership) for people with mental health problems would mean penalizing millions of people who pose no danger. It would also deter troubled gun owners from seeking help and treatment. One approach would be to develop a legal, practical system for preventing seriously mentally ill people from acquiring guns. On a local basis, consider the establishment of a panel of three qualified citizens that would include one mental health specialist. The panel would review a case brought before them by a concerned third party and then make a recommendation to a sitting judge.

In the aftermath of many high-profile shootings, we hear pundits and politicians call for the passage of laws that already exist. How many times have people clamored for machine guns to be banned? They essentially already are and have been for 80 years. Since the George Floyd riots in the Summer of 2020, many municipal law enforcement departments have been reluctant to arrest lawbreakers in certain geographic areas. This trend must be reversed. It starts with mayors and other community leaders showing support for their police departments. Besides the enforcement of existing laws, including gun laws, the duly elected District Attorneys and States Attorneys must prosecute individuals who have systemically violated the criminal code. It is an absolute travesty that some progressive prosecuting attorneys are undercutting the police and letting habitual criminals off the hook. This is both demoralizing to the police and dangerous to public safety.

As previously mentioned, there is no shortage of laws currently on the books that if enforced and prosecuted would go a long way in providing a safer environment for citizens. This would particularly be the case for the enforcement of laws prohibiting the "straw" purchases of handguns. A "straw" purchase is an illegal firearm purchase where the actual buyer of the gun, being unable to pass the required federal background check or desiring to not have his or her name associated with the transaction, uses another person who can pass the required background check to purchase the firearm. The argument can also be made for increasing penalties for stealing a gun and also for committing a crime with a gun.

Laws and the legal system can influence the number of gun-related homicides and crimes, but the solutions are to be found in the communities where these problems are most prevalent. Consortiums of parents, educators, clergy, community leaders, and police have had minor to moderate success in reducing local violence. Due to drugs, poverty, and fatherless households, it is a constant uphill battle to improve conditions that facilitate violence.

I will finish this section on guns with an opinion that some would consider runs contrary to my previous thoughts on the subject of guns. Although a proponent of carry-conceal laws, I do not support open-carry laws for private citizens. Research shows that the presence of a visible gun makes people more aggressive. Allowing guns to be carried openly in public also makes it very difficult to distinguish between the "good guys" and the "bad guys" during an active shooter incident.

CHAPTER SEVEN

HUNTING

FOR OVER 60 YEARS I have been an advocate and active participant in one of the more prominent "blood sports." My favored blood sport is not bullfighting, cock fighting, or even boxing. It is hunting. Unapologetically. I am a hunter of wild game and will be one until the day I either die or become physically incapacitated. Hunting has been a vital part of my existence and is an important component in a description of my essence. It is difficult, if not impossible, for a hunter to make a nonhunter understand his love of hunting. There is not just one aspect of the sport that appeals to a hunter. It is more a compilation of several traits that interact and conspire to facilitate an activity that for some people is immensely satisfying and borderline addictive.

I will attempt to describe why hunting appeals to me so much. First and foremost, although not always the case, hunting tends to be a social sport. Over the decades, the camaraderie with like-minded friends has been special, perhaps even a bit magical. The short list of my closest friends is 80% hunters. Thanks to hunting, my life is full of great friends and long-lasting memories we've created together. Those kinds of memories will stick with me throughout my life. Hunting brings you close to the wild and nature in multiple ways and requires physical exertion in the great outdoors. Even coming home from hunting empty-handed is rewarding due to the exercise and dealing with the elements. I will not deny that the killing game elicits a gratifying feeling and sense of accomplishment. Most hunters, myself included, consume the meat from the animals they harvest. I get excited about preparing and eating the meat from my prey. Lastly, hunting is a great stress relief. This is especially the case for those with sedentary, mental occupations conducted inside a building. One can temporarily escape from life's ordeals and problems. It's a perfect remedy for relaxing and clearing a cluttered mind.

Without walking upright on two legs and developing a large, high-capacity brain, Homosapiens would have never evolved into the apex predator on the planet. The hunting skills of early man allowed for survival at the subsistence level. Hunting by our ascendants has allowed me to write, and for you to read, this book. That fact has either never been learned or forgotten by current generations. The morality and ethics of hunting were never a concern when basic survival was the overriding issue at hand.

The history of hunting in the United States is rich and prominent in American culture. Hunting became ingrained in our national heritage and is part of a vast tradition that uniquely qualifies it as a classic American sport. In conscious contrast to the exclusionary hunting laws of the home country England, courts in America supported the doctrine of "free taking." This concept of "free taking" holds wild game to be the property of all, subject to regulation for the common good. English-style rules that reserved hunting for large landowners were rejected as "contrary to the spirit of our institutions." The hunter evolved into an emblem of self-reliance, a symbol of America.

The recreational hunting movement, hunting for sport, in the United States started in the second half of the 19th Century and became common by the early 1900s. This trend of hunting as a hobby was deeply entwined with a more general wave of enthusiasm for getting back in touch with nature and reversing what many influential Americans feared was a loss of manly virtue brought on by urban luxury, vice, and the meanness of "trade."

Hunting was proclaimed to offer wholesome outdoor exercise, a nearness to nature, and a cure for the perceived epidemic of "Miss Nancyishness" afflicting American manhood. Teddy Roosevelt extolled hunting as a way to put some backbone into perceived spineless American youth. Interestingly, recreational hunters laid the basis for a "consciousness of equilibrium and an ethics of restraint" toward nature that became the cornerstone of the modern environmental movement.

According to hunting proponents, hunting remains the "backbone" of wildlife conservation in the United States. Hunters do more to help wildlife than any other group in America. They not only provide financial support for state wildlife agencies, but they also play an important role in wildlife management activities. By the late 19th Century unregulated killing and habitat destruction pushed many species, including bison, white-tailed deer, and wild turkeys, to the edge of extinction. In response to the nation's declining wildlife populations, sportsmen began to organize conservation groups and advocate for hunting regulations. They realized that natural resources were not limitless and needed to be protected for future generations. For example, hunters could take an unlimited number of ducks until 1903 when a bag limit of 50 ducks was established. That was quickly reduced to 35 in 1905 and to 20 in 1907.

In the 1930s, Congress passed the Migratory Bird Hunting Stamp Act (Duck Stamp Act) and the Federal Aid in Wildlife Restoration Act (Pittman – Robertson Act). To date, the Duck Stamp Act has generated more than $1.1 billion for the preservation of over 6 million acres of waterfowl habitat. Also, to date, due to an 11% excise tax on firearms, ammunition, and archery equipment, the Pittman – Robertson Act has generated more than $12 billion for state conservation initiatives. State fish and wildlife agencies also rely heavily on hunting license sales, generating on an annual basis over $500 million in revenue for conservation. Memberships in national conservation organizations such as the National Wild Turkey Federation, Rocky Mountain Elk Foundation, Whitetails Unlimited, Pheasants Forever, and Ducks Unlimited serve a significant role in habitat creation and protection.

In addition to providing funds for conservation, hunters play an important role in helping state wildlife biologists manage the size of certain animal populations. Some prey animals such as elk or deer can become overabundant in their habitat. This is mostly due to a lack of predators or landscape changes. Regulated hunting is one of the most effective tools that state wildlife agencies can use to address the overpopulation of a species. Take deer, for example. Hunting proponents argue that killing deer is more humane than letting them starve to death. Also, hunting to control specific wildlife populations is relatively inexpensive for taxpayers. Hunters will kill the deer for free.

An activity that just a generation or two ago was a venerated part of American life - combining traditional virtues of independence and self-reliance, frontier spirit and wood lore, good sportsmanship and character-building for the young – has increasingly become stigmatized and detested by growing numbers of Americans. In 1955, roughly 10% of Americans hunted. Today, that number has dropped to just 6%. According to Mother Jones magazine, more Americans prefer birdwatching to hunting. I too enjoy watching birds, especially when they are falling from the sky after I shoot them. The primary reason for the steep decline in hunting is attributable to the continued march of urbanization. The interest and opportunities to hunt are not present for city dwellers. For the most part, hunters reside in rural areas across the country. The proportion of hunters in rural areas remains steady at 20% to 25%. Given the overwhelmingly male cast to the sport, this suggests that nearly half of the rural adult males hunt.

I have experienced my share of conversations with anti-hunters where I have defended my right to hunt and also attempted to explain why it is a passion and important to me. About 20 years ago I grudgingly accepted the fact that the hunting debate will probably never be resolved. Hunters and people who oppose hunting will never agree on the ethics of killing wild animals for food, trophies, or recreation. In the following paragraphs, I will detail some historical philosophical thoughts supporting the morality of killing animals. Since I am a hunter, and I am writing this book, elements of the counterargument will not appear here.

Animals are not human beings and thus do not enjoy the value and rights traditionally extended to the human animal. The view that animals were put on earth to solely serve human beings originated from the Christian Bible. This probably reflects a basic human attitude toward other species. I do not support that contention. On the other hand, I have no problem with people using animals as a source of calories, clothing, companionship, transportation, and recreation. Except for an animal's right to avoid cruelty and torture inflicted by people, I believe rights are unique to human beings.

It is generally accepted that animals lack the capacity for free moral judgment. An extension of that argument is that since animals don't behave morally, they do not qualify for moral treatment from other beings. St. Thomas Aquinas taught that animals acted purely on instinct while human beings engaged in rational thought. The great French philosopher, Rene Descartes, taught that animals were no more than complicated biological robots. Animals, argued by many then and now, inherently behave selfishly. They look after their interests, while human beings will often help other people. This is even the case if doing so is to their disadvantage. In theory, if all animals had a right to freedom to live their lives without molestation, then someone would have to protect them from one another. But that is an absurd proposition. Why should human beings have obligations towards animals if animals don't have obligations to other animals or human beings?

If it hasn't already happened, the day is not far off when the number of anti-hunters will exceed the number of hunters. This trend will continue to accelerate. Most of the general public, particularly millennials and Gen. Z'ers detests the practice of trophy hunting. Big game hunting on the continent of Africa is subject to a surplus of attention and press – about 99% of the negative nature. Cecil, the lion, became an Internet icon in 2015 when he was killed by Walter Palmer, a Minnesota dentist, on a trophy hunt. Dr. Palmer was subsequently attacked by a social-media mob and was met by a crowd of media and angry protesters when he returned to his dental practice in Bloomington, Minnesota. Besides online death threats, the group of protesters called for Walter Palmer's extradition to Zimbabwe to face trial. A reasonable person would ask, "Face trial for exactly what?" The authorities in Zimbabwe did not bring charges against the trophy-hunting dentist because in their words the hunt was "perfectly legal."

There will be dissent on the forthcoming opinion, but I'm sticking to my guns, figuratively and literally. Trophy hunting is essential to the conservation of African wildlife. It may seem counterintuitive to many, but banning the practice of trophy hunting in Africa would lead to the systemic slaughter of wildlife, trampling of unique ecosystems, and possible extinction of rare species. Sacrificing a quota of big game to hunters keep many others alive. Quotas are set below population growth rates. Outsiders need to understand that to people in many African villages, the wildlife is dinner or it is danger.

It is difficult, if not impossible, to convince poor Africans of the need to conserve animals when they don't have sufficient food, shelter, or financial stability. They want to do exactly what America's settlers did; Convert habitat to farmland and kill wild animals either for meat or as backyard pests. Who can blame them? After all, elephants trample crops and lions eat cattle. There are numerous conservation success stories in Africa. Nambia's wildlife numbers have grown sixfold since the 1960s when private landowners were given the right to use the animals for economic benefit. Since 1968, when regulated hunting of white rhinos was introduced in South Africa, the population has risen from 1,800 to 18,000.

The Save Valley Conservancy is one of the largest private game reserves in Africa. Located in the southeastern low veld of Zimbabwe, bordering on the Save River on its eastern side, the Conservancy comprises 750,000 acres of diverse wildlife habitat. Without hunting revenues, Save Valley would regress to what it was in 1990, a collection of overgrazed, dusty cattle farms with no elephants in sight. The anti-hunting backlash in rich countries leaves a sour taste in the mouths of many Africans. After centuries of Westerners telling them how to run their affairs, it understandably rubs them wrong. The conservation scientist, Rosie Cooney, refers to it as "green neo-colonialism."

Part of the reason for the growing movement of anti-hunting

activists is that they live in a world detached from both history and reality. Try taking a group of grade school children from urban environs on a field trip to an operating farm that includes livestock. The kids would struggle with grasping the fact that the cheeseburger they enjoyed for lunch and the bacon they devoured at breakfast is derived from Besse the Cow and Arnold the Pig. They just naturally assume that these tasty items magically appear at the local grocery store.

I don't believe in reincarnation. If I did, however, my overwhelming preference would be to come back in another life as a wild deer vs. a domestic cow or chicken. A deer that is ultimately killed by a hunter at least had the opportunity to escape and lived a free and wild life before ending up in somebody's basement freezer. The same cannot be said for a cow or chicken that is "processed" to provide calories for the masses. As I wrap up this section on hunting, I have one final observation. Before the end of the 21st Century, I would not be surprised to see recreational hunting close to extinction in the United States. Since I will be under the dirt well before that happens, my life will not be impacted whatsoever. I am appreciative and thankful for the numerous opportunities to participate in blood sports during the course of my lifetime. In some respects, I am a member of the "Last Generation" of American hunters who could enjoy hunting opportunities available to my ascendants, but will probably not be as nearly available to my descendants.

CHAPTER EIGHT

CLIMATE CHANGE

THE ISSUE

It is an unquestioned fact that the Earth is warming. Since 1850, there has been an uptick of 1.1 degrees Celsius (just under 2 degrees Fahrenheit). Carbon dioxide (CO2) is a chemical compound made up of molecules that each have one carbon atom covalently double bonded to two oxygen atoms. Carbon dioxide is transparent to visible light but absorbs infrared radiation, acting as a greenhouse gas. It is a trace gas in Earth's atmosphere, presently at 417 ppm (parts per million), or about 0.04% by volume. The ppm for carbon dioxide was 280 ppm at the onset of the Industrial Revolution (1760). The ppm for this molecule was measured at 310 in 1958. Once carbon dioxide is added to the atmosphere, it hangs around for a long time: between 300 to 1,000 years. Nature emits vastly more carbon dioxide and greenhouse gases (97% of the total) than human activities. Nature also absorbs vastly more carbon dioxide and greenhouse gases. The 3% generated by humans burning fossil fuels is suspected of distorting the natural carbon cycle enough to trigger increased carbon dioxide concentrations which in turn has led to global warming and climate change. That is the operating theory, anyway.

I can agree with the premise that fossil fuel-generated carbon dioxide emissions have likely contributed to the mild warming of our planet over the past couple of centuries, and also in all likelihood will continue to contribute to additional warming going forward. That said, besides the slight warming to date, I do not subscribe to the premise that the warming has unleashed the Four Horsemen of the Apocalypse or has materially changed the climate. Yet. Seemingly every natural disaster or severe weather event in the world is now blamed on climate change.

Besides consistently ignoring the distinct difference between weather and climate, the general fearmongering is absurd. I also do not concur with the assessment that any forthcoming climate change represents an existential threat to the future of mankind. I am not advocating sitting back and doing nothing. There is a lot to this issue. The biggest mistake we can make is to panic and implement irrational policies that destroy the world economy and plunge hundreds of millions, if not billions, of people back into poverty that they escaped not all that long ago. Cooler heads need to prevail.

Led by liberals on the far left, the public education system, the mainstream media cartel, and rabid climate activists, practically every young person in America has been inundated for a good part of their life about the need to eliminate dirty, evil fossil fuels if they hope to live a long and prosperous life. Second graders come home from school and inform their parents at the dinner table that they need to use less electricity in the home and less gasoline in the family car to "save the world." Are we surprised when the "2020 Survey of Americans" determined 71% of millennials and 67% of Gen. Z feel climate change has negatively affected their mental health? The militant climate activists are the most disconcerting and ridiculous participants in this global soap opera. They would rather cut carbon dioxide emissions at any cost than come up with a viable solution. Greta Thunberg and others like her are only intellectually capable of considering one aspect of an extremely complex issue. They are less concerned with reducing the rise in temperature than they are with eradicating the use of fossil fuels. One question I tender – why would anybody with a functioning brain give them the time of day?

The media, politicians, and other prominent voices have all but declared that the "science is settled" as far as climate change is concerned. In reality, core questions remain largely unanswered. I would not be classified as a hardcore climate change denier but count me as being a member of the group labeled as "climate change skeptics." I need to see more data and information and convincing evidence before jumping on board the climate change train. What's particularly disturbing is that anybody not blindly accepting the judgment of some "experts" holding a doctorate is relegated to pea-brain status and/or considered morally deficient. The arrogance on display is profound. This is especially the case when one reviews the "experts" previous track record in making climate predictions over the past 40 years. Spoiler alert: Not only have they not been right with their various predictions about climate, in particular the timing of predicted adverse consequences, but they have been 180 degrees wrong consistently. If they were in the for-profit business world, they would have been fired long ago.

When considering predictions, we must recognize that climate is difficult, if not impossible, to model and predict. All climate predictions are based on computer programs that perform mathematical simulations of the climate system. As University of Wisconsin statistician, George Box said famously in 1978: "All models are wrong, but some are useful." In theory, the models strive to help us understand how the climate system works, why it changed in the past, and how it might change in the future. As you might infer from the accuracy of weather forecasts, it is a daunting proposition to predict the future. Weather forecasts can be accurate only out two weeks or so. After that, good luck. No matter how precisely we might specify current conditions, the uncertainty in our assumptions and estimates grows exponentially as they extend into the future. One assumption of the future that is particularly challenging to accurately discern would be the numbers and types of clouds present in each of the layers of the Earth's atmosphere. Flows of sunlight and heat through the atmosphere are greatly influenced by the extent of cloud cover.

Climate computer models that are used to predict the future aren't able to accurately describe the past, suggesting they are deeply flawed. The fact that the models can't reproduce the past is a big red flag. This disturbing attribute also erodes confidence in the climate models' projections of future climates. The various models are unable to reproduce the strong warming observed from 1910 to 1940. On average, the models gave a warming rate over that period of about half what was observed. In so many words, the vaunted International Panel on Climate Change said they had no idea what caused the failure of these models. Likewise, despite a dramatic rise in greenhouse gas emissions, global temperatures decreased from 1940 to 1970. In the late 1960s and the 1970s, the "experts" were predicting catastrophic global cooling. Following are some headlines from the 1970s:

> The Guardian, 1974: "Space Satellites Show New Ice Age Coming Fast"
>
> Newsweek, 1975: "The Cooling World" – Climatologists are pessimistic that political leaders will take any positive action to compensate for the climate change, or even to allay its effects.
>
> N.Y. Times, 1978: "International Team of Specialists finds no End in Sight to 30-Year cooling trend in Northern Hemisphere"

It is evident to many that government and United Nations press releases and summaries do not accurately reflect the reports themselves. Distinguished climate scientists, some of whom contributed to the actual reports, are embarrassed by some media portrayals of the science. It should also be pointed out that assessment reports average results from an ensemble made up of a few dozen models from research groups around the world. The implication has traditionally been that the various climate models generally agree. That simply is not the case. Model results differ dramatically both from each other and from observations. Still, another concern is that some modelers have a propensity to "adjust" or "tune" their model to deal with troublesome inconsistencies or paper over irksome uncertainties. Is it possible they have an intrinsic bias to having their results fit a certain pre-ordained narrative? Just wondering.

I have lived long enough to have contracted a serious case of "The Boy Who Cried Wolf" syndrome. I'm sure it is an affliction shared with many of my peers who are closing in on long tooth status. Over the years we have witnessed a steady parade of doomsayers proclaiming the end is near due to some reason or other. The Reverend Thomas Robert Malthus deserves credit for being the founder and leading proponent of modern-day fearmongering. In his 1798 writings, "An Essay on the Principle of Population," he put forth the concept that population growth is potentially exponential while the growth of the food supply and other resources is linear, which eventually reduces living standards to the point of triggering a population collapse. Fortunately, Malthusianism has been discredited, primarily due to advances in agricultural techniques and modern reductions in human fertility. Will climate change suffer a similar fate? Time will tell.

THE MANY BENEFITS OF FOSSIL FUELS

Fossil fuels have received an unwarranted bad rap over the past couple of decades. Does it ever occur to anybody that fossil fuels have been a major, if not the major, contributor to the dramatic increase in the world's standard of living over the past couple of centuries, as well as a significant reason for the virtual eradication of organized mass human muscle power (slavery)? Following are comments from the British journalist, Matt Ridley – "Human enslavement was the most common way of getting other people to expend energy on your behalf until fairly recently. Now, our "slaves" are machines, powered by nonhuman energy. Current prosperity for much of the masses is made possible by the invention of energy- substitutes for slavery. Were it not for fossil fuels, 99% of people would have to live in slavery for the rest to have a decent standard of living."

124

Fossil fuels are a uniquely cost-effective source of energy. That can partly be attributed to the fact that in comparison to the predominant renewables, the energy offered by fossil fuels is concentrated and dense. A general rule of thumb in energy generation is that the more concentrated a source of raw energy, the better. Another advantage of fossil fuels is that energy is available to us in its naturally stored form and the source of this energy is mobile. It can be moved great distances for use in other locations. Also, unlike the sun and the wind, the energy derived from oil, coal, and natural gas is both consistent and controllable. There is no downtime when the wind stops blowing or the sun stops shining. Lastly, there is still a natural abundance of fossil fuels. We've only scratched the surface of what is available for extraction.

Fossil fuels have led to improved internal air quality in the parts of the world where it is used for cooking and heating a dwelling. Until approximately 100 years ago, the energy for cooking and heating was provided by burning wood and animal dung. Globally, wood went from providing nearly all primary energy in 1850 to 50% in 1920 to just 7% today. There are still places in the world where people breathe indoor smoke every day. According to the World Health Organization, indoor air pollution shortens the lives of four million people per year. The poor folks that suffer from this condition don't gripe about inhaling these fumes in their abodes. They complain more often about how much time it takes to chop wood, haul wood, start fires, and maintain them.

What is climate change doing to nature? Based on what we hear every day, it's turning green pastures and forests into dust bowls. The reality is the opposite. Warming and more carbon dioxide (plant food) in the atmosphere facilitate positives along with negatives. The overwhelming cause of global greening is carbon dioxide fertilizer. Roughly 40 percent of the planet has seen "greening" – the production of more forest and other biomass growth - between 1981 and 2016. New tree growth, primarily in North America and Europe, has exceeded tree loss on a global basis for the last 35 years. Crop yields have never been higher, and part of the credit can be given to the boost provided by carbon dioxide. Credit also should be given to one of the most important inventions in the 20th century – the "Haber- Bosch process." Through this process, we can transform natural gas into fertilizer. Artificially "fixing" nitrogen in this process feeds half the world.

As acknowledged, the planet is getting warmer. Historically, most human beings have wanted the world to be a warmer place. Cold weather is far more dangerous than hot weather. As the world gets warmer, people benefit. Heat kills within a few days, whereas cold kills over weeks. Carbon dioxide warming is occurring mostly in the northern latitudes (very cold places). It is more prevalent during the winter months (when people usually want to be warmer) than in the summer months. Lastly, the temperature change is more noticeable during the night compared to the day.

Electric Vehicles will become more and more common sight on our nation's highways and streets. It will undoubtedly take longer than many folks want and anticipate, but it is only a matter of time. The same cannot be said for the heavyweights, the workhorses of the global economy. I am referring to the ocean tankers and cargo ships, the towboats, airplanes, semi-trucks, and the oversized earth-moving machines. Something of that size does not currently lend itself to the battery technology that powers electric cars. Fossil fuels will continue to dominate the transportation of physical products. Also, sun and wind-generated electricity are not conducive to generating the very high levels of heat required in the process of making plastics, cement, and steel. Those are three of the four pillars of modern civilization according to Vaclav Smil. Professor Smil's fourth pillar is ammonia, the byproduct of the aforementioned "Haber-Bosch process" that "fixes" nitrogen from natural gas.

MYTHS SURROUNDING FOSSIL FUELS

The legacy media establishment habitually sensationalizes every weather incident and reinforces the concept that unprecedented weather events are transpiring before our very eyes. They go on to promote that any changes in the global climate system are

126

almost 100% due to man-made carbon dioxide emissions. In reality, there is nothing whatsoever "unprecedented" going on in terms of the amount of carbon dioxide in the atmosphere or the average temperature on Earth. Itemized below are four basic truths about the history of climate:

1. The global climate system is near historic lows in carbon dioxide and temperature.
2. By many estimates, the peak of historical carbon dioxide levels was 15 times today's level.
3. Life on Earth thrived at far higher CO2 levels in the past.
4. Planetary warming is concentrated in colder parts of the Earth.

One wonders if we are experiencing more extreme weather, or if are we suffering from extreme exaggeration. Whether it's drought, flooding, forest fires, or destructive hurricanes, serious weather events are inevitably cast by the media as evidence that climate change is not only real but also urgent and disastrous. The Intergovernmental Panel on Climate Change (IPCC) is a United Nations body of 195 scientists and other members from around the globe responsible for assessing the science related to climate change. Rightly or wrongly, it is considered the gold standard for climate assessment. The IPCC's most recent Assessment Report was issued in 2021. The language in the actual report in many cases runs contrary to what is expressed in the media.

The IPCC's 2021 Assessment Report shows that the legacy media purported link between man-made climate change and drought is weak: "There is low confidence in attributing changes in drought over global land areas since the mid-20th century to human influence." And, "Since 1895, the total area of the lower 48 states that have been very dry certainly has not increased." The same Report addresses flooding with this language: "Confidence is in general low in attributing changes to human influence." The United Nations has estimated the total amount of flooding around the world and found that it's not clear whether it is even getting more or less frequent. In the early part of the last century, when there were few and mostly cheap houses to be flooded, an average year of floods claimed about half a percent of GDP (United States) each year, with the Great Flood of 1913 costing a still unrivaled 2.2 percent of GDP. Today, with many more and more costly houses, average floods over a year cost just over 0.05 percent of GDP -10 times less. Flooding takes a far less toll than it did a century ago.

Hurricanes are the costliest weather catastrophe. U.N. climate scientists looked at the evidence and concluded that globally, hurricanes are not increasing in frequency or intensity. The 2021 IPCC Assessment Report specifically states, "There is low confidence in attributing changes in hurricane activity to human influence." From Texas to Maine, the number of housing units within 30 miles of the coast increased from 4.4 million in 1940 to 26.6 million in 2000. Exposure to damage is much greater now.

Wildfires and forest fires have garnered significant media attention over the past few years. On a global basis, the acreage burned each year now is dramatically less than 100 years ago. Most of the current increase in the American West has little to do with climate and everything to do with forestry management and residential development. The underbrush in forests out West is extensive and provides the ideal kindling for fires. It needs to be cleaned up. Also, the number of homes built in high-fire-risk zones has increased big-time from half a million in 1940 to almost seven million in 2010.

Every four years the United States government issues its "Climate Science Special Report" (CSSR). The most recent report released in 2018 states: "The annual number of high-temperature records set display no significant trend over the past century nor the past 40 years, but the annual number of record cold nights has declined since 1895, somewhat more rapidly in the past 30 years."

Rising sea levels might be one area of concern that retain some legitimacy. Even there, however, the "chicken little" crowd tends to get over their skis and exaggerates claims. Over the past 20,000 years, contrary to the idea that sea level rise is accelerating in unprecedented ways, it has dramatically decelerated. Sea level rises are so slow as to be nearly nonexistent, measured in millimeters per decade, not feet per decade. Sea levels have risen about a foot over the past 150 years. According to geological records, the sea level has risen by about 400 feet since the Last Glacial Maximum (20,000 years ago), as rapidly as 5 inches per decade, until about 7,000 years ago, when the rate slowed dramatically.

Over the past 100 years, there has been an inverse correlation between increased carbon dioxide levels and people dying due to weather-related natural disasters. Deaths caused by weather-related disasters have declined precipitously over the past century. In the 1920s, those disasters killed almost half a million people a year. Today – fewer than 20,000. Over the past hundred years, the number of deaths from these types of catastrophes has plummeted by 96%. The global population has increased fourfold. Thus, the average personal risk of dying in a weather-related disaster has declined by 99%.

WHY THE HATRED?

Supporting the elimination of cost-effective energy while ignoring its benefits cannot be explained by ignorance of facts alone, and it cannot be explained by pleading ignorance that this is an irrational method of evaluation – everyone knows you should not support the elimination of something without first considering its benefits. So, what can explain it? I don't know if I have the answers, but I'll take a stab at explaining the inexplicable.

With the evolving demise of organized religion, droves of people, in particular young people, are searching for purpose and for something to hold on to as they navigate their way through life in arguably turbulent times. The ardent believers of climate change have to some extent adopted this cause almost as a secular religion. As Gerard Baker puts it in an editorial for The Wall Street Journal, "The High Church of Environmentalism has acquired many of the characteristics of its ecclesiastical predecessor. An apocalyptic eschatology warns that we will all be consumed by fire if we don't follow the ordained rules." Sumantra Maitra, writing for The Federalist, describes what he calls "Climate Worship" with much less tact, though with the same insistence that responses to the global climate crisis are creating a new religion, in all the worst ways.

Many of the other "players" in the climate change saga were incentivized to adopt a position that elevates a potential future issue and problem to that of a full-fledged present crisis of off-the-charts magnitude. Of course, with the media, it is always "If it bleeds it leads." There is never a time when there is not an extreme weather story somewhere in the world to support a sensational headline. Newsrooms are shrinking, and serious in-depth reporting is becoming less common. Most journalists reporting on climate don't have a background in science. For some journalists, too many in my opinion – climate change has become a cause and a mission - to save the world from destruction by humans. Politicians play an oversized role in kindling fear. They win elections by arousing passion and commitment from voters by motivating and persuading them. H.L. Mencken's 1918 book, *"In Defense of Women"* noted: "The whole aim of practical politics is to keep the populace alarmed (and hence clamorous to be led to safety) by menacing it with an endless series of hobgoblins, most of them imaginary."

Scientific institutions have been disappointing. In the preparation of official assessment reports, they often describe the data in ways that are actively misleading. All too often they attempt to make the science fit a narrative rather than ensure the narrative fits the science. Many scientists have been equally disappointing, succumbing to massive peer pressure.

More than a few climate contrarians have suffered public opprobrium and diminished career prospects for publicizing data that doesn't support the "broken climate" model. Activists and NGOs (Non-Government Organizations) are deep down the rabbit hole. If you believe there is a climate emergency, have built an organization on that premise, and rely upon your donor's continuing commitment to the cause, projecting urgency is crucial. The public does not escape scrutiny. Many people increasingly get their news and information from social media sources. They tend to believe, and trust, their chosen media in areas outside their expertise. That is a terrifying proposition.

I also think some people oppose fossil fuels because they object to development and economic growth in general. They object to the significant impact that the various sources of energy have on the rest of nature. These folks who hold "Anti-impact" views are equal opportunity energy dissenters. They hate fossil fuels because they are considered "dirty" and spew carbon dioxide into the atmosphere. But they also dislike nuclear energy because of potential problems with radiation and waste. Hydropower received criticism from this group because it interferes with free-flowing rivers. Even solar and wind-generated energy ends up in the Anti-impactor's doghouse. This is because solar and wind require large-scale mining and extensive land use.

I grow weary of those who believe our planet is a pristine, perfect orb that is delicately balanced with nature that is at great risk due to violent attacks on the environment perpetuated by Homo sapiens. In many quarters, that is known as the "Delicate Nurturer" gospel, which I opine is a boatload of unadulterated crap. The Earth is not a naturally nurturing "delicate balance" best left untouched by man. It is rather a naturally dynamic, deficient, dangerous place that we must massively impact if we are to survive and flourish. I'm also going to go out on a limb and claim the most ardent supporters of the anti-impact movement are also anti-human. This is not a new phenomenon. Throughout history and today, some people support anti-human policies even when they have the factual and methodological knowledge to know they are supporting anti-human policies. Their primary moral goal is anti-human.

50 – 70 YEARS

Despite the excessive hand-wringing, claims the sky is falling, and melt-down in general, I have some discouraging news for stressed-out climate changers: The transition to Green Energy is not going to transpire over the next 10-20 years, and it's going to be a long time until global carbon dioxide emissions begin their gradual decline. A more reasonable estimate for the global economy to wean itself from fossil fuels would be in the 50 -70 year range. Fossil fuels currently supply 80% of the world's energy and remain the most reliable and convenient means of meeting growing energy demand. Renewable energy sources currently provide 20% of our planet's electricity, primarily from hydroelectric. When measured against all energy use, wind turbines provide only 3% and solar panels an anemic 1%. Energy demand is expected to grow by about 50% through mid-century as most of the world's inhabitants improve their lot. Because of this anticipated demand, it is highly likely our share of renewable energy in 2050 will still be around 20%, not 100%.

Most of the world desperately needs more energy. Residents of the United States are fortunate to be part of the 2 billion people who reside in what is considered the "empowered world." Approximately 3.5 billion people live in the "barely empowered world." That leaves 2.4 billion people who call the "unempowered world" home. There are five times as many people "developing" as there are "developed." Presently, total emissions from the developed vs. the developing world are equal. That will change over the course of the century. Combined, China and India represent just under one-third of the world's population. They would both fall into the category of "developing" countries. China is the undisputed leader in carbon dioxide emissions, with the United States a distant second. Of the top 10 countries with the highest emissions, the cumulative emissions of countries 2-10 approximate that of China unilaterally. By 2030, India will probably displace the U.S. for the number two spot. China is leading the world in new coal power plants, building more than three times as much new coal power capacity as all other countries combined in 2020. India expects their power demand to more than double in the next 10 years and is looking at new coal-fired plants as the primary source of meeting demand.

PARIS AGREEMENT

In December 2015, leaders from almost every country in the world approved the Paris Agreement on climate change. French President Francois Hollande said: "This is a historic moment, not just for us but for our children, our grandchildren, and future generations." Al

Gore saw it as "bold and historic." Unfortunately, they are wrong. The Paris Agreement will cost a fortune to carry out and do almost no good. It is not a binding agreement with enforcement parameters. Each country simply declared how much carbon dioxide emissions it would reduce until the year 2030. Some countries made ambitious promises, while others made far easier to achieve-vows.

Supporters of the Paris Agreement sometimes accept that promises through 2030 will achieve next to nothing, but then argue that further down the road, the pact has the potential to achieve much more. So, do we give the politicians the benefit of the doubt and believe that governments will break with historic precedent and honor their commitments? I for one say, "No. Hell no!" The two previous global climate agreements in Rio de Janeiro in 1992 and Kyoto in 1997 came to virtually nothing at the end of their deal periods. To think Paris is different would be unrealistic and display extreme naivety. Leaders of various nations will blow a surplus of verbal hot air and expect the handful of large, wealthy nations to fund the entire enterprise estimated at $1 - $2 trillion each year. If fully implemented to that extent, it will do almost nothing for the climate. All of the Paris Agreement's promises will reduce the temperature rise by the end of the century by an almost imperceptible 0.05 degrees Fahrenheit. Spending trillions to achieve virtually nothing is a bad idea.

HURTING THE POOR

Climate policy places an unfair burden on poor countries and poor people. The inevitable higher energy prices have a disproportionately negative impact on the poor. Climate policies often make life needlessly challenging for the poor. Poor countries need much more power at a low cost, not fickle power at a high cost. Today's nonsensical climate policies are putting the world's worst-off countries on a slower path to progress and prosperity. For the poorest regions the best policies should focus on economic growth and development, not climate. Resources are needlessly consumed that could have been spent making people's lives healthier, longer, and more prosperous. Rising prosperity means more money to spend on adaptation – building better homes, building improved transportation, and infrastructure systems in vulnerable parts of the world. It also means more money for fighting malnutrition and improving education.

In a comprehensive study published in 2018 in "Nature Climate Change," results indicated that strong global action to reduce climate change would cause far more hunger and food insecurity than climate change itself. The huge growth in biofuels mightily contributed to a reduction in food and an increase in food prices; a confidential World Bank report obtained by the "Guardian" found that biofuels had forced global food prices up by 75 percent. The charity "ActionAid" calculated that the number of crops needed to fill an SUV's fuel tank with biofuel would feed a child for an entire year, and every gallon of biofuel wiped out 40 meals.

The truth is that climate policies hurt the poor everywhere, even in wealthy countries like the United States. One 2019 study showed that U.S. low-income consumers spend 85% more on electricity as a percentage of total expenditures than high-income consumers. Rich elites have no problem saying we should increase gas prices to $20 a gallon – they can easily afford it. Many people are struggling to pay their energy bills. The International Energy Agency estimates that 10 percent of Americans, or thirty-two million, are "energy poor," spending more than 10 percent of their income on energy. This means poor Americans often literally have to forgo other basics to heat (or cool) their homes sufficiently.

NUCLEAR POWER

Nuclear power is a promising alternative to fossil fuels. It is clean, carbon-free, 24/7 power, 365 days a year. It's scalable more quickly than other carbon-free sources and takes up far less space. Nuclear energy could get us to the cleaner future that proponents of green energy want – without wrecking the global economy. In terms of efficiency, nuclear power blow competing energy sources out of the water. Below is an itemization of power sources and their respective "capacity factors:"

Nuclear	-	92.5%
Geothermal	-	74.3%
Natural Gas	-	56.6%
Hydropower	-	41.5%
Coal	-	40.2%
Wind	-	35.5%
Solar	-	24.9%

In other words, nuclear power plants operated at full capacity 92.5% of the time during the year. Whereas wind turbines and solar panels bring up the rear at 35.5% and 24.9%, respectively. Nuclear power has the safest track record of any major source of energy. The only major nuclear accident in the U.S. – Three Mile Island in 1979 – caused neither death nor increase in cancer areawide. The 2011 "disaster" at the Fukushima plant in Japan also directly caused neither deaths nor disease from radiation exposure. Worldwide, there have been fewer than 150 deaths from nuclear plants, mostly from the 1986 Chornobyl accident, in which bad design and a series of operator errors led to a significant release of radiation. Detractors of nuclear power maintain that the "resulting waste disposal problem has become a major challenge for policymakers." In reality, as energy and environmental expert Michael Shellenberger has pointed out, "If all the nuclear waste from U.S. power plants were put on a football field, it would stack up just 50 feet high. In comparison to the waste produced by every other kind of electricity production, that quantity is close to zero." Given how little waste there is, it can be safely and affordably stored on-site, as it is today – and eventually used as fuel for more advanced nuclear plants.

We need to stop wasting trillions of dollars on strategies that punish American citizens and businesses while China and India increase their greenhouse-gas emissions. Massive subsidies for electric vehicles, wind turbines, and solar panels are a huge waste of money. The obvious solution is nuclear energy and there is no logical reason to explain why we are not aggressively moving in that direction. The anti-impact knowledge system has demonized nuclear energy using the rationalization of "safety" – even though in theory and practice nuclear energy is the safest form of energy. They hate nuclear energy because it impacts nature in ways they consider morally unacceptable, dealing with "unnatural" high-energy, radioactive materials and processes. This vilification of nuclear power, including the shutdown of existing nuclear plants that remain serviceable is a crime against humanity. Until so-called climate activists incorporate nuclear energy in their list of solutions to the problem, I am unable to take anything they say seriously.

As noted earlier in this chapter, fossil fuels have the advantage of being a naturally stored, concentrated, abundant source of energy. Nuclear energy has these advantages to a greater degree. Oil's amazing energy density makes it the fuel of mobility and is arguably the most valued material in the world. Well, the concentration of energy in uranium is more than a million times that of oil and two million times that of coal.

It is inexcusable that since the 1980s it has been virtually impossible to build new nuclear reactors in the U.S. Even with that ludicrous history, nuclear power has roughly supplied a fifth of America's power each year since 1990. Assuming common sense makes a return to the energy sector, nuclear energy can provide more low-cost, on-demand energy that can meaningfully supplement and someday even replace fossil fuels. Significant advances in nuclear power plant design that have improved efficiency and safety should no longer be ignored. One interesting approach is to replace large-scale nuclear facilities with many smaller, but safer, cheaper, and more manageable units known as Small Modular Reactors (SMRs).

It's time to start building.

ADAPTATION AND PROSPERITY

A number of those who predict terrible loss of life and unprecedented property damage over the remainder of this century due to climate change overlook a rather obvious factor.

Humanity has historically demonstrated an amazing capacity to adapt when circumstances dictate such. That ability to adapt will not simply evaporate as we move forward. There are intelligent ways at a reasonable cost to mitigate global warming in the event problems arise. Adaptation is a simple but effective first line of defense. Fossil fuels provide the ability to significantly neutralize any climate danger caused by carbon dioxide emissions. That would include combating heat waves with fossil-fueled air conditioning, and neutralizing drought with fossil-fueled irrigation and food transport. This has allowed and will continue to allow large swaths of our nation's population to live comfortably in hotspots such as Southern California, New Mexico, Arizona, Texas, and Florida.

Rising temperatures will have the biggest human health impact in urban environments. Black roofs can be deadly in a prolonged heat wave. White, reflective surfaces added to rooftops can dramatically lower the effects of a sustained heat wave. More urban vegetation and oases of green would help diminish temperatures in urban centers. Another idea is to paint streets and other areas of black asphalt with a cool, gray coating. People talk about rising sea levels in apocalyptic terms, but the truth is that there are proven and cost-effective ways to defend coastlines to ensure that more people and property are protected. Coastal defense in many cases will mean dikes but also measures like adding sand to beaches and the restoration of mangrove forests as is being done in Indonesia and elsewhere. It is estimated that each dollar spent on protection will avoid more than $100 of damage. Much can be learned by looking at the Netherlands' relationship with water. About one-third of Holland lies below sea level.

The left considers mere "adaptation" ignoble and cosmetic in nature. Al Gore, in his 1992 book, *"Earth in the Balance,"* mocked the idea that we can adapt effectively to rising carbon emissions, saying it reflected a "kind of laziness and arrogant faith in our ability to react in time to save our skins." Adaptation is casually dismissed, including assessments used by the U.S. Environmental Protection Agency that projected a future in which humans will fail to adapt to a gradually warming environment. This led to the absurd prediction that if northern cities like Chicago warm to the level of certain southern cities today, they will experience mass heat deaths that the southern cities don't experience today.

Increasing prosperity on a global level should be an important component of climate policy. Though it's often the opposite of traditional climate policy, promoting prosperity is likely the best way to protect the world's poor from global warming, and it improves their quality of life in countless other ways too. The United Nations estimates that even if no country does anything to slow global warming, the annual damage by 2100 will be equivalent to a 2.6% reduction in global gross domestic product. Given that the United Nations also expects the average person to be 450% as rich in 2100 as today, that figure falls only to 434% if the temperature rises unimpeded. This is a problem – but not the end of the world.

As indicated previously, for some reason the focus is always on the potential havoc rising temperatures could wreak, but none on that created by various mandated climate regulations. Only one side of the ledger is taken into account before knee-jerk policies are implemented. Policies to address global warming create more expensive energy and slow economic growth. Although there is one potential regulation for which I opine should be given consideration - a Carbon Tax. If it could be universally and equitably implemented, it could be beneficial. The tax would be introduced at a relatively modest level and then gradually increased over time. The fact that a Carbon Tax would be a market-based program appeals to me.

REASONABLE FUTURE ALTERNATIVES

Until we find a green energy source that is cheaper (without subsidies) than fossil fuels, it will be hard to convince the world to fundamentally turn away from fossil fuels. Whatever approaches are taken, I advocate making low-risk changes until we have a better understanding of why the climate is changing and how it might change in the future. It would behoove our leadership structure to make realistic and prudent choices in this area. The following are four possible sources of future energy. They would be hydrogen, nuclear fusion, air capture, and deep geothermal. Air capture is not technically a source of energy, but it would reduce carbon dioxide in the atmosphere.

Hydrogen is a naturally occurring gas that is also the most abundant element in the universe. It has enormous potential as an environmentally friendly alternative to fossil fuels because it only emits water when it is burned. That said, some hurdles still need to be overcome. The biggest issue is that hydrogen that leaks into the atmosphere can exacerbate the level of greenhouse gases in the atmosphere. In addition, hydrogen is a much lighter gas than gasoline which makes it difficult to store and transport. To be able to store it we need to compress it into a liquid and store it at a low temperature. The high amounts of pressure needed to store hydrogen make it a difficult fuel to transport in large quantities.

If ever mastered, nuclear fusion promises a virtually limitless form of clean energy. The operative word in the previous sentence is "if." The scientific community has been working on fusion for 90 years. Atomic experts rarely like to estimate when fusion energy may be widely available, often joking that, no matter when you ask, it is always 30 years away. If it is ever eventually mastered, fusion energy will power the world. Just one gram of fuel as input can create the equivalent of eight tons of oil in fusion power. To date, the most successful fusion experiment produced 59 megajoules of energy over five seconds (11 megawatts of power) - only enough to boil about 60 kettles worth of water. It has a way to go before coming to fruition but keep an eye on this possibility.

Industrial facilities are popping up around the world that remove carbon dioxide from the air and put it underground. The main challenges are scale and cost. It is even feasible to pull CO2 from the air and use it to make synthetic fuel. Instead of adding more carbon dioxide to the air from fossil fuels, we can simply recycle the same carbon dioxide molecules over and over. Currently, such technology is expensive – about $600 per ton of carbon dioxide. In a recent study, however, scientists say future chemical plants could drop that cost below $100 per ton.

I find the concept of energy produced by deep geothermal extremely interesting. Dig deep enough and, no surprise, it's hotter than hell down there. Typically, the temperature rises about 75 degrees Fahrenheit for each mile, and more the deeper you go. The steam wafting out of hot springs in Yellowstone National Park or other places where the Earth's crust is thin shows how much heat the mantle gives off. Scientists at NASA's Jet Propulsion Laboratory (JPL) have a strong interest in what is going on underneath Yellowstone. They have evaluated the caldera system under Yellowstone as well as the potential damage and probability of a super-volcanic eruption, which has happened at Yellowstone three times previously. The last such eruption was 631,000 years ago; the one before that was 669,000 years prior. It's not a matter of if it'll erupt, but when. The JPL determined that the devastation of such an eruption would exceed that of an asteroid 1.5 miles wide hitting Earth. Say hello to "volcanic winter" and mass starvation if this happens. Fortunately, the JPL also points to a potential solution – horizontal drilling for geothermal energy extraction – that would siphon off excess energy, providing enough electricity to power as many as 20 million homes for a few thousand years.

Fracking techniques would be used to generate energy with no carbon emissions. There is a huge upside to digging down miles and injecting water into underground reservoirs and then the heated water is pushed back out to generate steam and electricity. Why are so few talking about deep geothermal? Maybe because anything having to do with drilling is considered dirty and unsavory. Critics go on about the risk of seismic activity. But seismic activity from fracking oil and gas wells is fairly uncommon. It would be even less so with deep geothermal because the wells are much deeper and you're merely circulating fluids after the initial drilling to create the underground hot reservoir.

Improving the alternatives just detailed or coming up with entirely new alternatives will not happen without increased emphasis on research and development. Over the next five to 10 years, the United States and other nations need to significantly increase research and development expenditures to push down the price of alternatives or come up with concepts entirely new and viable expense-wise. When we invest in innovation, most ideas fail. An abundance of new technologies to power the world is not requisite. One or two would be game changers if carbon dioxide emissions are drastically reduced and the expense to achieve that goal on a global level is reasonably priced.

GEOENGINEERING

This is a controversial topic and it needs to be researched in great detail if and when any of the more aggressive measures are ever deployed. Geoengineering would be Plan "B" if conditions quickly went south, and temperatures escalated more rapidly than anybody anticipated. It is always wise to have a backup plan, and for that reason, we should start researching geoengineering technologies before we start playing God with the atmosphere. Geoengineering is the only approach that allows us to make fast, dramatic cuts in global temperature at a relatively low cost. There is also the possibility that a single nation, a rogue billionaire, or even a highly energized NGO could deploy the technology on their own with disastrous results. For that reason, the more we know about the inherent risks the more unlikely that will happen.

We already know how to cool the Earth expeditiously. History tells us that past volcanic eruptions of major magnitude have dropped temperatures a few degrees for a year or two. The abundant amounts of ash spewed into the atmosphere effectively reduced the amount of sunlight reaching the planet's surface. The additional particles in the atmosphere reflect sunlight and thus increase the Earth's albedo. We don't want to generate volcanic eruptions, but the same principle would work with a systemic seeding conducted by airplanes around the world. Other possibilities include engineering crops that would be more reflective of sunlight and installing giant mirrors in space that would divert sunlight from reaching the Earth. Another concept that has been considered is to brighten the oceans by creating microbubbles on the surface. Again, until we have a better understanding of the risks involved with these ideas, implementation should be deferred until it is imperative and we have a good handle on the likelihood of adverse consequences.

CLOSING COMMENTS

Humans appear to be exerting a growing, but physically small, warming influence on the climate. We would be remiss not to treat it as a potential problem. However, fixating on scary stories about climate change leads us to make poor policy decisions. It is important to make sure a preoccupation with climate change doesn't distract us from other crucial problems. Well-researched, emotionless policies need to be put in place that will both limit the extent of climate change and enable the world to best manage its impact. The move away from fossil fuels will not happen overnight. It must be gradual evolution and it should be acknowledged that any negative climate impacts of fossil fuels have and will continue to be outweighed by benefits. Fossil fuels have been essential to human flourishing and progress. Over the past century, the world has become a better place, thanks to human ingenuity and innovation. Call me an optimist, but I expect that pattern to continue.

RECOMMENDED BOOKS ON THE SUBJECT

There are numerous good books by authors who refuse to drink the climate Kool-aide. I've listed four below that I deem exceptionally relevant on the subject of climate change:

1. *"Unsettled"* by Steven E. Koonin
2. *"Apocalypse Never"* by Michael Shellenberger
3. *"False Alarm"* by Bjorn Lomborg
4. *"Fossil Future"* by Alex Epstein

CHAPTER NINE

RACE IN AMERICA

SLAVERY

It would be egregious to begin a discussion on "Race in America" without first addressing the history of the chronically evil practice of slavery. This history spans many cultures, nationalities, and religions from ancient times to the present day. The practice of slavery has existed in many – if not most- cultures. The victims of slavery have come from many different ethnicities and religious groups. The social, economic, and legal positions of enslaved people have differed vastly in different times and places. Slavery was widespread in the ancient world. It was found in many ancient civilizations, including the Roman Empire. Both Christians and Muslims captured and enslaved each other during centuries of warfare in the Mediterranean regions. Beginning in the 16th century, European merchants, starting with Portugal, initiated the transatlantic slave trade, purchasing enslaved Africans from West African kingdoms and transporting them to Europe's colonies in the Americas. The transatlantic slave trade was eventually curtailed due to European and American governments passing legislation abolishing their nation's involvement in it. Although slavery is no longer legal anywhere in the world, human trafficking remains an international problem. An estimated 25-40 million people are presently enslaved, the majority in Asia.

Slavery was endemic in Africa and part of the structure of

everyday life throughout the 15th to the 18th century. During that period, it is estimated that anywhere between one-third and one-half of the entire population of various African states consisted of enslaved people. Slavery in Ethiopia persisted until 1942. The Atlantic slave trade peaked in the late 18th Century when the largest number of people were captured and enslaved in raiding expeditions into the interior of West Africa. These expeditions were typically carried out by African states. Europeans rarely entered the interior of Africa, due to fear of disease and fierce African resistance. The enslaved people were brought to coastal outposts where they were traded for goods. The people captured in these expeditions were shipped by European traders to the colonies of the New World. It is estimated that over centuries, 12-20 million enslaved people were shipped from Africa by European traders. The majority were shipped to the Americas. Selling captives or prisoners was a common practice among Africans, Turks, Berbers, and Arabs during that era. African chieftains would barter their enslaved people to Arab, Berber, Ottoman, or European buyers for rum, spices, cloth, or other goods.

SLAVERY IN AMERICA

The legal institution of human chattel slavery, comprising the enslavement of Africans and African Americans, existed from 1619 until 1865, predominantly in the South. Before the nation's birth in 1776, approximately 125,000 slaves were shipped to the Thirteen Colonies that ultimately formed the United States. The last 25 years of the 18th century and the first 25 years of the 19th century saw another 175,000 slaves shipped to the United States. Under the law, an enslaved person was treated as property that could be bought, sold, or given away. Slavery existed in about half of the U.S. states until abolition.

During and immediately following the American Revolution (1775-1783), abolitionist laws were passed in most Northern states and a movement developed to abolish slavery. The role of slavery under the United States Constitution (1789) was the most contentious issue during its drafting. Although the creators of the Constitution never used the word "slavery," the final document, through the three-fifths clause, gave slave owners disproportionate political power. All Northern states had abolished slavery in some way by 1805. The Atlantic slave-trade was outlawed by individual states starting during the American Revolution.

The rapid expansion of the cotton industry in the Deep South after the invention of the cotton gin greatly increased demand for slave labor, and the Southern states continued as slave societies. The United States became ever more polarized over the issue of slavery, split into slave and free states. The total slave population in the South eventually reached four million. By 1850, the newly rich, cotton-growing South was threatening to secede from the Union and tensions continued to rise. When Abraham Lincoln won the 1860 election based on a platform of halting the expansion of slavery, seven slave states seceded to form the Confederacy. Shortly afterward, on April 12, 1861, the Civil War began when Confederate forces attacked the U.S. Army's Fort Sumter in Charleston, South Carolina. Four additional slave states subsequently joined the Confederacy. The Civil War was long and bloody. The most-accepted estimate was about 620,000 dead, with 360,000 Union deaths and 260,000 Confederate deaths. Within months of the Union victory, the Thirteenth Amendment to the United States Constitution was ratified on December 6, 1865, prohibiting "slavery and involuntary servitude, except as a punishment for crime."

There is a persistent myth in some historical circles that contends slavery was essential for industrialization and American economic hegemony. Both of those claims are unequivocally false. In 1847, the famous political philosopher, Karl Marx, wrote: "Without slavery, you have no cotton; without cotton, you have no modern industry... cause slavery to disappear and you will have wiped America off the map of nations." As with most of his postulations concerning economics, Marx was proven wrong. Following the Civil War and the abolition of slavery in 1865, historical data show there was a recession, but after that, post-war economic growth rates rivaled or surpassed the pre-war growth rates, and America continued on its path to becoming the number one political and economic superpower, ultimately superseding Great Britain. Slavery was neither a central driving force nor economically necessary for American economic dominance.

While slavery was an important part of the antebellum economy, claims about its central role in the Industrial Revolution and in America's rise to power via export-led growth are exaggerated. While cotton exports comprised a tremendous share of total exports prior to the Civil War, they accounted for only around 5 percent of the nation's overall gross domestic production, an important contribution but not the backbone of American economic development. One can certainly argue that slavery made the slaveholders and those connected to the cotton trade extremely wealthy in the short run, but the long-term impact of slavery on total American economic development, particularly in the South, is undeniably and certainly negative. As David Meyer of Brown University explains, in the pre-war South, "investments were heavily concentrated in slaves, failing to build a deep and broad industrial infrastructure," such as railroads, public education, and a centralized financial system. A logical conclusion would be that slavery in the first 90 years of our country's existence was a national tragedy that also inhibited economic growth over the long run and created social and racial divisions that still haunt the nation.

JIM CROW

Jim Crow laws were state and local laws enforcing racial segregation in the Southern United States. These laws were enacted in the late 19th and early 20th centuries by white Southern Democrat-dominated state legislatures to disenfranchise and remove political and economic gains made by African Americans during the Reconstruction period. Jim Crow laws were enforced until 1965. In practice, Jim Crow laws mandated racial segregation in all public facilities in the states of the former Confederate States of America and some others, beginning in the 1870s. Jim Crow laws were upheld in 1896 in the case of Plessy vs. Ferguson, in which the Supreme Court laid out its "separate but equal" legal doctrine concerning facilities for African Americans. Although in theory, the "equal" segregation doctrine was extended to public facilities and transportation too, facilities for African Americans were consistently inferior and underfunded compared to facilities for white Americans; sometimes there were no facilities for the black community at all. Far from equality as a body of law, Jim Crow institutionalized economic, educational, political, and social disadvantages and second-class citizenship for most African Americans living in the United States.

The origin of the phrase "Jim Crow" has often been attributed to "Jump Jim Crow," a song-and-dance caricature of black people performed by white actor Thomas D. Rice in blackface, first performed in 1828. As a result of Rice's fame, Jim Crow had become by 1838 a pejorative expression meaning "Negro." When Southern legislatures passed laws of racial segregation directed against African Americans at the end of the 19th century, these statutes became known as Jim Crow laws. Among those blatantly racist acts were laws to make voter registration and electoral rules more restrictive, with the result that political participation by most black people began to decrease. As a result, voter turnout dropped dramatically throughout the South. In Louisiana, by 1900, black voters were reduced to 5,320 on the rolls, although they comprised the majority of the state's population. By 1910, only 730 black people were registered, less than 0.5% of eligible black men. Schools were another area of glaring differences. While public schools had been established by Reconstruction legislatures for the first time in most Southern states, those for black children were consistently underfunded compared to schools for white children, even when considered within the strained finances of the postwar South where the decreasing price of cotton kept the agricultural economy at a low.

The advent and enforcement of Jim Crow laws in the South should not be considered a surprising development. Bigotry was widespread in the South after slavery became a racial caste system.

White Southerners deeply resented African Americans, who represented the Confederacy's Civil War defeat and humiliation. They exerted their political power to segregate public spaces and facilities in law and reestablish social dominance over black people. The decline of Jim Crow started slowly in the early years of the 20th century and picked up steam in the 1950s. In the landmark case Brown vs. Board of Education (1954), the United States Supreme Court ruled unanimously (9-0) that public school segregation was unconstitutional. This decision had far-reaching social ramifications. Meanwhile, racial integration of all-white collegiate sports teams started to evolve during the 1950s. The cynic in me thinks that alumni demanding top players to win games superseded the concept of racial equality – at least initially. In 1955, Rosa Parks refused to give up her seat on a city bus to a white man in Montgomery, Alabama. This act of civil disobedience was chosen, symbolically, as an important catalyst in the growth of the Civil Rights Movement and the ultimate destruction of Jim Crow laws between 1964 and 1968.

CIVIL RIGHTS MOVEMENT

The civil rights movement was a political movement and campaign from 1954 to 1968 in the United States to abolish institutional racial segregation, discrimination, and disenfranchisement throughout the United States. The movement made its largest legislative gains in the 1960s after years of direct actions and grassroots protests. The social movement's major nonviolent resistance and civil disobedience campaigns eventually secured new protections in federal law for the civil rights of all Americans.

The Supreme Court made a series of rulings in the 1950s and 1960s that struck down many of the laws that had allowed racial segregation and discrimination during the Jim Crow era. Besides banning segregation in public schools and public facilities, a ruling struck down all state laws banning interracial marriage. In the 1960s the United States Congress passed several significant pieces of federal legislation that authorized oversight and enforcement of civil rights laws. The Civil Rights Act of 1964 explicitly banned all discrimination based on race, including racial segregation in schools, businesses, and in public accommodations. The Voting Rights Act of 1965 restored and protected voting rights by authorizing federal oversight of registration and elections in areas with historic under-representation of minority voters. The Fair Housing Act of 1968 banned discrimination in the sale or rental of housing.

Preceding the flurry of civil rights legislation in the 1960s, multiple major events contributed to the ultimate fruition of these new federal laws. One such event was the brutal murder of Emmett Till, a 14-year-old African American from Chicago visiting relatives in Money, Mississippi, during the summer of 1955. Following an alleged incident with a white woman, young Till was beaten and mutilated by the woman's husband and brother (both later acquitted) before being shot in the head and dumped in the Tallahatchie River. After Emmett's mother, Mamie Till came to identify the remains of her son, she decided she wanted to "let the people see what I have seen." Till's mother then had his body taken back to Chicago where she had it displayed in an open casket during the funeral services. Many thousands of visitors arrived to show their respects. "Emmett's murder," historian Tim Tyson writes, "would never have become a watershed historical moment without Mamie finding the strength to make her private grief a public matter." The visceral response to his mother's decision to have an open casket for Emmett's funeral mobilized the black community throughout the United States. The incident involving Rosa Parks in 1955 was brought up in the previous section. Her arrest led to a boycott of public buses that lasted 381 days and was supported by 90% of Montgomery's (Alabama) 50,000 black residents. The boycott reduced bus revenues significantly, as Blacks comprised the majority of the riders. The local ordinance segregating African Americans and whites on public buses was repealed.

A crisis erupted in Little Rock, Arkansas, when Governor Orval Faubus called out the National Guard on 9/4/57 to prevent entry to nine African American students who had successfully sued for the right to attend an integrated school, Little Rock Central High School. President Dwight D. Eisenhower then federalized the National Guard in Arkansas and ordered them to return to their barracks. Eisenhower then deployed elements of the 101st Airborne Division to Little Rock to protect the students.

Martin Luther King Jr. is often cited as the most visible leader of the civil rights movement. Under King's leadership, the predominant use of protest was nonviolent, or peaceful. Often referred to as pacifism, the method of nonviolence is considered to be an attempt to impact society positively. The philosophical method of nonviolence employed in the American civil rights movement was largely inspired by Mahatma Gandhi's "non-cooperation" policies during his involvement in the Indian independence movement. The strategy was to gain attention so that the public would either "intervene in advance," or "provide public pressure in support of the action to be taken." During the 1950s and 1960s in America, the nonviolent protesting of the civil rights movement caused definite tension, which garnered national attention.

One form of nonviolent protesting involved "sit-ins" at lunch counters at diners and restaurants. The protesters were encouraged to dress professionally, to sit quietly, and to occupy every other stool so that potential white sympathizers could join in. Freedom Rides were journeys by civil rights activists on interstate buses into the segregated South. Activists traveled through the Deep South to integrate seating patterns on buses and desegregate bus terminals, including restrooms and water fountains. These Freedom Rides were not without risk and beatings were not uncommon.

Martin Luther King was among many protesters arrested and jailed during a peaceful protest in Birmingham, Alabama, on April 12, 1963. While in jail, King wrote his famous "Letter from Birmingham Jail" on the margins of a newspaper, since he had not been allowed any writing paper while held in solitary confinement. Supporters appealed to the Kennedy administration, which intervened to obtain King's release. Walter Reuther, president of the United Auto Workers, arranged for $160,000 to bail out King and his fellow protesters. King was also a prominent figure in the

"March on Washington" (8/28/63). An estimated 200,000 to 300,000 demonstrators gathered in front of the Lincoln Memorial where King delivered his famous "I Have a Dream" speech. After the march, King and other civil rights leaders met with President Kennedy at the White House. At the time, there were not enough votes in Congress to pass the Civil Rights Act. However, when President Kennedy was assassinated on November 22, 1963, the new President Lyndon Johnson decided to use his influence in Congress to bring about much of Kennedy's legislative agenda – starting on July 2, 1964, when President Johnson signed the Civil Acts Right of 1964. A year later, on August 6, 1965, Johnson signed the Voting Rights Act of 1965, which suspended literacy tests and other subjective voter registration tests. Within four years of the bill's passing, voter registration in the South had more than doubled. The Fair Housing Bill was the most contentious civil rights legislation of the era. It was the most filibustered legislation in U.S. history.

A day after delivering his stirring "I've Been to the Mountaintop" sermon, which has become famous for his vision of American society, Martin Luther King was assassinated on April 4, 1968. Less than a week after King was murdered, Congress passed and Johnson signed the Civil Rights Act of 1968 that dealt with fair housing. The Act prohibited discrimination concerning the sale, rental, and financing of housing based on race, religion, and natural origin. It also made it a federal crime to "by force or by the threat of force, injure, intimidate, or interfere with anyone… because of their race, religion, color, or natural origin."

THE 1619 PROJECT

For those not familiar with this work of journalism, "The 1619 Project" is a series of ten written essays compiled by a writer at The New York Times named Nikola Hannah – Jones. The first edition appeared in a 100–page issue of The New York Times Magazine on August 14, 2019. The publication was timed to coincide with the 400th anniversary of the arrival of the first enslaved Africans in colonial Virginia. In 1619, a group of 20 or so captive Africans arrived in the Virginia Colony. An English privateer operating under a Dutch letter of marque, "White Lion," carried the slaves who had been captured in joint African – Portuguese raids against the Kingdom of Ndongo in modern-day Angola, making its landing at Point Comfort in the English Colony of Virginia. The creator of "The 1619 Project" attempts to replace the actual 1776 founding of our country with the arrival of a couple of dozen slaves in Virginia in 1619 as noted above.

Furthermore, "The 1619 Project" maintains that slaves are responsible for everything that made America prosperous. A consistent theme running through "The 1619 Project" is that white Americans were universally oppressors, immoral and evil. While black Americans were universally victims, moral and good. Needless to say, this work sparked a tidal wave of controversy. It is my opinion that Hannah – Jones' creation distorts, even fictionalizes, history to suit the Marxist ideology that traces every ill in society back to capitalism. The questionable claims of the author are so lacking facts, details, and evidence that a reasonable person could only conclude that there are either nefarious motives at play or a profound ignorance of accepted history.

Nikola Hannah – Jones postulates that our Declaration of Independence was drafted primarily to protect the institution of slavery. In 1776, she maintains, Great Britain was on the verge of abolishing slavery and the slave trade, thus provoking the colonists into independence. This claim is patently false. In 1776 Great Britain was not threatening to abolish slavery in its empire. Few if any British colonists in 1776 were frightened of British abolitionism. It was the American colonists who were interested in abolitionism in 1776. Far from protecting slavery, the American Revolution inflicted a massive blow to the entire slave system of the New World. Not only were the Northern states the first slave-holding governments in the world to abolish slavery, but the United States became the first nation in the world to begin actively suppressing the despicable international slave trade.

Hannah – Jones laid another egg when she claimed the slaves in Thomas Jefferson's Monticello "struggled under a brutal system of slavery, unlike anything that had existed in the world before." What?! As pointed out earlier in this chapter, since the advent of civilization, slavery has existed across the world and throughout history, in many cases much more oppressive and brutal than slavery in North America. Slavery was a commonly accepted practice at that time and more of the rule than the exception.

There are also some significant misdirects and omissions in "The 1619 Project." For instance, the prose gives the impression that packs of white men retained by slave traders commonly ventured into the interior of West Africa and kidnapped Africans from their idyllic farms and villages. This is far from the case. There was constant warfare between the tribes along the west coast of Africa. Strong, victorious tribes, when they did not kill, took captives, made slaves, and sold those slaves to white slavers for transport to the New World. "The 1619 Project" also conveniently forgot to mention the fact that it was not exceptionally rare for there to be black slave owners in 19th Century America. Some free African Americans had no reservations about buying and selling their fellow African Americans at the block.

GEORGE FLOYD AND SUBSEQUENT RIOTS

It's not often that an abuser of illegal drugs who was also a convicted felon with an extensive rap sheet can suddenly morph into an international martyr and hero to many. This rare feat was accomplished, posthumously, by George Perry Floyd, Jr. Mr. Floyd was a 46-year-old African American man who was killed by a white police officer in Minneapolis, Minnesota, during an arrest after a store clerk suspected Floyd may have used a counterfeit twenty-dollar bill. On May 25, 2020. Derek Chauvin, one of four police officers who arrived on the scene, knelt on Floyd's neck and back for somewhere between eight and nine minutes which facilitated Floyd's death. After his death, protests against police brutality, especially toward black people, quickly spread across the United States and globally. George Floyd's dying words, "I can't breathe," became a rallying cry.

Between 1997 and 2005, Floyd served eight jail terms on various charges, including drug possession, theft, and trespass. In 2007, Floyd faced charges of aggravated robbery with a deadly weapon; according to investigators, he had entered an apartment by impersonating a water department worker and barging in with five other men. He then held a pistol to a pregnant woman's stomach while his co-robbers searched for money, drugs, and items to steal. Floyd was arrested three months later during a traffic stop, and victims of the robbery identified him from a photo array. In 2009, Floyd was sentenced to five years in prison as part of a plea deal and subsequently paroled in January 2013.

George Floyd had been fired from his delivery driver job in January 2020 and was looking for another job when the Covid-19 pandemic hit Minnesota. In March (2020) Floyd was hospitalized after overdosing on drugs. The following month he contracted Covid-19 but recovered a few weeks later. On May 25, 2020, police were called by a Cub Foods grocery store employee who suspected Floyd had used a fake $20 bill. Floyd was sitting in a car with two other passengers when the police arrived. The officers forcibly removed Floyd from the car and handcuffed him. Before ending up handcuffed and face-down on the pavement with Chauvin on top of him, Floyd resisted arrest. George Floyd was a big man – at the time of his autopsy, he was 6 feet 4 inches tall and weighed 223 pounds. The drama surrounding Floyd's arrest and subsequent death was recorded via a video on a witness's cell phone. The entire world would soon see this video.

The medical examiner found that Floyd's heart stopped while he was being restrained and that his death was a homicide, caused by "cardiopulmonary arrest, complicating law enforcement subdual, restraint, and neck compression," though fentanyl intoxication and recent methamphetamine use may have increased the likelihood of death. Officer Chauvin was ultimately found guilty by a jury of his peers. He was sentenced to 22.5 years in prison with the possibility of supervised release after 15 years. Floyd's family was able to alleviate some of the pain of George's demise when they settled a wrongful death lawsuit for $27 million with the City of

Minneapolis. I found George Floyd's death both unfortunate and unnecessary. That said, upon conducting an internal search for any remnants of empathy, I found none.

A series of protests and civil unrest against police brutality and racism started in Minneapolis within 24 hours of Floyd's death and continued through the summer of 2020. Protests quickly spread nationwide and to over 2,000 cities and towns in over 60 countries in support of the Black Lives Matter (BLM) movement. It is estimated that upwards of 20 million people participated at some point in the demonstrations in the U.S. While the majority of protests were peaceful, demonstrations in some cities featured looting, arson, and street skirmishes with police and counter-protesters. When all was said and done, over 15,000 people had been arrested and more than 20 people had died due to the unrest. Furthermore, the riots were responsible for $2 billion of property damages nationwide. For political reasons, Democratic governors and mayors were hesitant to crack down and thus allowed the violence and damage to property to be perpetuated. The protests also led to a wave of monument removals and institutional name changes. Without a doubt, the ongoing Covid-19 pandemic and emotions associated with the 2020 U.S. presidential election were also contributing factors to the civil unrest.

"Defund the police" is a slogan that supports removing funds from police departments and reallocating them to non-policing forms of public safety and community support, such as social services, youth services, housing, education, healthcare, and other community resources. Among some liberal politicians and activists, this slogan became common during the George Floyd protests. Among the general public, however, the concept of defunding is unpopular. A 2021 Gallup survey found that 81% of African Americans wanted police to spend the same amount of time or more time in their neighborhoods, as did 86% of the sample as a whole. For that reason, it is unlikely defunding the police will come to fruition. Criminals usually weigh the possibility of getting caught when committing a crime. If there is a low likelihood of apprehension there will be more crimes committed – more people victimized.

Despite outlandish claims of police actively "hunting" Blacks and all African Americans living in constant fear of the police, there is no significant evidence of antiblack disparity in the likelihood of being fatally shot by police. The video of George Floyd's arrest is not representative of the 375 million annual contacts and 10 million annual arrests that police officers have with civilians. In 2019 police officers fatally shot 1,004 people, most of whom were armed or otherwise dangerous. African Americans were about a quarter of those killed by police officers   that year (235). The share of black victims is less than what black crime would predict. The police fatally shot nine unarmed blacks and 19 unarmed whites in 2019. A police officer is 18.5 times more likely to be killed by a black male than an unarmed black male is to be killed by a police officer. Police shootings are not the reason that blacks die of homicide at eight times the rate of whites and Hispanics combined; criminal violence is.

There is no question that a low percentage of police officers are "bad apples" and should not be wearing a badge. The police officer responsible for George Floyd's death had been the subject of more than a dozen complaints about his conduct. How can such men be allowed to "serve and protect"? Unions. Public-sector unions, particularly police unions, will do almost anything to protect their members. These unions create a culture of impunity. It is time to rethink public-sector unions, in particular police unions. Increasing turnover of public-sector jobs could help root out toxic employees. Officials need the ability to fire low-performing officers. That would help ensure that the most violent, disrespectful, and incompetent officers are dismissed each year. Conversely, it would also make sense to reward the top-performing police officers who go above and beyond the call of duty.

Another area of concern that needs to be addressed is the "blue wall of silence," also referred to as the "blue code" or the "blue shield." These are terms used to denote the informal code of silence among police officers in the United States not to report a colleague's errors, misconduct, or crimes, especially as related to police brutality. If questioned about an incident of alleged misconduct involving another officer, while following the code, the officer being questioned would perjure themselves by feigning ignorance of another officer's wrongdoing. Officers who follow the code are unable to report fellow officers who participate in corruption due to the unwritten laws of their "police family." This needs to stop. Officers who do not lie in court may sometimes be threatened and ostracized by fellow police officers. This also needs to stop. At a minimum, officers who falsify documents such as arrest reports, warrants, and evidence to provide cover for an illegal arrest or search need to be fired.

George Floyd, and many others that have suffered his fate, would probably be alive today if they had simply refrained from resisting arrest. Whether it be a police officer or any other armed individual, remedial common-sense dictates that you are assuming great risk if you initiate violence against him or her. The television personality, Mike Rowe, hit the nail on the head when he made the following comment: "I support peaceful protests, and I'm all for rooting out bad cops," Rowe concluded. "But let's not stop there. If we're serious about saving lives and eliminating the confrontations that led to the demise of Eric Garner and Michael Brown, let's also condemn the stupidity that leads so many Americans to resist arrest. I don't care if you're white, black, red, periwinkle, burnt umber, or chartreuse - resisting arrest is not a right, it's a crime. And it's never a good idea."

BLACK LIVES MATTER

The words "Black Lives Matter" represent both a concept and an organization. The organization came into existence shortly after the death of Michael Brown in August 2014 in Ferguson, Missouri. The concept, or the statement or slogan, "Black Lives Matter", is unassailable and probably affirmed by over 99% of the nation's population. The same cannot be said, however, for the organization. The racially tinged socialism and radical, extremist positions espoused by the organization, "Black Lives Matter," should concern everyone who cherishes freedom. The mainstream media has been negligent in not reporting BLM's policy platform and true aims.

Americans need to be made aware that BLM is a revolutionary political organization with an agenda no less comprehensive than reshaping the entire world. This movement seeks not to reform, but to pursue societal transformation under the guise of racial reconciliation.

The killing of George Floyd in May 2020 provided the "spark point" for BLM activists to take their cause, their movement, to the next level. So, what exactly do the leaders of BLM espouse? Following are the various policy platforms and demands endorsed by the organization, Black Lives Matter:

- Reparations for past and continuing harms, including both corporate and government reparations for a litany of ills that include "food apartheid" and "racialized capitalism." Government reparations will take the form of "a guaranteed minimum livable income for all black people."
- BLM's "universal health care" policy mandates that wealthy residents pay for a portion of health care services while low-income workers receive free services.
- Black people would be entitled to full and free access to lifetime education at any university, community college, or technical education facility, as well as retroactive forgiveness of student loans.
- Public schools would be transformed from centers of education to the delivery points of intersectional/multicultural studies and comprehensive welfare programs, including free abortions for minors.
- BLM proposes an end to arrests of any black students, and an end to all jails, detention centers, youth facilities, and prisons as we know them.
- BLM looks forward to the destruction of the traditional family: "We disrupt the Western-prescribed nuclear family structure requirement by supporting each other as extended families and "villages" that collectively care for one another, especially our children, to the degree that mothers, parents, and children are comfortable."

- BLM proposes to start a "global liberation movement" to overthrow capitalism. The specific policy states: "As oppressed people living in the U.S., the belly of global empire, we are in a critical position to build the necessary connections for a global liberation movement. Until we can overturn U.S. imperialism, capitalism, and white supremacy, our brothers and sisters around the world will continue to live in chains."
- According to BLM, America's alliance with Israel makes the U.S. complicit in the genocide taking place against the Palestinian people. It makes U.S. citizens complicit in the abuses committed by the Israeli government.
- BLM demands lawmakers cut the U.S. military budget by 50%.
- It (BLM) believes the federal government should focus on taxing "bads", not "goods." BLM would increase the death tax, the capital gains tax, impose new taxes on real estate transfers and financial "speculation," and create a national wealth tax.
- BLM would legalize prostitution and the possession and sale of all drugs, no matter the quantity. Prisoners convicted of these crimes would be released and their records retroactively expunged. Also, any government savings "must be invested into reparations to all people who have been adversely impacted by the war on drugs."
- The BLM manifesto insists the U.S. make reparations to countries and communities devastated by American warmongering, such as Somalia, Iraq, Libya, and Honduras.
- BLM's voting reforms demand universal voter registration, as well as pre-registration for 16-year-olds, the enfranchisement of formerly and currently incarcerated people, local and state residents voting for undocumented people, and a ban on all disenfranchisement laws.

BLM has more "demands," but this gives an accurate flavor of the platform Black Lives Matter would implement if given the opportunity. Before giving money or time to Black Lives Matter, I would suggest reviewing the policy positions just detailed above.

As previously mentioned, BLM hit the financial jackpot when George Floyd was killed in 2020. Due to the largesse of ultra-woke, virtue-signaling corporations and well-healed individuals, Black Lives Matter's internal reporting said it raised $93 million in 2020. BLM is registered as a 501(c) (3) entity (tax exempt) with the Internal Revenue Service. When you are granted this tax status, you are required to file Form 990 on an annual basis with the IRS. A Form 990 shows what the tax-exempt entity is doing with the money. BLM was delinquent in filing this form and its tax-exempt status was put on hold and not allowed to raise funds until it submitted the delinquent Form 990 for the 7/1/20 – 6/30/21 period. In May of 2022, the "missing" Form 990 was filed. It showed revenues of $80 million. Grants paid in the amount of $26 million, "other" expenses for $11 million, and a fiscal year-end (6/30/21) balance of $43 million in assets. BLM's finances have been subjected to criticism both from proponents and opponents. In April 2021, New York Magazine reported that funds were used to buy a house in California for $6 million in cash in October 2020 used by one of BLM's three founders. In January 2022, The Buffalo Tribune reported that BLM paid $8 million in cash to purchase a mansion in downtown Toronto. There are numerous other questionable financial transactions. Jacob Harold, a non-profit expert, said he was struck in particular by the number of paid employees listed on the aforesaid Form 990, which was just two, versus the number of volunteers, which was 49,275. He concluded by saying, "This 990 tells a story of weak non-profit governance."

Lastly, we will look at the three founders of Black Lives Matter. This trio is self-described "radical black organizers." Their names are Patrisse Cullors, Opel Tometi, and Alicia Garza. Cullors earned her bachelor's degree in religion and philosophy from UCLA. For the epigraph for her 2017 memoir, Cullors chose lines penned by Assata Shakur that echo Marx's "Communist Manifesto": "We must fight for our freedom/we must win/ We must love each other and support each other/We have nothing to lose but our chains."

Tometi attended the University of Arizona, where she earned her bachelor's degree in history and her master's in communication and advocacy. According to her BLM biography, Tometi "is a student of liberation theology." Alicia Garza may be the most radical of the BLM founders. When Verso Books decided to publish a third edition of "Revolution in the Air: Sixties Radicals Turn to Lenin, Mao, and Che," they asked Garza to write the forward. Garza has tattooed on her chest six lines from June Jordan's "Poem About My Rights:"

> I am not wrong: Wrong is not my name
> My name is my own my own my own
> And I can't tell you who the hell set things up like this
> But I can tell you that from now on my resistance
> My simple and daily and nightly self-determination
> May very well cost you your life

CRITICAL RACE THEORY

Like most bad and subversive ideas, Critical Race Theory (CRT) sprang from academia, specifically the American university system. In the 1970s, a coalition of leftist scholars argued that American law was just politics in disguise, a way for the powerful to control the weak. True to their Marxist roots, these professors proclaimed that our society was divided into two distinct groups – the oppressors, and the victims of the oppressors. It didn't take long for Critical Theory in law to find its way to the subject of race relations. Still in the 1970s, a professor at Harvard Law School, Derrick Bell, embraced the cause with great vigor. Professor Bell is often described as the godfather of Critical Race Theory. His work explored what it would mean to understand racism as a permanent feature of American life. He wrote that racial equality is "impossible and illusory." According to Bell, civil rights legislation will not on its own bring about progress in race relations. He went on to say that alleged improvements or advantages to people of color "tend to serve the interests of dominant white groups." In other words,

161

instead of explicit and intentional prejudices of individuals, CRT postulates that racism and disparate racial outcomes were a direct result of a rigged "system."

For two score years, Critical Race Theory remained practically dormant as a niche academic theory fashionable mostly in the halls of Ivy League law schools. All that changed in May 2020 when police officer Derek Chauvin killed George Floyd. Floyd became far more than the victim of murder – he was turned into a martyr, one who becomes a victim to further a cause. To turn the victim into a martyr, liberal politicians portrayed Floyd as a Christ-like figure who'd sacrificed himself for racial justice. As activists turned Floyd's death into a potent symbol, public interest in CRT skyrocketed. Suddenly, the term was everywhere. It made national and international headlines and became a target for cable news talking heads. Culture wars over CRT have turned school boards into battlegrounds. Almost overnight, a once-niche academic theory became prevailing "wisdom" and a crucible for the vanguard of woke warriors. Without truly understanding, corporate boardrooms and universities caved and jumped on the bandwagon for this bizarre explanation of the current status of race in America.

Until writing this section of the book, I had a weak grasp and understanding of what constituted Critical Race Theory. Thus, I elected to take a "deep dive" into this hot-button subject. What I discovered was disturbing, if not outright disgusting, at least to me. As you will soon see, I disagree with 100% of the assumptions and tenants espoused by Critical Race Theory.

The fundamental tenant of CRT is that racism is present in every aspect of life, every relationship, and every interaction. No exceptions. Every. It is a belief that everything that happens in the social world and beyond that results in any disparity is a result of favoritism for the "racially privileged" at the expense of the "racially oppressed." These assumptions lead people who take up CRT to look for racism in everything until they find it. That is, after all, the job of a "critical" activist: to look for the hidden problems that they assume must be present. In a workplace that adopts CRT, this means that it's only a matter of time until someone with that worldview finds out how your entire company and its culture are racist. At that point, they will cause a meltdown that forces everyone to take sides and demand a reorganization of the entire office culture and management. In schools, it will mean teaching our children to think this way and always looking for racism in every situation and interaction. In our relationships, it means that friends and even family members will eventually call each other out and reject one another because tolerating racism is also considered a form of racism that would have to be discovered and stopped.

One of the central ideas of CRT is the "Interest- Convergence Thesis." The premise of this thesis is that white people only give black people opportunities and freedoms when it also serves their interests. It goes on to say that because racism advances the interests of both white elites (materially) and working-class people, large segments of society have little incentive to eradicate it. The Interest-Convergence Thesis makes it impossible for anyone considered to have the racial privilege to do anything right because anything they do right must also have been self-interested. By giving people no way out, CRT becomes deeply manipulative and unable to be satisfied due to its excessive lists of demands.

At its core, Critical Race Theory is against freedom and free societies. CRT perceives a free society as a way to structure and maintain inequities. It also sees free societies and ideals that make them work – individualism, freedom, peace – as a kind of tacit conspiracy theory that we all participate in to keep racial minorities down. When its advocates accuse people of being "complicit in systems of racism," this is part of what they mean. They would prefer that we do not have free societies and would rather arrange society as they see fit and make us all go along with their ideas.

Critical Race Theory isn't just against free societies and the individualism that enables them, but it also doesn't even believe individuals meaningfully exist at all. In Critical Race Theory, every person has to be understood in terms of the social groups they are said to inhabit, and these are determined by their identity, including race. In CRT, the goal of ideally treating every person as an individual who is equal before the law and meant to be judged upon the contents of their character and merits of their work is considered a myth that keeps racial minorities down. Instead, it sees people only according to their racial grouping.

Critical Race Theory believes science, reason, and evidence are a "white" way of knowing and that storytelling and lived experience are a "black" alternative. CRT is not particularly friendly to science, residing somewhere between generally disinterested in science and openly hostile to it. Since modern science was predominately produced by white, Western men, CRT, therefore, maintains that science encodes and perpetuates "white dominance" and thus isn't fitting for black people. Because science believes in objectivity, in the CRT world, it (objectivity) is referred to as an oppressive myth.

Critical Race Theory is completely against the common-- sense idea that race becomes less socially relevant and racism is therefore diminished by not focusing on race all the time. CRT rejects all potential alternatives, like colorblindness, as forms of racism. They insist the concept of "colorblindness" is one of the most racist things possible because it hides the real racism from view.

Critical Race Theory acts like anyone who disagrees with it must do so for racist and white supremacist reasons. Proponents of CRT have outlined what the essential experience of each racial group is. It then judges individual people on how well they give testimonial to that experience – which is to say, they judge individual people based on how well they support Critical Race Theory. This makes it impossible to disagree with Critical Race Theory, even if you are black.

Critical Race Theory can never be satisfied. It is, in this way, like a black hole. No matter how much you give to it, it cannot be filled and only gets stronger – and it will tear apart anything that gets too close to it. Although giving in to a demand made by CRT cannot appease it, it can signal that you will give in to their demands, which will then continue to come and escalate. As we witnessed in countless examples across the corporate world, this will include demands for you to step down from your job and give it to activists, and even that won't satisfy them. And if the venture fails as a result of all of this disruption, racism was the cause of that failure too.

There are additional disturbing tenants of Critical Race Theory, but I believe you have been sufficiently enlightened and get the picture. Critical Race Theory is truly a dreadful way to deal with race issues and racism. This theory needs to be shoved back into the hole it escaped from practically 50 years ago.

BLACK CRIME

The reality is both stark and troubling. Both in terms of victims and perpetrators, the black community displays violent crime statistics and data that should be of great concern to everybody. Before speculating on possible reasons for these disturbing numbers, I will provide some of the cold, hard data: According to the FBI's database, in 2018 – 2020, African Americans made up more than 50% of known homicide offenders and committed more than 60% of the robberies. These are not good numbers, especially when you take into account that African Americans represent approximately 13% of the nation's population. Reviewing the FBI's crime data from 2011 to 2020, showed that African Americans bear an increasingly large share of the harm from crime. African American offenders, meanwhile, are committing an increasingly large share of violent crimes. For other racial groups, the numbers are either decreasing (in the case of both white victims and offenders), increasing by much smaller amounts, or holding constant. The most striking figure in the data is the spike in overall (all races) reported homicides, which tripled from 3,549 offenses in 2011 to 10,440 offenses reported in 2020.

Following is an excerpt from a speech made on Father's Day in 2008 by the 44th president of the United States: "Of all the rocks upon which we build our lives, we are reminded today that family is the most important. We know the statistics – that children who grow up without a father are five times more likely to live in poverty and commit crimes. They are more likely to have behavioral problems, run away from home, or become teenage parents themselves.

And the foundations of our community are weaker because of it."
Half of the political spectrum – the left half – too often dismisses
the importance of family structure in direct contradiction to
Barack Obama's previous quote above. As New York Times
columnist David Leonhardt notes in one of his columns: "Partly
out of a worthy desire to celebrate the heroism of single parents,
progressives too often downplay family structure. Social science is
usually messy, with correlation and causation difficult to separate.
But the evidence, when viewed objectively, points strongly to the
value of two-parent households." Close to 60% of black children
are living in a household absent their biological fathers. Certainly
not in all cases, but this can be a recipe for disaster. Comparatively,
30% of Hispanic and 20% of white children are living absent their
biological fathers.

Besides fatherless homes, a share of the source of the crime
problem in urban enclaves can be attributed to failing public school
systems. By any objective measure, these schools consistently fail to
provide their African American students with the fundamentals of
a basic education. In a number of these school districts, proficiency
rates for black eighth graders are down in the single digits (see
Detroit's 4% for math and 5% for reading, or Milwaukee's 5% for
math and 7% for reading). Most are in the low teens. Embarrassed
by the way our big city public school systems are failing black
children, progressives answer not by making it easier for these kids
to get into schools where black children are achieving, whether
this be charter or parochial schools. Instead, they focus on getting
rid of the embarrassment by getting rid of the achievement tests
that expose it, doubling down on race preferences, and trying to
hamstring the schools that show black children can and do learn in
the right environment.

Many knowledgeable people believe that the surge in race-
essentialist rhetoric is playing a role in the upswing of black
crime rates. There is precedent for this trend. The increase in
black offenders and black victims is reminiscent of the fallout
from the Black Power movements of the 1960s. Back then (the
1960s), radicals began to reject the approach of "the old civil

rights movements," which called for peace, equality, and integration. The radicals favored racial separatism and black nationalism, which gave way to surges of frustration, disorder, and black violence. The violence occurred primarily in black neighborhoods and the primary victims were working-class black people. As with the riots of the 1960s, the anti-police riots of 2020 caused significant harm to black neighborhoods and black-owned businesses. Also similar to the 1960s Black Power movement, the trendy race rhetoric of today is more focused on calling out and rebuking the supposed omnipresent specter of white supremacy than it is on peace, equality, and integration. I don't believe the specter of widespread white supremacy still exists. It is being used as a facade and an excuse to pursue political and economic gains.

Without question, the high rates of poverty in some black communities adversely affect the crime rate in those areas. The hopelessness and lack of opportunity that characterize many disadvantaged settings are conducive to an increased level of crime. Residents are more ambivalent about the law and social norms deteriorate to a great extent. Disadvantaged neighborhoods are also ripe for the trafficking of drugs by competing street gangs. There is a street culture that in many respects supersedes the influence of family, church, and schools. This street culture can best be described as a set of informal rules governing interpersonal public behavior, particularly as concerns aggression and violence.

As such, the neighborhood street culture outlines the proper way to present oneself in a manner that demands respect and deters acts of victimization from others as well to negotiate respect on the street. At the heart of the street culture is an emphasis on respect, toughness, retribution, and ultimately, violence. The street culture maintains that a violent response when someone initiates disrespect is necessary to elicit respect from others. The use of violence, even at the risk of going to the slammer for an extended period, allows those participating in the street code to achieve social status among peers. This type of culture in my mind is the primary reason for the high black crime rate.

REPARATIONS

Race hustlers and grifters like Al Sharpton and Ta-Nehisi Coates have claimed for years that the only way for whites to truly atone for slavery in America's past is to pay off black people now. Some politicians, I'm looking at you, Gavin Newsom, champion this idea to advance their ambitions. The concept of reparations in the form of financial compensation is nothing more than a political weapon proponents can wield to assert their will on feckless white leaders who don't want to be called racist. The results of a 2021 Associated Press – NORC poll indicated 74 percent of African Americans now favor reparations payments, while 85 percent of white Americans oppose them. The split is staggering.

The idea of paying off a current generation of black people for the sins committed by white people – and others – over 150 years ago makes absolutely no sense. None. To be clear, slavery remains the great moral and spiritual failing of the United States. Acknowledging that failing, or the role of racism in American history, is overwhelmingly the proper treatment of this failure. However, there is no good argument for reparations and numerous reasons why reparations would represent a massive policy mistake, encourage divisiveness, and in all probability push the country to even angrier extremes on either side of the argument. The conversation over reparations will further divide Americans at a time when we more than ever need to come together. Based on both principle and practicality, as with slavery, it's time to leave the notion of reparations in the past.

Before attacking the very principle behind reparations, we will look at the total impracticality surrounding reparations. It would present an insurmountable, logistical nightmare. Tens of millions of today's non-black Americans are descended from people who arrived in the country after slavery ended. The two great waves of American immigration occurred after 1880 and then after 1960. These descendants cannot be held responsible for America's crimes or its legacy. Additional tens of millions of citizens are descended from people who did not own slaves.

Only a tiny percentage of the total American population were slave owners. Further, some blacks and some Native Americans owned slaves. It is estimated that there were 3,000 black slave owners in the antebellum United States. Are reparations to be paid to their descendants too.

There are no historical precedents that justify the reparations claim. This would be the only case of reparations to people who were not immediately affected and whose sole qualification to receive reparations would be racial. It also should be noted that there is evidence the hardships perpetuated over 150 years ago were hardships that individuals could and did overcome. The black middle class in America is a prosperous community that is now larger in absolute terms than the black underclass. Does its existence not suggest that economic adversity is the result of failures of individual character rather than the lingering after-effects of slavery and racial discrimination? West Indian blacks in America are also descended from slaves, but their average incomes are equivalent to the average incomes of whites (and nearly 25% higher than the average incomes of American-born blacks). How is it that slavery adversely affected one large group of descendants but not the other?

If attempted, reparations would raise expectations to an unreasonable pitch and then would become hopelessly tangled up in politics and bureaucracy. The possibilities for corruption would be endless. The potential for resentment would be profound. Poor whites paying reparations to rich blacks would create a breeding ground for new racial resentments. Moreover, it's a laughable idea that simply writing a check to every black person in America suddenly will make the condition of black people here better forever. The Civil War was fought over the practice of slavery. The price tag was high. Approximately 360,000 Union soldiers died to free the slaves. They gave their lives. What possible moral principle would ask them to pay (through their descendants) again?

The reparations cause is an illogical attack on all Americans – especially African Americans. It is still another assault on America, conducted by racial separatists and the political left. A heightened sense of grievance – which is what the claim for reparations will inevitably create – is neither a constructive nor a helpful message for black leaders to be sending to their communities and others. To focus the social passions of African Americans on what some Americans may have done to their ancestors sixty or a hundred and sixty years ago is to burden them with a crippling sense of victimhood. In summary, acknowledging and apologizing for the institution of slavery on American soil is essential and absolutely the right thing to do. But adding a price to that apology would be sheer folly and create (by a power of at least 10) more problems than it solves.

WHITE PRIVILEGE AND WHITE GUILT

It seems to be ebbing somewhat recently, but for a bit, the term "white privilege" was thrown around frequently by those of the left, particularly the mainstream media cretins. I consider the term an inane generalization that serves no purpose and is insulting to a large portion of the population. As a white man, I concede the good fortune of being born in the right country at the right time to the right parents. I am the product and beneficiary of hard-working parents who stressed the importance of education, avoided the pursuit of criminal behavior, and instilled in me a universally acknowledged positive set of values for which to navigate life. Others may feel differently and apologize for it, but I am proud of my heritage and will not bend a knee to any ethnic group or individual. That said, I concur that black Americans have historically been confronted with extra layers of hurdles and challenges. There are currently significantly fewer obstacles than ever before, but some still exist, as do random acts of overt racism.

In retrospect, "white guilt" in many respects would be considered a first cousin to "white privilege." If somebody elects to feel guilty for the conditions in parts of our country several generations past, that would be their prerogative. However, those who are guilt-ridden due to certain past actions of their ancestors more often than not fall into the "presentism" trap. Presentism is a historical term meaning judging past actions by today's standards, or uncritical adherence to present-day attitudes, especially the tendency to interpret past events in terms of modern values and concepts. People need to be mindful that attitudes, accepted standards, and cultural values are subject to change (often dramatically) over time. To me, it seems nonsensical to accept and bear the burden of the sins of my ascendants, or the peers of my ascendants. I'm sorry, but if I am to assume some guilt, it's damn well going to be restricted to my actions and behavior.

I can understand the emotions behind the removal of Confederate monuments and the renaming of certain public places related to leaders of the Confederacy. Instead of a mob tearing down a statue, it would be preferable to move the monument to a museum where it could serve as a reminder of our ancestors, moral warts and all. This would also invite us to consider the degree to which we, too, are ethical works in progress. There is one historical racist symbol, however, that the culture warriors want to give a pass and not relegate to destruction or a dusty wing of a museum – The Democratic Party. The Democratic Party was the party of slavery. The Democratic Party was the party of Jim Crow laws. The Democratic Party fought civil rights advances for a century. The Democratic Party's military arm in the South was the Ku Klux Klan. The Democratic Party opposed the 14th and 15th Amendments to the Constitution, making former slaves citizens of the United States and giving them the vote. Perhaps we could put Democrats in museum exhibits, behind glass, watching white political bosses chomp cigars and pass out goodies for votes, as minorities were relegated, as they are today, to failing schools and lost educational opportunities and neighborhoods that have become killing fields for the young and old. Of course, I am being sarcastic to point out the hypocrisy that all too often is forthcoming from the denizens of the far left. Oh, and did I mention that it is also a historical fact that the Republican Party was the party of abolitionists?

The left strategically created and deployed "white guilt" to effectuate ridiculous policies like "Quotas," "Affirmative Action," and "Diversity, Equity, Inclusion" (DEI). The big push now from the left is to replace "equal treatment under the law" with "equity." The difference between equality and equity is similar to the difference between night and day. Fundamentally, it is the difference between equal treatment and equal outcomes. Equality means equal treatment, unbiased competition, and impartially judged outcomes. Equity means equal outcomes, achieved if necessary by unequal treatment, biased competition, and preferential judging. Extensive measures would be needed to pull off an equal outcome coup. Only a powerful central government combined with an intrusive bureaucracy could impose the intensive – and expensive – programs of social intervention, ideological re-education, and economic redistribution.

Since the New Deal, most Americans have supported some form of social safety net for the poor and disadvantaged. What we are seeing now is different. It is a claim that the unfair treatment of previous generations or perhaps a disadvantaged childhood entitles one to special consideration today as an adult. Most Americans, who are both generous and pragmatic, have been willing to extend some of these benefits, at the margins and for limited periods. However, they don't want to turn these concessions into large, permanent entitlement programs, giving substantially different treatment to different groups, even if those groups have suffered historical wrongs. When you think about it, isn't equity just a new name for the oldest program of achieving equal outcomes? Its name is socialism.

AMERICA IS NOT SYSTEMICALLY RACIST

I grow weary of the constant clamor from the political left that America is "systemically racist." It inarguably was at one time but is no longer the case. Racism still exists randomly and in pockets, but it is no longer systemic in nature. Those who claim racism is widespread and "everywhere" today are delusional. Many of the authors, commentators, and journalists who spend all of their energy thinking and talking about race these days fail to acknowledge how much has improved in the matter of race relations in this country. My own family represents a microcosm of this subtle transition. As concerns race, my parents were more tolerant than my grandparents, I am more tolerant than my parents, my children are more tolerant than me, and I expect my grandchildren will be more than my children. In my mind, that is positive and the natural evolution of progress in a multi-racial society. Another sign of progress in race relations would be interracial marriages. The number of interracial marriages as a proportion of new marriages increased from 3% in 1967 to 19% in 2019. Public approval of interracial marriage rose from around 5% in the 1950s to 94% in 2021.

Shortly after George Floyd died in 2020, my daughter asked me if I was a "racist." My response went something like this: Twenty years past I would have been considered progressive in terms of tolerance and acceptance in the realm of race relations. Ten years ago, I still would have been considered a "respectable" human being on this issue. In 2020 and today, many on the left would conclude that a white robe and hood hung in my closet, and in my spare time, I joined my peers and burned crosses in the front yards of African Americans. Through the process of introspection, I came up with ten questions, and answers, to determine the extent of my racism. Itemized below are these questions and my honest responses:

1. Would you be uncomfortable if a black family moved into a residence across the street? - No
2. Do you believe that in general blacks have been atrociously and then poorly treated in America for the good part of 300 years? – Yes
3. Do you believe that racial tolerance and acceptance are accelerating and progressing on a generational basis? – Yes
4. Do you believe that a black person should have 100% of the opportunities that were available to you? – Yes
5. Do you believe that "Affirmative Action" is wrong and unconstitutional? – Yes
6. If you owned a business, would you have any reservations whatsoever about hiring an African American if he/she was qualified to do the job? – No

7. Would a friend that occasionally made off-the-cuff racist comments preclude your friendship from continuing? – No
8. Would you have been upset, at least initially, if your daughter married a black man? – Yes
9. Have you ever treated a black person, either in business or in personal interaction, differently than a white person? No
10. Do you have any black friends in the inner circles of your closest and dearest friends? – No I honestly don't know what the net result of my responses above says about me. I'll leave it to the readers to pass judgment and then live with their opinions; whether they be positive, negative, or somewhere in between.

It's probably not an accurate and fair comparison, but Irish immigrants and the plight of African Americans share some historical similarities. The Irish peasants fleeing the potato famine in the late 1840s had a shorter life expectancy than slaves in the United States, many of whom enjoyed healthier diets and better living quarters. In 1847, 19% of the Irish emigrants died on their way to the U.S. or shortly after arriving. By comparison, the average mortality rate on British slave ships of the period was 9%. Slave owners had an economic incentive to keep slaves alive. No one had such an interest in the Irish. In the antebellum South, the Irish took jobs – mining coal, building canals and railroads – considered too hazardous for slaves. The Irish were known for drinking and brawling. Irish gangs were common. When an Irish family moved into a neighborhood, property values declined and other residents fled. Political cartoonists gave Irish men dark skin and simian features. Anti-Catholic employers requested "Protestant" applicants only. Want ads said: "Any color or country except Irish." None of these obstacles proved insurmountable. It took several decades, but eventually, the Irish were able to break through and achieve acceptance and prosperity. The modern attitudes toward assimilation notwithstanding, hopefully, the struggles and challenges of Blacks will have a similar outcome.

Next, I would like to level some overdue criticism on the vastly subjective concept of "hate speech." The only speech that I believe is deserving of this description is speech where one individual either verbally or in writing threatens physical harm to another individual. Everything else in my mind has the full protection of the First Amendment of the U.S. Constitution. "Sticks and stones may break my bones, but words will never hurt me." The time is at hand for that adage to make a comeback. A physical attack may injure somebody, but a verbal attack cannot injure somebody. This blathering about words being violence and the concept of semantical microaggressions is a bunch of baloney. Are we intent on creating a country of frail, sensitive souls who fall apart when somebody insults them or uses a word they don't like? Language and words are not akin to a punch in the nose or being struck by a high-velocity chunk of lead.

I also am troubled by certain ethnic groups believing they, and they alone, "own" certain words and terms. No words should be banned by use by the general public. Although certain words may encumber users with adverse consequences. User beware. I don't see a lot of parties pushing for a ban on the various "N" words used internally in the black community, or by black role models like rap and hip-hop stars. Chinese don't usually use "chink" or "China man" to refer to each other; Mexicans don't use "wetbacks" and Sikhs don't use "towelheads" to refer to each other. I also find claims of "cultural appropriation" baseless and silly. Similar to a word, an ethnic group does not "own" the various elements of their culture. Anybody is free to extract any parts they so desire from any culture. Whatever happened to the thought, "Imitation is the sincerest form of flattery?"

The following is an excerpt from an article written by the author, Shelby Steele: "What they missed is a simple truth that is both obvious and unutterable: The oppression of black people is over with. This is politically incorrect news, but it is true nonetheless. We blacks are today, a free people. It is as if freedom sneaked up and caught us by surprise. Of course, this does not mean there is no racism left in American life. Racism is endemic to the human condition, just as stupidity is. We will always have to be on guard against it. But now it is recognized as a scourge, as the crowning immorality of our age and our history."

One-hundred years ago, the socialist elements of American society who subscribed to the theories of Karl Marx, attempted a total transformation of the American economic system. The vehicle they utilized for this coup attempt was class division and the labor movement. As history shows, that attempt failed. Miserably. Instead of leveraging class differences, the current attempt to disrupt and change America is using race as the spearhead. The very definition of racism has been altered by the far left in an effort to attain their nefarious goals. Fortunately, the absurd notion that racism is about institutionalized white power simply doesn't compute for most Americans. I know it doesn't compute for me. I require definitive proof of "systemic racism." Until somebody can show me an existing written law, regulation, or policy issued by any private or public entity in the country, I categorically reject the claim of "systemic racism" in contemporary America.

CHAPTER TEN

OTHER RELEVANT TOPICS OF INTEREST

ABORTION

IN MY LIFETIME, the United States Supreme Court has issued multiple monumental rulings that profoundly liberalized the nation's social order. Those high court decisions would include the desegregation of schools, elimination of prayer in schools, interracial marriage, and gay marriage. Although somewhat unpopular at the respective times of issuance, these rulings were eventually followed by widespread public acceptance. Roe vs Wade adjudicated in 1973, however, was an outlier in terms of acceptance and soundness of legal logic and Constitutional interpretation. Why was this landmark case (1973) so singular, unique, and divisive? Quite simply – because all of the other decisions were about how to live, and Roe was about death. It involved death, inescapably and at its heart. This decision in 1973 affirming that women have a constitutional right to an abortion has roiled our country for half a century.

The issue of abortion has split the country down the middle for numerous decades. The vast majority of people on both sides of the issue are utterly sincere and operating out of their best understanding of life. Sure, some people over the past 50 years used this issue to accrue money and power. It took a toll on the well-being of each of our major political parties. The Democrats adopted abortion as one of the main pillars of their very foundation. They let dissenters know they were unwelcome. In addition, they caved to the vociferous activists ever pushing for more extreme measures. Large campaign donations from the abortion industry itself flowed to the Democratic Party. Many Republican politicians were both insincere and hypocritical when endorsing the Pro-Life position. They took for granted and covertly disrespected the Pro-Life groups, which consultants shook down for campaign cash.

Abortion supporters consistently claim that abortion has been legal on a federal level for almost 50- years and it thus should be considered established law. They hang one of their hats on the legal principle of stare decisis, which means to "stand by things decided."

In other words, precedent should carry significant weight. I would counter with the argument that historically (for 200 years) abortion was not looked at favorably by the great majority of citizens and was not accepted at the cultural level. Insofar as stare decisis, the precedent has been overturned before in important and dramatic cases, especially when a precedent's validity is so hotly contested. There was a general view among the conservative justices that Roe was wrongly decided in 1973, a bad decision that should be overturned. Many staunch legal minds on the left also questioned the intellectual "leap" made by the high court with the Roe decision in 1973. Archibald Cox wrote in 1976 that the court had failed to consider "the most compelling interest of the State in prohibiting abortion: the interest in maintaining respect for the paramount sanctity of human life." Ruth Bader Ginsburg also questioned its reasoning and observed in 1985 that Roe appeared "to have provoked, not resolved conflict."

At approximately the halfway mark for 2022, the U.S. Supreme Court voted to strike down the landmark Roe vs. Wade decision. It is without question the proper legal decision. The Constitution is quite obviously silent on the matter of abortion rights. The Tenth Amendment of the U.S. Constitution stipulates that the federal government has only those powers delegated to it by the Constitution and that all other powers not forbidden to the states by the Constitution are reserved to each state. Thus, the 50 state legislatures will have the authority to determine their abortion policies. We are a large and diverse country. Having the individual states determine abortion rights is preferable to a national edict of "one size fits all."

As indicated earlier, many on the political left perceive the prohibition of abortion as a sin against women. Whereas many on the political right perceive abortion on demand as a sin against life. The overturning of Roe is the closest America will get to justice and democratic satisfaction on the abortion issue. It may seem chaotic for a bit, but the liberal states will have their liberal decision and the conservative states their conservative ones. Instead of nine-robed jurists making a monumental determination, the responsibility for solving the dispute will be shifted closer to the people and the democratic process will play out based on the preferences of the electorates of the various states.

Looking back in a review of my thoughts on abortion over the past 50 years, I see a gradual evolution. In 1973 I was 18 years old. At that time, I didn't give a second thought to abortion and believed it should be universally available to women on demand. That changed and I'm sure receiving the gift of children and grandchildren was the primary reason for the modification of my views. If pinned into a corner and given a binary choice restricted to either Pro-Life or Pro-Choice, I would opt for the Pro-Life side of the argument. However, my personal preference at this point is to allow abortion during the first 16 weeks of pregnancy and also in cases of rape, incest, medical emergency, and severe fetal abnormality.

AFGHANISTAN

Americans have notoriously short memories, although few will forget the absolute debacle when our involvement in Afghanistan unraveled in 2021 – the Taliban seized Kabul, the Afghan government collapsed, and President Joe Biden ordered a hasty and chaotic evacuation of troops in August 2021. Biden's mismanagement of the withdrawal from Afghanistan ending a 20-year occupation is so egregious that future historians will have a field day detailing the layers and depths of incompetence. Most Americans understood and agreed with the policy of removing most if not all, American soldiers from the country known as the "Graveyard of Empires." The criticism comes from the timing and manner of the withdrawal, which needlessly put at risk the lives of thousands of Afghan citizens.

In a July (2021) interview, President Biden said a collapse of the Afghan government and a Taliban takeover of the country was "highly unlikely." Yet, a memo sent that same month from the Kabul Embassy reportedly warned that the withdrawal as planned would result in the very disaster that unfolded. Bottom line – either the President knew about the coming disaster and lied to the American people, or the President's advisers never informed him about it. Either conclusion is deeply disturbing. President Biden further asserted he ordered the withdrawal from Afghanistan based on the advice of senior U.S. military advisers. However, in September 2021, top Pentagon officials testified under oath that they advised the President to keep 2,500 troops on the ground and were not asked for advice on the withdrawal until August 26th (2021), directly contradicting the President's claim.

President Biden presented his choice in Afghanistan as between remaining indefinitely or completely withdrawing. A third choice existed: making the American withdrawal contingent on an intra-Afghan peace deal and doing more to secure Afghan women's rights. There is no guarantee this would have succeeded, but the U.S. had a moral obligation to attempt such a third path. This is especially the case due to expending U.S. blood (2,000 lives) and treasure (over $1 trillion), and over 65,000 Afghan citizens losing their lives in the 20-year conflict.

In my opinion, the most disturbing dereliction of duty involving our hasty and disorganized exodus was the total abandonment of tens of thousands of Afghans who worked for and helped the American government. It is estimated that only about 3 percent of Afghans who helped the U.S. and applied for special visas were evacuated, leaving behind close to 80,000. These Afghans stuck in the Taliban-ruled country face desperate circumstances with a high probability of execution. According to a report issued by the nonprofit "Association of Wartime Allies,": "Their lives have been devastated by being left behind with seemingly no verifiable path to safety." In a Wall Street Journal article written by Karl Rove and published one year after our departure, Mr. Rove is quoted as: "President Biden destroyed the value of America's word, diminished our global influence, and made the world more dangerous when he surrendered in Afghanistan a year ago this week. The Taliban, a jihadist terror movement and avowed enemy of the U.S. could claim to have defeated the world's mightiest nation."

AMERICAN EXCEPTIONALISM

The term "American exceptionalism" has different meanings for different people. Parts of American exceptionalism can be traced to American Puritan roots that took hold in the first half of the 17th century. Thousands of English Puritans colonized North America, almost all in New England. They believed that God had made a covenant with their people and had chosen them to provide a model for the other nations of the Earth. With this mindset went feelings of specialness and superiority. In other words – God's chosen people. I do not agree with this contention and find it both arrogant and narrow-minded. My definition of American exceptionalism is based on the premise that the United States is inherently different from other countries and its accomplishments accrued over the past 250 years are indeed exceptional. A person would have perpetually had their head stuck in the sand not to see and acknowledge the sheer magnitude of significant accomplishments that appear on the credit side of America's historical balance sheet. Those making a counterargument would maintain that it is human nature to express a bias that cultures and groups within various cultures commonly consider themselves exceptional. That argument against American exceptionalism falls apart, however, when statistics, data, and cold, hard facts are introduced to the equation.

On an economic basis, there has never been a more productive economy and prosperous society in the history of the world than the United States of America. There are a few countries with higher per capita Gross Domestic Product (GDP) than the U.S. A couple of examples would be Switzerland and Norway. Those nations, though, have populations of 8.7 million and 5.4 million people, respectively. The U.S. is a rich, developed country that is home to 330 million people. It is a big country that is simultaneously wealthy. China is closing in on the U.S. in terms of raw GDP. Insofar as per capita GDP, China lands somewhere between 20% and 25% of the per capita GDP of the U.S. It should also be noted that besides being the wealthiest nation on the planet, the U.S. leads the world in charitable giving. Unlike any other large country, for most of its history, the U.S. has been known as the "land of opportunity." In that sense, it has prided and promoted itself on providing individuals with the opportunities to escape from the confines of their class and family background. America is home to more immigrants (45 million) than any other country. There are about 80% as many Norwegian-Americans as people are living in Norway. There are more than 80% as many Jews as there are in Israel. And there are six times as many Irish- Americans in the U.S. as there are citizens of Ireland.

Americans in the past have not played it safe compared to their peers in other countries. When given a choice – Americans have typically taken more risks and opted for more individual freedom when presented with the opportunity. The U.S. is the most individualistic country in the world. Polls consistently show Americans are among the most likely to say that hard work is the key to getting ahead in life or that people are in control of their fates. The same can be said for competitiveness. Americans have a competitive streak and strive to win at just about everything. American culture, fueled in large part by capitalism and economic resources, has proven a particularly fertile environment of innovation of all kinds. That is reflected in the fact the U.S. has more Nobel Prizes than the next five countries combined.

Theories abound as to the source of exceptionalism associated with the American experiment. Political scientist Seymour Martin Lipset traces the origins to the American Revolution, from which the U.S. emerged as "the first new nation" with a distinct ideology. This ideology is based on liberty, egalitarianism, individualism, republicanism, democracy, and laissez-faire economics. Thomas Paine's "Common Sense" for the first time expressed the belief that America was not just an extension of Europe but a new land and a country of nearly unlimited potential and opportunity that had outgrown the British mother country. Some argue that the American political tradition lacks the left-wing/socialist and right-wing/aristocratic elements that dominated throughout Europe. They felt that colonial America lacked feudal traditions such as established churches, landed estates, and a hereditary nobility. As a result, American politics developed around a tradition of "Lockean" liberalism. In addition, the national government that emerged in America was far less centralized or nationalized than its European counterparts.

French political scientist and historian Alexis de Tocqueville was the first writer to describe America as "exceptional" following his travels there in 1831. Although ironically, the term seems to have originated with American communists in the late 1920s. They argued that the United States is independent of the Marxist laws of history "thanks to its natural resources, industrial capacity, and absence of rigid class distinctions." In 1989, Scottish political scientist Richard Rose noted: "America marches to a different drummer. Its uniqueness is explained by any or all of a variety of reasons: history, size, geography, political institutions, and culture. Explanations of the growth of government in Europe are not expected to fit the American experience and vice versa."

In 2012, the conservative historians, Larry Schweikart and Dave Dougherty, argued that American exceptionalism is based on four pillars: 1.) common law; 2.) virtue and morality located in Protestant Christianity; 3.) free-market capitalism; 4.) the sanctity of private property. Yale Law School Dean Harold Hongu Koh argues: "To this day, the United States remains the only superpower capable, and at times willing, to commit real resources and make real sacrifices to build, sustain, and drive an international system committed to international law, democracy, and the promotion of human rights."

It remains without question that certain aspects of American history were exceptionally bad, and shameful. At the top of the heap of course would be the enslavement of Africans and African Americans until the time of the Civil War. This atrocity cannot be swept under a rug and casually ignored. At the same time, all issues need to be judged with some degree of relativism. It is wrong to think every culture at every time saw things the same way. Failing to put the past in context – or worse yet, denying its reality is not good. Also, invalidating the entire American experience based on deplorable previous actions, morally objectional as they are, doesn't make sense in the global historical context.

Some proponents argue that the U.S. is exceptional in that it was founded on a set of republican ideals rather than on a common heritage, ethnicity, or ruling elite. While I agree with this to a certain extent, there are other aspects that I was remiss in not mentioning earlier. From the get-go, our religious freedoms were unique when most major nations had state religions. Struggles and hardships on the frontier as pioneers pushed west were conducive to shaping the American spirit and individualism in the minds of many. It should be noted before wrapping up this subject that America stands as the world's oldest constitutional republic. In closing, I quote talented Wall Street Journal columnist, Peggy Noonan: "America is not exceptional because it has long attempted to be a force for good in the world, it tries to be a force for good because it is exceptional."

COVID-19

In terms of blockbuster events and factors that have impacted the entire world, the Covid-19 pandemic is inarguably the biggest story thus far in the 21st century. There is a general agreement that the novel coronavirus originated in Wuhan, China during the last couple of months of 2019. Wuhan is a city of 11 million inhabitants located in the central part of China. When the Chinese Communist Party belatedly informed the world about this new virus, they claimed that the source of the deadly pathogen was a "wet market" in Wuhan. A wet market is an outdoor marketplace selling fresh foods such as meat, fish, produce, and other consumption-oriented perishable goods. Some, but not all, also sell exotic types of dead animals for consumption. While the virus may very well have organically originated in the Wuhan wet market, whatever is proclaimed by the CCP needs to be taken with a grain of salt. There is another possible explanation for a source that has gained traction over time and which many believe to be the more likely story of how the pandemic started.

It just so happens that the Wuhan Institute of Virology, a research institute focusing on the study of coronaviruses, is located in Wuhan. It isn't unheard of for a virus to escape from a government-funded lab, and some evidence suggests that's what happened in Wuhan. As it turns out, the Wuhan lab in question appears to have operated, in part, with U.S. government grant funding, although American scientists had no oversight role. Chinese scientists allegedly pursued gain-of-function research, increasing the virulence and transmissibility of certain viruses. China continues to bar access to the Wuhan lab and its records, effectively blocking any possible investigation in its tracks. Even if the virus did not escape from this lab, China's behavior and lack of transparency have been deplorable. Beijing covered up evidence of the virus's early spread and allowed international flights from Wuhan during January and February 2020, while locking down domestic travel. Chinese officials spread lies, deception, and disinformation that kept the United States and the world in the dark during this critical period.

Once the Wuhan Bat Flu reached American shores, our response to the virus invasion was less than stellar. Our government's smartest medical minds expected this outbreak to be like SARS, avian flu, swine flu, MERS, Zika, and Ebola outbreaks that came before it – a serious public health emergency to be sure, but one we could handle. On 1/21/20, Anthony Fauci, the director of the National Institute of Allergy and Infectious Diseases, said in an interview, "This is not a major threat for the people of the United States, and this is not something that the citizens of the United States right now should be worried about." Fauci and practically everybody else, including me, were wrong with our optimistic predictions.

As President, Donald Trump received his share of criticism. Although it should be noted that despite some bellyaching, Trump heeded the advice of our public health experts every step of the way. Decisions that slowed the U.S. response the most were not made by Trump. The FDA refused to allow private and academic labs to develop coronavirus tests, costing six crucial weeks in ramping up testing. The CDC's sloppy laboratory practices contaminated the only approved test kits, rendering them ineffective. We should not have been surprised. The evidence of much of history is that the failure to respond adequately to a looming threat is embedded in our nature.

Among a long list of Covid mistakes, the most glaring was the failure to understand and act on the virus's propensity to kill the old and vulnerable. Policymakers failed to understand the enemy. In New York State this was taken to the extreme when hospitals released Covid-positive elderly patients and sent them to rehab in nursing homes. On the flip side, the restrictions placed on young adults and children were cumbersome, unnecessary, and frequently counterproductive. With the luxury of hindsight, it would have made the most sense to have narrowed protections of the most vulnerable 20% of the population while freeing the remaining 80% from wasteful burdens.

Comparisons are often made between the Covid-19 pandemic and the Spanish Flu pandemic 100 years ago. In reality, there is no comparison. The 1918-1920 flu pandemic was much worse, probably by a power of four or five. The reason, simply, is that the Covid pandemic killed old people and the Spanish Flu pandemic killed young people. It is estimated that 675,000 Americans died of the Spanish influenza. At the time, the country's population was 106 million and life expectancy was 54 years. The death toll of 675,000 represented .64% of the national population. The flu pandemic hammered young people in the prime of their life. The average age of flu deaths was 28. The difference between life expectancy and those succumbing to the flu was 26 years (54 − 28 = 26).

To date, Covid-19 has killed just under 1.1 million people in the U.S. according to the CDC. With a current population of 330 million, this figure represents .33% of the national population. The average age of Covid fatalities is approximately 72 years, with 50% over age 80. The country's life expectancy in 2020 stood at 77 years. The Covid pandemic hammered old people already near the end of their life. The difference between life expectancy and those succumbing to Covid was 5 years (77 − 72 = 5). The following example may further encapsulate the point I'm trying to make: If an 18-year-old dies of Covid (which is rare), he loses 61.2 years of expected life. If an 85-year-old dies of Covid, he will lose 6.4 years of expected life.

Comparisons are often made between Covid-19 fatality numbers and those deaths caused by seasonal influenza. In reality, there is no comparison. The risk of death presented by Covid infection is much worse, probably by a power of five to ten. One statistic used by epidemiologists is the Infection Fatality Rate (IFR). This is the probability that a person will die once becoming infected with a virus or other pathogen. The global average Infection Fatality Rate of SARS-Cov-2 (Covid-19) is roughly 0.30%. The average U.S. fatality rate is higher, probably 0.40% or 0.50%, because Americans are older, fatter, and in general less healthy than those in most other countries. Obesity may triple the risk of hospitalization if infected with the virus. Being fat is linked to impaired immune function and reduced lung capacity. Diabetics and those suffering from hypertension are also prone to a higher level of risk. Americans' proclivity to a poor diet and lack of physical activity contributed to the severity of the pandemic in the United States.

There is a growing consensus that lockdowns were not effective and possibly even counterproductive. The costs of "protection" via the lockdowns included: reduced schooling, reduced economic activity, increased substance abuse, more suicides, more loneliness, reduced contact with loved ones, delayed cancer diagnoses, delayed childhood vaccinations, increased anxiety, lower wage growth, travel restrictions, reduced entertainment choices, and fewer opportunities for socializing and building friendships. One possible silver lining with the pandemic is that the experience with Covid-19 may prove educational and helpful when our leaders, government agency bureaucrats, and populace encounter the next deadly microbe that comes down the pike. If mistakes are to be made, there is no question it is preferable with something like Covid-19 with a 0.50% IFR vs. a nasty bugger with a 5.0% IFR.

In both a backseat and retroactive manner, admittedly an advantageous position, I hereby tender a few more observations of the recent pandemic. Masks probably provided some marginal, incremental benefits to adults through indoor usage if the masks worn were of the N95 variety. I will not back the same claim for outdoor usage or for when sitting alone in your car. Children never should have been required to wear masks. Due to the number of asymptomatic and mild cases, utilizing the data of "confirmed cases" for policy decisions was a mistake. The actual cases were no doubt double or even triple the confirmed cases. Another statistical inaccuracy would be fatalities attributed to the virus. Patients that died of other causes that were simultaneously infected with Covid were included in the death count.

People are dreaming if they think "Zero Covid" is feasible. Similar to seasonal flu, Covid-19 will be with us on an indefinite basis. Also, as with climate change, the media has fully embraced the opportunity to sensationalize and politicize the virus. We witnessed the tendency of people to be more fearful of novel risks or inspire dread. An example of this would be the public perception of children contracting and dying of Covid. According to the CDC, three times as many children died of the flu between February and July (2020) as died of Covid-19, but the flu is familiar to parents and other adults, and Covid-19 is not.

In my humble opinion, the majority of Covid policy decisions pertaining to children ages 2-12 will ultimately prove to be mistake-laden and in some cases even harmful. Except for March–May of 2020, elementary schools should never have been closed to in-school learning. Grade school children should not have been required to wear masks in classrooms and other locations on school properties. In that same light, there is no logical reason for vaccinating healthy children from a pathogen that poses a risk to children that falls somewhere between zero and negligible. I fundamentally have a problem with actions that stunt the social and educational development of children combined with these same children being exposed to a vaccination that for children carry with it more potential risks than potential benefits.

The "Great Barrington Declaration" was an open letter published in October 2020 in response to the Covid-19 pandemic and subsequent lockdowns. It claimed that harmful Covid-19 lockdowns could be avoided via "focused protection," by which those most at risk could be kept safe. The declaration said that lockdowns have adverse effects on both physical and mental health. The three authors of the controversial open letter were portrayed as "repeatedly dismissed as fringe or pseudoscience." This characterization is patently false. The three authors were world-renowned scientists, at the pinnacle of their fields working at upper echelon research universities. Disgustingly, this "hit job" was a joint effort between government bureaucrats, social media platforms, and mainstream media outlets to discredit and silence an opinion that ran contrary to the prevailing political winds. This was only one of many examples and represented the tip of the iceberg. Censorship of dissenting viewpoints was rampant during the pandemic.

As with practically everything concerning the pandemic, even the introduction of the vaccines stirred controversy and vehement disagreements. It is generally considered miraculous that the approved vaccines were developed and distributed as rapidly as they were. There is risk involved with so expeditiously advancing this approach to dampening the viral fire. So far, the data tells us that the benefits of getting vaccinated outweigh the risks. The CDC maintains they are safe, with the risk of serious side effects associated with these vaccines very small. However, it is early in the game and we probably won't have a complete picture for a decade. The Covid vaccines actually should be labeled a therapeutic and not a true vaccine. We have learned that the primary benefit of getting vaccinated is not protection from infection – it is keeping more people alive who contract the virus. In my situation, I elected to receive the two initial jabs (Pfizer) followed by a brace of boosters.

If I had been 25 years of age or younger, I would not have received any jabs whatsoever. At the age of 65, however, I thought vaccination avoidance carried too much risk. On a final note, I respect the right of anybody to flatly refuse to get vaccinated and although they had the legal right, I did not approve of employers mandating that all employees be vaccinated.

DEMOCRACY VS. REPUBLIC

The word "democracy," especially used in the context of a phrase like "a threat to our democracy," appears frequently in our era's political commentary and dialogue. The Founding Fathers were well-acquainted with world history and thus harbored grave concerns about democracy. To put it more bluntly, they consistently expressed a strong distaste and distrust for pure democracy. Following are some historical quotes from a handful of the more prominent Founders that are less than flattering in terms of the form of government commonly known as democracy:

- "Democracy is like two wolves and a lamb voting on what to eat for lunch, but a republic is well-armed lamb contesting the vote." – Benjamin Franklin
- "One of the worst forms of government is a pure democracy, that is, one in which citizens enact and administer the laws directly. Such a government is helpless against the mischief of faction." – James Madison
- "The democracy will cease to exist when you take away from those who are willing to work and give to those who would not." – Thomas Jefferson
- "Real liberty is neither found in despotism or the extremes of democracy, but in moderate governments." – Alexander Hamilton
- "Remember democracy never last long. It soon wastes, exhausts, and murders itself. There never was a democracy yet that did not commit suicide." – John Adams
- "The republican is the only form of government which

is not eternally at open and secret war with the rights of mankind." – Thomas Jefferson

With the possible exception of George Washington, one would be hard-pressed to identify any other individuals who were more influential and important in the creation of our country and form of government than the historic figures quoted above.

In a democracy, the majority has total power and is thus in a position to strip the minority of their rights and deny the minority group any respect or consideration. James Madison and his compatriots were greatly concerned about the potential abuse posed by "the tyranny of the majority." The people in "flyover country" are deprived of enough attention as it is, but with a strict democracy, they would be completely at the mercy of the majority. That's not a great place to be. As the Austrian political philosopher Erik von Kuehnelt-Leddiln observed in his book "Leftism," the crucifixion of Jesus was "a democratic event." What the wolves want matters, but so does what the sheep wants."

John Adams knew that democracy is fragile, difficult to maintain, and fraught with the potential to devolve into rule by "mob action." Because of this, democracy often leads to a government takeover of the people, organized by the people. The French Revolution in 1789 is a classic example. After the working class had overthrown the monarchy in a quest for democracy, the majority immediately established a new man to rule over them: Napoleon Bonaparte. Democracy is arduous to organize and often leads to political suicide. History also shows that in many cases a democracy will not last long before someone new becomes appointed to rule over the masses. Thomas Jefferson recognized that a "secret war" naturally occurs under a democracy, a war for power and control. There is a reason Plato said, "Dictatorship naturally arises out of democracy."

The Founders came up with an answer to bypass the risks inherent in a strict democracy. The solution, both brilliant and fortuitous in its inception, was to design a form of government known as a constitutional republic - a system of government that separated the powers of three distinct branches and provided a series of checks and balances between the branches of government. If you recall your civics class in high school, the three branches of our government are legislative, judicial, and executive. Each of these branches has been given a distinct role and each role differs for each branch. The legislative branch is further divided into two separate chambers. The House of Representatives, where the number of members is greater for the more populous states. And the Senate, where each of the 50 states has two representatives (which helps keep less-populated states from being steamrolled). The quest for absolute power is voided when there is no absolute power to achieve. The American Republic is a system of government carefully balanced to safeguard the rights of both the majority and the minority.

I, for one, am extremely grateful the Founders had the foresight to bypass a pure democracy in favor of a republic. The profound differences between a democracy and a constitutional republic are crucial to every aspect of American life. The majority and minority can have their voice heard by representatives who pursue legislation for those they represent. So, the next time somebody starts waxing eloquent, or ineloquent, about our democracy, set them straight and remind them: "We're not a democracy, we're a constitutional republic!"

ELECTORAL COLLEGE

I am a strong proponent of the Electoral College system of electing U.S. presidents. The system is inarguably cumbersome, misunderstood, and awkward, but also ingenious in its concept and a time-tested mechanism for stability in a democracy. The political left does not agree with my contention and conviction. They want to do away with the Electoral College and have presidents elected by a simple majority of votes (the popular vote) on a national basis. Forthcoming I will attempt to convince the reader that it would be an egregious error to replace the Electoral College with the popular vote system.

It happens, but it is uncommon for the Electoral College to elect a president that didn't win the popular vote. Our country has only experienced five occasions when a closely divided popular vote and the electoral vote have failed to point in the same direction. The benefits of the Electoral College system far outweigh the handful of times the national popular vote is superseded.

First and foremost, the Electoral College system contributes to the cohesiveness of the country by requiring a distribution of popular support to be elected president. Without such a mechanism, presidents would be selected either through the domination of one populous region over the others or through the domination of large metropolitan areas over the rural ones. Now, politicians seeking the presidency have to stop in Iowa and stand by hogs and hay bales and wear jeans. But without the Electoral College, they wouldn't come near an Iowa hog. The same would apply to numerous other states of lesser populations in the Union. The candidates would fly to the coasts where the population is centered, spending all of their time and money in large urban areas. The people in "flyover states" would be diminished and irrelevant. When people are diminished, they grow sullen and their anger builds. Although fictional, I refer you to the "Hunger Games" as an example.

Proponents also point out, far from diminishing minority interests by depressing voter participation, the Electoral College enhances the status of minority groups. This is because the votes of even small minorities in a State may make the difference between winning all of that State's electoral votes or none of that State's electoral votes. And since ethnic minority groups in the United States tend to concentrate in those States with the most electoral votes, they assume an importance to presidential candidates well out of proportion to their number. The Electoral College also protects the minority of thought and belief. There is always potential for abuse and a risk to liberty when simple majority rules and 50.1% of the electorate has total control over 49.9% of the electorate.

Proponents further argue that the Electoral College contributes to the political stability of the nation by encouraging a two-party system. A practical effect of our current system is to virtually force a third-party movement into one of the two major political parties. Conversely, major parties have every incentive to absorb minor party movements in their continual attempt to win popular majorities in the States. In this process of assimilation, third-party movements are obliged to compromise their more radical views if they hope to attain any of their more generally acceptable objectives. Thus, we end up with two large, pragmatic political parties which tend to be the center of public opinion, rather than dozens of smaller political parties catering to divergent and sometimes extremist views. Lastly, and most importantly in my opinion, I favor the Electoral College because it is at the very core of our system of federalism. It is doubtful we would even have a constitution or a country without federalism. If the Electoral College were abolished, I fear that the 50 individual States would eventually disappear along with the U.S. Senate. It would strike at the very heart of the federal structure laid out in the Constitution. Furthermore, it would lead to the nationalization of our central government – to the detriment of the States. Soon after, we could have immediate national referendums on almost every important issue, swinging one way or another depending on the country's mood at the time. The populated coasts would become supreme. And if California got passionate and wanted Great Lakes water, we would have a quick national vote on it probably followed by the construction of a pipeline to drain the lakes.

The Founders designed the operation of the Electoral College with unusual care. The language of Article 2, Section 1 of the Constitution describing the Electoral College is longer and descends into more detail than any other single issue in the document. It was a contentious issue at the Constitutional Convention and was finally settled by compromise when James Madison "took out a pen and paper and sketched out Electing the president" by a "college" of "Electors... chosen by those of the people in each State, who shall have the qualifications requisite." In conclusion, whether attributable to intellectual brilliance, blind luck, or a combination thereof, I am one citizen who is grateful for the structure of government established by our country's Founders and will vigorously defend both the Electoral College and federalism.

FIRST AMENDMENT

The Constitution of the United States is the supreme law of the United States of America. It superseded the Articles of Confederation, the nation's first constitution, in 1789. There are currently 27 amendments to the Constitution. In 1791, a list of ten amendments was added to the Constitution. The first ten amendments to the Constitution are called the Bill of Rights. Following are the specific words of the First Amendment: "Congress shall make no law respecting an establishment of religion, or prohibiting the free exercise thereof; or abridging the freedom of speech, or of the press; or the right of the people peaceably to assemble, and to petition the Government for a redress of grievances."

There is a reason why the First Amendment was designated the first amendment to the Constitution. It is vitally important and essential to the existence of a free country. Although the First Amendment applies only to state actors and government censorship, there is a common misconception that it prohibits anyone from limiting free speech, including private non-governmental entities. Moreover, the Supreme Court has determined that the protection of speech is not absolute. As evidenced by history, the parameters established by the First Amendment can be gray, blurred, and subject to mixed interpretations.

Throughout history, many kingdoms and nations have closely aligned themselves with religion by establishing official, government-endorsed faiths. Even today, more than 80 countries either have an official religion or favor one or more religious groups over others. The First Amendment precludes that situation from occurring in the United States. America's Founders were averse to creating a society where all were forced to worship the God of one particular religion. The separation of church and state was first broached by Thomas Jefferson. Separation helps to prevent the government from promoting one religion or sect over the others. The "wall of separation between church and state" is an American original. The idea was born during the Enlightenment. But it was first implemented in the "American Experiment." Until then, no other nation had sought to protect the people's right to think freely by separating religion and government. We should be proud of that fact.

As mentioned earlier, the protection of speech is not absolute and unlimited. The Supreme Court has carved out exceptions to First Amendment protections. Those would include speech that incites listeners to riot or to conduct other illegal activities, threatens someone with violence, or is harmful in certain other ways. The government has the power to prevent speech that displays a clear and present danger of riot or another immediate threat to public safety, peace, or order. At the same time, people have a constitutional right to advocate violence in general, even for abhorrent reasons. The First Amendment does not give you the right to make a direct, "true threat." A true threat is meant to communicate a serious intention to carry out imminent violence against someone. Whether something you say is considered a true threat or protected free speech often depends on the courts where you live, as well as the individual circumstances.

Direct personal insults aren't protected free speech if they're so offensive that they're likely to provoke the listener to resort to immediate violence. Pornography is protected free speech unless it fits within the Supreme Court's strict definition of obscenity or it involves children. Perjury (lying under oath) is not protected by the First Amendment. The same would apply to plagiarism – copying other people's writing, art, or music without their permission. And lastly, soliciting someone else to commit a crime and the act of blackmail are also exempt from First Amendment protections.

Elon Musk's purchase of the social media platform Twitter in late 2022 has pushed to the forefront various opinions and dialogue concerning the present state and future of free speech in the United States. To no one's surprise, records and evidence are surfacing and being made public that show Twitter was an important ally of the Democratic Party. Conservatives and their viewpoints were consistently censored on this platform. Contingent to the government not being involved, I have no problem with this approach. Social media platforms are private companies and thus censor what people post on the platform as they see fit.

We are learning, however, that it might not be that cut and dried and there may be complicated issues that are problematic. It appears that the executive branch of the federal government may have violated First Amendment provisions by directing or influencing Twitter to censor specific content on their platform. It will be interesting to see how this shakes out. I would not be surprised if a legal case involving this matter eventually finds its way to the docket of the Supreme Court.

I am a fan, an advocate, of the First Amendment. That would particularly be applicable insofar as free speech and freedom of the press. I find it ironic that in contemporary America, the greatest threat to these important freedoms is coming from the left. This is the exact opposite of the 1960s when elements of the right were hell-bent on restricting free speech. I guess if you live long enough you see about everything. Although it cannot be unfettered, when it comes down to either having too little freedom or too much freedom, my preference is to error on the side of too much freedom.

IMMIGRATION

The immigration debate in the United States has been contentious for decades, and if anything, is more politically divisive now than at any time in the last 50 years. Like most major issues, there are pros and cons involved with people immigrating to the U.S. from other countries. I will attempt to share some of those benefits and costs. I will also go on record and state we should adopt dual policies that expand legal immigration while at the same time reducing levels of illegal immigration.

The United States has always been considered a nation of immigrants. Continuous waves of immigration helped form the landscape, culture, and economy Americans are familiar with today. The U.S. has been built on the hard work of hungry migrants willing to make sacrifices for future generations. They are ambitious risk-takers like none other. Immigrants have played a vital role in shaping the U.S. as a leading innovator. They are much more likely to embrace the entrepreneurial spirit and start a business compared to native-born Americans. The percentage of our population that is foreign-born approximates 13.5%. This translates into about 45 million people out of a total population of 330 million.

A Gallup poll a few years ago found that 750 million people worldwide would permanently leave their countries if they could, with the U.S. as the top choice of destination. A great many migrants to the U.S. are fleeing insufferable conditions, driven by poor, corrupt governance. People tend to vote with their feet. They feel so strongly about it that they've left loved ones, gambled life savings, and set off on precarious journeys to secure better lives. The squalor of their homelands is not for them. They believe they can do better. Those who decide to come here mostly admire American institutions or have opinions on policies that are in many respects similar to those of native-born Americans.

One huge benefit of increased immigration is that it offsets declining birth rates in the United States. As various global economies and their populations age, that combination can become a serious social problem. The primary concern with declining birth rates is that future generations will have smaller pools of workers who struggle to support larger, aging populations. A stark example of this would be our social security benefits system. The number of workers contributing to the system is growing more slowly than the number of beneficiaries receiving monthly benefits. In 1960, there were 5.1 workers per beneficiary; that ratio has dropped to 2.8 today. The U.S. birth rate has fallen by 20% since the 2008 Great Recession. In 2008, there were 2.12 births per woman, compared to 1.64 births per woman in 2020. This is unsustainable. There need to be 2.1 children per woman to ensure a stable population. Bottom line -immigration can help nations increase or maintain their population numbers.

There is no question that anti-immigration advocates have some legitimate concerns and reservations regarding our country admitting immigrants, especially of an illegal nature. One frequent argument from the right is that importing large numbers of people from abroad depresses the wages of workers already here. The left counters with the claim that native-born workers don't compete for jobs with immigrants because the two groups are in different occupations – "jobs Americans won't do is the shorthand term" – are not without basis. It's just that immigrants are more likely to compete against other immigrants so the effect on less-skilled native-born Americans might be relatively small.

Other variables make the immigration proposition less than favorable in the eyes of many. Large influxes of immigration can stir social conflict within host countries. Limits on immigration contribute to the stability of social arrangements. To be successful and harmonious, any society needs to cultivate a sense of fellowship and solidarity among its members. There is no avoiding the reality that admitting large numbers of poor people into the U.S. inevitably strains the resources of our institutions and creates costs for . The majority of illegal immigrants don't pay income taxes while still using public services such as schooling and healthcare. The economist, Milton Friedman, made an astute observation when he was still alive. Professor Friedman maintained that a country can't have both a relatively open immigration system and a generous welfare state.

Besides valid concerns, there are a few myths surrounding immigration to the United States. One myth is that it is easy to immigrate (legally) to the U.S. The process is anything but easy and takes on average 2-3 years. Based on government data, about 900,000 immigrants became U.S. citizens during the 2022 fiscal year (10/1/21 – 9/30/22). That is not a lot of new citizens when you take into account that the population of the U.S. is 330 million. Another prominent myth is immigrants are a major source of crime. Just the opposite is true, native-born Americans, both on a per capita basis and in raw numbers, are the major source of crime. Another interesting tidbit that surprises most people is that immigrants consume 28 percent less welfare and entitlement benefits than native-born Americans on a per capita basis.

Under the utterly inept leadership of President Joe Biden, the worst border crisis in our country's history is currently ongoing with no end in sight. Due to the terrible policies and publicizing such, the southern border is a sieve with several thousand aliens illegally entering the U.S. daily. Border security and thus national security is exposed to risk. Based on Biden's track record while in office, many of his detractors believe it has slipped the President's mind that America has a southern border. These same detractors opine that an open border is exactly what Democrats desire to change the demographic composition of the country. As conservative, older Republicans kick the bucket, the theory is that young immigrants who become citizens tend to vote for liberal candidates. The Left is counting on this shift to keep them in power for the indefinite future.

As I wrap up this section on immigration, I'll specify what I would do if suddenly a magic wand was waved and I was named Czar of Immigration with the power to implement policies I saw fit. Number one would be to act aggressively, maybe excessively aggressively, to close the door and plug the leaks on the porous southern border. The situation has reached the point where it is both ridiculous and dangerous. Word has to be disseminated that anybody caught attempting to enter the country illegally will be immediately detained, identified, and then returned to the non-American side of the border. They will further be informed that they have broken U.S. law and that action may preclude them from ever being considered for U.S. citizenship in the future.

At the same time, I would liberally expand the legal immigration parameters. Instead of 1 million new citizens each year, I would triple that number to 3 million. A merit-based system that would award points for attributes like education, vocational skills, and English language proficiency would be introduced. The spouse and young children of existing U.S. citizens would be prioritized. Besides considering the vocational skills of prospective immigrants, those with technological skills or other skills in high demand in our economy would move to the front of the line. Contrary to current practice, I would sparingly grant political asylum only to the small number of refugees whose situation is factually both genuine and extraordinary. Both Reagan and Bush (H.W.) signed reform bills that increased enforcement while providing pathways to citizenship for millions of undocumented immigrants. Now is as good a time as ever for similar action.

JANUARY 6

As I write these words on the above-referenced topic, I note with irony that today's date is January 6, 2023 – two years to the date that a mob of Trump supporters raised havoc at the United States Capitol Building in Washington, D.C. The mob was seeking to keep Donald Trump in power by preventing a joint session of Congress from counting the electoral college votes to formalize the election victory of President-elect Joe Biden. More than 2,000 rioters entered the Capitol Building, many of whom occupied, vandalized, and looted the structure. Multiple Capitol Police officers were physically assaulted. January 6 was a shameful, horrible, embarrassing event. It gave our country a black eye and was a gift of significant magnitude to the Democratic Party that they will milk for eternity. People who trespassed, damaged property, or behaved violently on that infamous day should be prosecuted. The news media and the Left use the word "insurrection" to describe January 6. They are wrong. It wasn't even close to an insurrection.

Both in dictionary terms and legal terminology the events of January 6 fall short of being considered an insurrection. The Merriam-Webster Dictionary defines insurrection as "an act or instance of revolting against civil authority or an established government." A usage note adds that the term implies "an armed uprising that quickly fails or succeeds." As noted above, the word insurrection is a legal term and is defined as "a violent revolt against oppressive authority" and "requires an organized group that plans an attack to overthrow the government."

The following comments were extracted from an article drafted by Jeffrey Scott Shapiro and which appeared in the Op-Ed section of the 1/5/22 Wall Street Journal: "Other near-synonyms (to insurrection) include rebellion, revolution, uprising, revolt, and mutiny. All require two elements, neither of which was present in the Jan. 6 breach – the organized use of violent force and the aim of replacing one government or political system with another."

"The demonstrators who unlawfully entered the Capitol during the Electoral College count were unarmed and had no intention of overthrowing the U.S. constitutional system or engaging in a conspiracy against the United States, or to defraud the United States. On the contrary, many of them believed – however erroneously – that the U.S. constitutional system was in jeopardy from voter fraud, and they desperately lashed out in a dangerous, reckless hysteria to protect that system."

Mr. Shapiro goes on to write: "A real insurrection would have required the armed forces to quell an armed resistance. Actual insurrections – apart from the Civil War – include Shays' Rebellion in 1787, in which thousands of insurrectionists tried to seize weapons from a Massachusetts armory after months of planning to overthrow the new revolutionary government, and the Whiskey Rebellion in 1794, in which 500 armed men attacked the home of a U.S. tax inspector in Western Pennsylvania. Both events required President Washington to quell the insurrections with thousands of armed troops who killed numerous resisters.

Shapiro finishes up his well-written article with the following tidbits: "The media's mischaracterization of these events created a moral panic that unfairly stigmatized Trump supporters across the nation as white supremacists conspiring to overthrow the U.S. government, resulting in the unnecessary mobilization of armed U.S. troops in Washington." "Those who violated the law inside the U.S. Capitol should be prosecuted and, if convicted, sentenced accordingly. But dramatizing a riot as an organized, racist, armed insurrection is false reporting and dangerous political gaslighting."

"The misuse of words, especially involving criminal accusations, can easily result in overreaching enforcement of the law and a chilling effect on free speech, all of which already happened – and in this case, endanger the very system the rioters' accusers purport to protect." In the days, weeks, months, and even years following the 1/6 riot, there have been almost 1,000 arrests made in connection with the storming of the Capitol. Of those nearly 1,000 defendants, not a single one was charged with insurrection under 18 U.S.C. 2383. It should be noted this was under the tenure of a Department of Justice controlled by a Democratic administration. To date, only a small percentage of those charged have been accused of violent crimes. The vast majority of those arrested have been charged with trespassing violations. Despite what was often reported, only one person was killed that day (1/6/21). A 14-year military veteran named Ashley Babbitt was shot and killed when a Capitol Police officer discharged his weapon as a throng of rioters attempted to overpower a closed entryway. That was the only shot fired during the melee.

The applicable FBI investigation has yielded little evidence of a coordinated and organized attack. There were a couple of dozen members of anti-government groups charged with seditious conspiracy to stir up trouble but with no intent to topple the government. Video footage shows people walking single file past idle officers as they entered the building. Afterward, most exited on their own accord. Most of those who breached the Capitol stood around taking pictures. Based on comments made by participants during court appearances, none of them stated the event was planned. Furthermore, most indicated they didn't know why they did it. At times an impassioned mob will defy individual thought and logic and assume an irrational mind of its own.

Both Trump's lawyers and the DOJ concluded within two weeks after the election (11/3/20) that legal challenges to the election results had no factual basis or legal merit. Despite those analyses, Trump sought to overturn the results by initiating the filing of at least sixty lawsuits, including two brought to the Supreme Court. Those challenges were all rejected by the courts for lack of evidence or the absence of legal standing. Trump then mounted a campaign to pressure Republican governors, secretaries of state, and state legislatures to nullify results by replacing slates of Biden electors with those declared to Trump. Former President Trump deserves a significant portion of the blame for the January 6 debacle. On the day of the riot Trump, despite urgent pleas from close family members and advisers, resisted sending the National Guard to quell the mob at the Capitol. It was almost like he was mesmerized by the enfolding train wreck and didn't snap back to reality until it was over. A week after the riot, the House of Representatives impeached Trump for incitement of insurrection, making him the only U.S. president to have been impeached twice. As with the first impeachment, Trump was acquitted for a second time. The House then passed a bill to create a select committee to investigate the attack on the Capitol Building.

Most conservatives, including myself, considered the 1/6 Commission a sham, a Kangaroo Court, political theatre to the extreme, and an 18-month infomercial for the Democrats in anticipation of the 2022 midterms. The select committee had nine members, seven Democrats and two Republicans that despised Trump – Adam Kinzinger and Liz Cheney. The Committee held nine televised hearings in 2022 to railroad Trump and damage the GOP's prospects in the midterms. As much as they tried, they were unable to uncover evidence that would place Trump in jeopardy of being convicted of inciting a riot. I will acknowledge that Trump's actions that day (1/6) were morally reprehensible. That said, his words and actions fall short of being legally accountable for inciting a riot. It will be interesting to see if the Justice Department pursues any criminal charges vs. Trump. I would be surprised if the DOJ files charges.

Arguments that January 6 was a failed coup attempt and that democracy was teetering on the brink of destruction are hyperbolic to the extreme and not supported by reality. I say this because of the overwhelming domination of our nation's major institutions by progressives. I maintain the following institutions are controlled by self-proclaimed liberals: 1.) The White House; 2.) Congress; 3.) Television; 4.) Large Corporations; 5.) Major Newspapers; 6.) Organized Labor; 7.) Silicon Valley; 8.) Education; 9.) Military; 10.) Hollywood; 11.) Professional Sports; 12.) Pop Culture & Entertainment; 13.) Wall Street; 14.) Social Media Platforms; 15.) Federal Bureaucracy. It appears to me that the Left holds a strong poker hand.

SENATE AND SCOTUS

I am mentioning the U.S. Senate because the composition of the Senate has come under criticism from progressives over the past decade. Unlike the House of Representatives, the upper chamber of Congress, the Senate, is not representative of the population of the various States. California is the most populous State. As a result, it has the most representation in the United States House of Representatives with 52 Representatives. Wyoming is the least populous State in the nation. It is represented by one Representative in the House. Wyoming has more U.S. Senators than U.S. Representatives, two vs. one. Every State has two Senators, with 50 States, which translates into 100 U.S. Senators. The Senate is widely considered the more deliberative and more prestigious body of Congress – primarily due to its longer terms and smaller size. The Senate also has several powers of advice and consent which are unique to it. These include the approval of treaties, and the confirmation of Cabinet secretaries, federal judges, flag officers, regulatory officials, ambassadors, other federal executive officials, and federal uniformed officers.

As indicated earlier in this section, progressives despise the format that determines Senate membership – basically for the same reasons they hate the Electoral College. Since the left is presently in power, they desire to forsake the principles of our constitutional republic and adopt a pure democracy. They fail to realize they probably won't always remain in power and the rights of the minority are important and relevant as well. Each State allocated two Senators also distributes power and influence on both a geographical and ideological basis. For an expansive, diverse country like the U.S., this is beneficial. The filibuster is a political procedure utilized by a Senator(s) in which a vote is delayed or blocked on a piece of legislation or a confirmation. The procedure to end a filibuster is known as "cloture." In 1975 the Senate reduced the number of votes required for cloture from two-thirds of Senators voting to three-fifths of all Senators, or 60 of the 100-member Senate. Both Republicans and Democrats have a love/hate relationship with the filibuster. They love it when they are in the minority in the Senate, and they hate it when they are in the majority. I believe the filibuster is an excellent rule. It is beneficial to the country in its entirety when the Senate reaches a consensus and bi-partisan action is taken.

The Supreme Court of the United States (SCOTUS) has also found itself in the crosshairs of the progressive left. Former president Donald Trump appointed three conservative judges to the Supreme Court during his tenure in office. This gave the Court a decidedly conservative tilt, with the Court one of the few national institutions to lean right. Not satisfied with controlling only the vast majority of American institutions, a conservative Supreme Court drives progressives absolutely bonkers. Historically, if the left did not have the votes to advance their liberal agenda via the legislative route, they attempted to bypass Congress by utilizing the judicial branch. Fortunately, this is not possible with the current Court.

Although there have been nine high court judges since 1869, in recent years Senate and House Democrats have introduced legislation to "pack" the Supreme Court, expanding the number of justices from nine to 13 to guarantee liberal victories at the Court. To date, this legislation has languished. The Biden administration created (in 2021) a 36-member, heavily left-wing commission comprised almost entirely of law professors – to consider and recommend changes to the Supreme Court. A ruling party packing the nation's highest court is a rare national embarrassment even in less developed countries. If Democrats ever manage to pack the Supreme Court, our country will join the august ranks of Venezuela in 2004 and Argentina in 1989. That any Democrats are seriously considering a plan to pack the Supreme Court is a profoundly sad development for the United States.

SOCIAL MEDIA

It would be interesting to have the ability to look a century into the future and see what historians have to say and write about the ubiquitous phenomenon we commonly refer to as social media. One of the first aspects noted by those 22nd-century historians would be the unbelievable growth in usage from 2005 until 2022. In 2005, only about 5 percent of users in the United States were involved in social media. By 2020, that number grew to about 70 percent. The internet has become a significant part of our daily lives. So too has social media. It has reached the point where many individuals cannot imagine life without it. Since the inception of social media, I have taken the position that social media is a net positive for society. In other words, the benefits and advantages offered by social media outweigh the costs and disadvantages. Today, I'm not confident making that identical claim. The argument can be made that neutral or even net negative has been reached in terms of social media's overall influence on our culture. Before looking at some of the harmful effects of social media, we'll first explore some of the beneficial aspects of social media.

First and foremost, social media provides the means to connect people. For example, we get the opportunity to see what our family and friends are doing regardless of where they live in the world. Social media can be a powerful tool to help us maintain relationships with individuals from our past and provides us with opportunities to develop new personal and professional relationships. Another benefit is that it can facilitate the distribution of information quickly to large amounts of people. A couple of examples of this would be invitations to a party or updating the status of an individual that is either sick or recovering from an injury. In a similar light, a connection can be established between people who are suffering and provide them with an opportunity for social support. Education around health issues can also be enhanced. In the workplace, a platform like LinkedIn is used to find employment opportunities and connect professional communities. Social media can be an effective marketing tool, provide quick access to information and research, and provide an avenue for civic engagement. We should also note that social media platforms allow for rapid communication in times of crisis. There are additional positives offered by social media, but those just mentioned are some of the more significant ones.

And then there is the dark, disturbing underbelly of social media platforms. Because social media is relatively new from a historical perspective, we are still evaluating some of the negatives of using it. But we already know enough to be concerned. A significant con of social media is that it has taken away privacy. Today, privacy is nothing more than an illusion. If someone takes an unflattering picture of another, it can quickly be disseminated to thousands of people in an instant. One does not always know who is on the other end of a social media account. Fake social media accounts are easily created and false information and statements are easily circulated without proper verification. It is often used to snoop on others as well. Ironically, excessive social media usage can contribute to social isolation. Research has shown that it can increase feelings of depression and anxiety. One-on-one communication has been dramatically reduced for many people due to social media usage. This is not a healthy trend. One study indicated that 32% of the people in a survey were either texting or on social media sites, instead of communicating with each other during family gatherings. Another concern is that it appears to some people that social media can become addicting. Research demonstrates that the first time we begin responding to social media notifications, dopamine is released in the brain which makes us feel good. Dopamine boosts mood and motivation and assists in regulating movement, learning, and emotional responses. It is part of our brain's reward system. This might be one of the many reasons that heavy social media users have to increase using it more often to get the same pleasurable sensation they had when they first started using it.

The hits just keep on coming. The primary sources of print news information that people read are no longer newspapers such as the *New York Times*, *Washington Post*, or *Wall Street Journal*. Yes, it would be social media websites. I find this trend downright scary. Employers are not fond of social media. Platforms like Facebook and Twitter are a direct cause of productivity loss in the workplace. Since their brains are still in development, children and teenagers are especially susceptible to the influences of social media. Fear of Missing Out (FOMO) leads young people to continually check social media sites. The possibility that you might miss out on something if you're not online can affect mental health. There can also be self-image issues, particularly for young girls. It is unhealthy to link self-worth to the comparison of one's physical attributes to that of others. Cyberbullying is still another issue. Kids have always been cruel to some of their peers, but social media can take bullying to a whole other level. Suicide rates among 10-to-14-year-olds have grown by more than 50% over the last three decades.

To a certain extent, social media networks and guns have similarities. Both are inanimate tools that are in the total control of human beings. Both come with aspects that could be considered good, bad, or ugly. Many people enjoy both guns and social media responsibly, but in the wrong hands, they have the potential to be dangerous. Guns are heavily regulated by the majority of countries. I foresee the federal government eventually enacting legislation and regulations that will restrict and perhaps even ban certain facets of social media.

Nevertheless, social media is here to stay. Learning to use it well and in positive ways is important to our mental and emotional well-being. No doubt due to my certified "old coot" status and personality characteristics, I have for the most part kept my distance from social media platforms. I allowed a friend to talk me into getting on Facebook in either 2008 or 2009. My involvement was consistently at a minimal level – signing on to the account on a quarterly or semi-annual basis. Shortly after the 2016 election, I exited stage left. The constant liberal blathering from certain Facebook "friends" was not conducive to my hypertension issues. I realize "de-friendling" was a route to take, but I was done with the whole medium. Unless I'm physically incapacitated to a great extent, I don't see that changing at any point up to when I'm pushing up daisies and therefore moot. There are too many other rewarding and interesting activities to pursue.

THE RISE OF CHINA

For almost 2,000 years, from before the birth of Jesus Christ up until the 18th century, besides being the planet's most populous political entity, China featured the world's richest economy and one of our most advanced civilizations. For various reasons, including the Industrial Revolution not being embraced by isolationist ruling elites, China descended into general poverty with little or no economic growth. Ultimately this once proud nation was torn apart by civil war and revolution. China was humiliated and not taken seriously by the world's powers. In 1949, the Chinese Communist Party (CCP) led by Mao Zedong emerged victorious in the Chinese Civil War and became the sole ruling party of the People's Republic of China. For the next three decades, China languished as a Third World nation while many nations realized economic growth and prosperity.

Led by Deng Xiaoping, often credited as the "General Architect," economic reforms were launched by reformists within the Chinese Communist Party starting on December 18, 1978. The CCP allowed the economic system to open up from total state control and unleashed powerful elements unique to capitalism. Individuals in China were not allocated political freedom, but they were allowed to enjoy the fruits of economic freedom. The transformation was nothing short of amazing. By the 1990s, China's economy was in high gear, growing annually at double-digit rates. Over the course of 40 years, this country of 1.2 billion inhabitants experienced remarkable economic gains with over a half billion people lifted out of debilitating poverty. By 2020, China was rapidly approaching equality with the United States in terms of Gross Domestic Product. It was also considered on equal footing with the U.S. insofar as military capability. If it hasn't already, it looks like China will soon be joining America in the world's superpower club.

Its history, its size, and the feeling of potency brought on by the remarkable growth of the past three decades push China to want something more and to take back the place that they feel foreigners stole from them. China's people and leaders believe their nation's time has come once again. The Chinese government remains staunchly communist and steeped in a belligerent form of nationalism and ruled over by men who respond to every perceived threat or slight with disproportionate self-assertion. China's leaders are convinced that America is determined to contain China. A combustible situation appears to be brewing. The combination of China's desire to re-establish itself and America's determination not to let that desire disrupt its interests and you have the sort of ill-defined rivalry that can be dangerous.

China's economic gains were predicated on taking an extremely aggressive posture with the rest of the world, particularly the U.S. China is doubling down on a reluctance not to share reciprocal trade arrangements with their trading partners. Many sectors are still closed to foreign competition. China maintains numerous tariffs as well as non-tariff barriers that block foreign access to its domestic markets. They are engaged in rampant intellectual property theft through either direct corporate espionage or forced transfer of technology. Threatened with expulsion or encountering costly disruptions to services or market access, many Western firms have reluctantly agreed to form joint ventures that favor China. There is no doubt that President Trump's trade war started in 2018 against China harmed U.S.-China relations. In addition to massive tariffs imposed on U.S. imports from China, Trump implemented an array of measures to curtail China's technological advancements.

As is typically the case with a communist government, China's citizens have virtually zero political freedom and are subject to a police state that exists to internally keep an eye on and control the behavior of the masses. Any dissent carries with it great risk. Political activists or suspected enemies of the CPC are detained without legal grounds and subjected to harassment, arrest, inadequate healthcare, and even torture. The CPC engages in extensive surveillance – relying on the use of facial recognition software and big data for increasingly pervasive spying and control. A social credit system is being developed by the government. The social credit initiative calls for the establishment of a record system so that businesses, individuals, and government institutions are tracked and evaluated for trustworthiness. The Chinese government habitually imposes political education on its citizens, sometimes to the extent of detaining them in re-education camps. The most blatant example of this would be the holding of hundreds of thousands of Uyghurs in Xinjiang internment camps.

In recent years China has also flexed its military muscles outside its borders and now is poised to challenge the territorial status quo as perceived by the United States. In the South China Sea, China has engaged in island construction, reclamation, and development. The rise of China threatens to undermine the U.S.-led security order in Asia. Chinese military modernization, particularly in the maritime sphere, has begun to shift the regional balance of power. Beijing has taken increasingly provocative actions against its neighbor, Taiwan, officially the Republic of China (ROC). These actions include flying fighter jets near the island and conducting naval drills and games in the proximity of the island nation of Taiwan.

Taiwan has been governed independently of China since 1949, but Beijing views the island and its 23 million inhabitants as part of its territory. Communist China has publicly vowed to eventually "unify" Taiwan with the mainland, using force if necessary. Everyone acknowledges that China is as serious as a heart attack in pursuing this endeavor. Most people in Taiwan support maintaining the status quo, but that is not relevant to China. For now, China's objective is to wear down Taiwan and prompt the island's people to conclude their best option is unification with the mainland. Through its policy of strategic ambiguity, the U.S. has for decades attempted to maintain a delicate balance between supporting Taiwan and avoiding war with China.

Many in the U.S. intelligence community believe China will attack Taiwan in the next decade, maybe as soon as 2024 when Taiwan has national elections. Instead of an amphibious assault, the attack may take the form of a naval blockade and quarantine to choke off the island's trade. Taiwan is the world's top contract manufacturer of semiconductors – generating 50% of the world's chip revenues. For this reason and others, some analysts fear the U.S. and China could go to war over Taiwan. Unlike Japan and South Korea, the U.S. has no mutual defense treaty with Taiwan. I hope that the United States restricts its involvement in the Taiwan conflict. Doing something similar to what we are presently doing for Ukraine would be acceptable in my opinion. The best thing we could do is get our act together and begin producing more semiconductors and microchips, sooner rather than later.

TRUMP

Trump. If there is another name, word, or term that has been bandied about more frequently over the past decade, I'm not aware of it. Suffice it to say that the discussions surrounding this mere human being that goes by the name of Trump have sucked an inordinate amount of oxygen out of the arena where we talk and write about current affairs. According to Wikipedia, Donald John Trump (born June 14, 1946) is an American politician, media personality, and businessman who served as the 45th president of the United States from 2017 to 2021. He came into the world via the silver spoon express, was born into a wealthy family, and inherited about $40 million from his late father, New York City real estate developer Fred Trump.

Trump graduated from the Wharton School of the University of Pennsylvania with a bachelor's degree in 1968. There have been claims he graduated at or near the top of this class, but the relevant records do not substantiate that claim. He avoided serving in Vietnam courtesy of five military draft deferments – four times for college and once for bad feet. Democratic Senator Tammy Duckworth, a Purple Heart recipient, once called him "Cadet Bone Spurs." At any rate, after graduation, Trump went to work for his father. He became president of his father's real estate business in 1971 and renamed it The Trump Organization. Trump expanded the company's operations to building and renovating skyscrapers, hotels, casinos, and golf courses and later started side ventures, mostly by licensing his name. From 2004-2015 he co-produced and hosted the popular reality television series "The Apprentice." Trump and his businesses have been involved in more than 4,000 state and federal legal actions, including six bankruptcies.

History informs us that Mr. Trump is somewhat of a flip-flopper when it comes to his affiliation with political parties.

Trump registered as a Republican in Manhattan in 1987. He then switched to the Reform Party in 1999. In 2001, it was time to try the Democratic Party. After eight years with the blue donkeys, it was back to the red pachyderms in 2009. Trump and his most loyal followers have always loosely thrown around the pejorative term RINO – an acronym standing for "Republican In Name Only." In my estimation, it is Trump who is the RINO. He has successfully hijacked the G.O.P. and the conservative cause, which many Republicans fail to grasp. Trump is not a true conservative. This is especially the case in matters concerning economics. I've concluded that the Orange Man is the founding father of the Trump Party – a transaction-based political party untethered to many of the traditional values and principles of the conservative base in America.

I also hold the theory that Trump ran for the presidency in 2015-2016 primarily to obtain free publicity and advertising to enhance the monetary value of his brand. Although he is exceedingly arrogant, I would be surprised if he anticipated winning the Republican nomination, let alone the presidency. In the G.O.P. primaries, Trump was one of 17 candidates. Until the 2020 Democratic primary race, it was the largest field in the history of U.S. politics. The size of the field helped Trump immensely, spreading the vote between many different candidates. Besides the large field, Trump's name recognition, uniqueness, and anti-establishment attitude contributed to securing the nomination. I favored Ohio Governor John Kasich and was disappointed when the Trump juggernaut rolled over Kasich and several other qualified Republican candidates.

Trump's narrow win over Hillary Clinton in 2016 stunned the world. The various pollsters and pundits were universally wrong with their predictions of a cakewalk for Clinton. The results should not have been as surprising as they were. Hillary Clinton was a candidate with no shortage of flaws, including the fact she lacked magnetism and in general had an unlikeable personality. She made a mistake when she took Wisconsin and Michigan for granted and didn't campaign in those states. In addition, she made a huge mistake by verbally categorizing a large segment of the electorate as "deplorables." Trump was the right candidate at the right time. He appealed to the deplorables and others that were sick and tired of conventional politicians and globalization. Populism and nationalism were making a comeback in the developed world. Trump rode this wave. He was able to secure a majority of Independent voters – a requirement for a Republican win on the national level.

It would have been impossible for a man of Trump's character to win a presidential election in 1980, or 2000 for that matter. The evolution of the American public experienced a waning of Puritanism and less sensitivity to the morality of their elected officials. They prioritized a candidate who could get the job done and most aligned with their ideology. All these factors aside, Hillary Clinton would have probably been president if FBI Director James Comey had not sent a letter to Congress ten days before the election. The letter, which said the FBI had "learned of the existence of emails that appear to be pertinent to the investigation" in the private email server that Clinton used as secretary of state, upended the news cycle and soon halved Clinton's lead in the polls.

Regardless of political affiliation, I've always granted a new president a 6-12 month "honeymoon" or grace period. Before leveling criticism, I thought it only fair to give the new president, any new president, an opportunity to govern and lead our nation. This attitude appears to be rare these days and certainly wasn't the case for the tens of millions of people who refused to accept Trump based on principle. A quasi-formal "Resistance," both inside government and outside government, was established even before Trump took the oath of office. There was resistance to many Trump policies for the sole reason that Trump implemented said policies. The viability, merits, and logic of the policies were not considered relevant. As we will soon see, some parties inside government were not simply part of the Resistance, they became activists bent on sabotaging the Trump presidency by any means they deemed necessary.

The anti-Trump activists inside government sometimes referred to as "Permanent Washington" or "The Deep State," pulled out all of the stops to destroy Trump. It was like something right out of the "Dirty Political Tricks" playbook compiled by Richard Nixon. Timely leaks to the press starting in 2016 implied that the Trump campaign illicitly colluded with Russia to win the presidential election in November 2016. Some in the media and the permanent D.C. bureaucracy went so far as to declare Trump a Russian agent. This was something more than disingenuous – it was a bald-faced lie. An extensive investigation headed by Robert Mueller found no evidence of collusion or even a connection between Russia and the Trump campaign/administration. On top of that, the infamous Steele dossier used to justify the Trump investigation was an opposition research report funded by the Clinton campaign and the DNC. This shoddily constructed and unverified dossier was used to hoodwink the FISA court to authorize spying on the Trump campaign. Bottom line - some prominent employees in the FBI attempted to influence the election outcome. News reporters and Democratic Congressmen bombarded the news cycle with untrue claims of Russian involvement. This became known as the "Russian Collusion Hoax."

On the cusp of the 2020 presidential election, the New York Post published an unflattering article concerning the contents of Joe Biden's son Hunter's computer laptop. The mainstream corporate media, Big Tech, and the Deep State elites worked in concert to bury the story. The reason given for suppressing this true and accurate reporting – is "Russian misinformation." More than 50 former senior intelligence officials signed a letter outlining their belief that the October 2020 disclosure of emails in Hunter Biden's laptop "had all the classic earmarks of a Russian information operation." The FBI had possession of the laptop for almost two years before finally acknowledging the information on the computer was not planted by the Russians but 100% attributable to Hunter Biden. Some of the contents of the laptop cast a shadow on the international business dealings of the Biden family, including the "Big Guy" – Joe.

I'm not sure which scandal is worse; the Russian Collusion Hoax, or the Hunter Biden Laptop Coverup. Both are disturbing.

Trump holds the ignoble distinction of being the first president ever impeached twice by the House of Representatives. The first time was in 2019 over the dealings with aid to Ukraine. The second time was shortly after the 1/6/21 riots at the Capitol. The charge was "incitement of insurrection." On both occasions, he was acquitted by the U.S. Senate. Both impeachments were political in nature and did not enjoy bi-partisan support. Why the hatred for Trump? The left hates Trump for myriad reasons, some of the same reasons being what it hates about America. They hate Trump's vulgarity, his unwillingness to walk away from a fight, his bluntness, his certainty that America is exceptional, his mistrust of intellectuals, his affinity for simple ideas that work, and his refusal to believe that men and women are interchangeable.

There are multiple reasons why Trump lost a tight election to Joe Biden in 2020. The obvious reason would be the Covid-19 pandemic. Besides a clumsy response by the government, the pandemic facilitated many states to modify their election procedures. Suffice it to say these procedural changes benefited the Democrats to the detriment of the Republicans. Unlike in 2016, Trump did not win the Independent vote. Many considered him too divisive for the country and others were tired of his personality and antics. What did him in was the "soccer moms." These suburban women did not vote for him. Their vote was based more on emotions than logic and policy positions. The soccer moms considered Trump to be: a womanizer, blowhard, consummate narcissist, obnoxious, crude, bombastic, rude, and needlessly contentious.

It's time to put a fork in the myth that the 2020 election was stolen from Trump. Based on what we know, he lost. No evidence has ever been produced that shows there was sufficient voter fraud to materially alter the Electoral College count. Compared to Trump, down-ballot Republicans did relatively well in the 2020 election. This fact is not consistent with the massive voter fraud contention. Post-election there were over 60 legal challenges to the election outcome. Every single one failed. Trump's refusal to accept the outcome was detrimental to the country. The 1960 election between

John Kennedy and Richard Nixon was an exceptionally close race, much tighter than Biden vs. Trump in 2020. Widespread fraud was suspected in Illinois and Texas, which had enough electoral votes to be decisive. Chicago had a well-earned reputation for election fraud. Mayor Richard J. Daley called Kennedy in Hyannisport and said, "Mr. President, with a little bit of luck and the help of a few close friends, you're going to carry Illinois." Many in Nixon's camp wanted to fight the results. The man who would go on to occupy the White House in 1969 flatly refused, saying: "Our country cannot afford the agony of a constitutional crisis," and "It'd tear the country to pieces. You can't do that." So, he didn't.

U.S. presidents are historically measured under the broad criteria of prosperity and peace. Under both of those categories, the Trump administration did quite well. We'll first take a look at the state of the U.S. economy during Trump's four-year term. Basically, for the first three years, 2017,2018, and 2019, the economy was humming. Growth was higher than at any time in the previous decade, unemployment was at or near record lows, and inflation was practically non-existent. Percentage-wise, the biggest beneficiaries of the strong economy were the lowest quintile of wage earners. The tax rate for corporations was smartly lowered and other changes to the tax code allowed for accelerated depreciation of certain business assets. This led to increased business investment in fixed assets such as equipment and machinery. A couple trillion dollars of monies held overseas by American companies were repatriated back to the U.S. A record number of cumbersome regulations were eliminated. The U.S. became a net exporter of oil and natural gas, becoming energy independent once again. The economy fell off a cliff in early 2020 when the pandemic hit home. Within one- year Americans were receiving emergency authorized vaccinations courtesy of "Operation Warp Speed." Lastly, Trump nominated, and the U.S. Senate confirmed, three highly qualified, bright conservative justices to the Supreme Court. This may one day be considered Trump's most significant accomplishment.

Trump's record was not exactly chopped liver on the foreign

policy front either. Peace prevailed. Trump did not start any new wars and started the process of ending our longest war.

Using a rather direct approach, he either convinced or shamed several of our NATO partners into increasing defense expenditures. Trump directed the U.S. military to put an end to ISIS. He withdrew the U.S. from the unenforceable Iran nuclear agreement while tightening sanctions against that murderous regime. He ordered a successful attack on Iran's chief terrorist, General Qassem Suleimani. Trump fulfilled the promises of his predecessors by moving the U.S. Embassy to Jerusalem. The Trump administration was the driving force behind the first peace agreement in decades between Muslim nations and Israel.

I didn't maintain a running tally, but I would hazard a guess that I approved of 90% of the Trump administration policy positions. The two significant decisions that I thought were bad would have been our withdrawal from the Trans-Pacific Partnership (TPP) and the imposition of tariffs in the trade war he started with China.

Trump's behavior and actions between 11/3/20 and 1/6/21 are the primary reason he will never again garner my support and vote. Denying he lost the election led directly to the debacle at the Capitol. Additional negative factors, at least in my book, are the fact that he is too old, too divisive, has the wrong temperament for the most important job in the world, and has a leadership approach that is not respected by the majority of U.S. citizens. The presence of Trump hurt the Republican Party in the 2022 midterms. The slating of his favored Senate candidates and constant election result denials turned off most moderate Republicans and Independents. Trump claims he is running for president in the 2024 election. God forbid he wins the nomination once again in 2024 because he is unequivocally unelectable in the general election. Trump needs to ride his golf cart off into the sunset.

UKRAINE

The argument can be made that Russia's war with Ukraine has been ongoing since February 2014. Following Ukraine's "Revolution of

Dignity" when they overthrew the corrupt regime of the Moscow-friendly Victor Yanukovych, Russia responded by annexing Crimea from Ukraine and supporting pro-Russian separatists in the war in Donbas against Ukraine government forces. A limited number of Russian troops were also involved in Russia's 2014 foray into the far eastern region of Ukraine. The Kremlin escalated the conflict drastically on February 24th (2022) with an invasion of the entire country. It is thought to be the largest military conflict in Europe since the end of World War II. Most of the world was surprised, if not shocked, by Russia's invasion of Ukraine. They should not have been.

Vladimir Putin's worldview emphasizes a deep-seated unity among the Eastern Slavs -Russians, Ukrainians, and Belarusians. All three of these ethnic groups can trace their origins to the 10th-century Kyivan Rus commonwealth. In Putin's mind, due to shared history, religion, and culture, these groups should be united as a single sovereign entity. The corollary to that view is the Russian claim that distinct Ukrainian and Belarusian identities are the product of Western manipulation and therefore their respective national identities are artificial. The ideological cornerstone of Putinism is the vision of a state locked in a struggle for survival. The desire to reunite the "Russian world" became an obsession with Putin and fueled his brutal invasion of Ukraine in February 2022. The consensus among historians is that Putin wants to reconstitute the Russian Empire and promote Russia's differences from the West and flatten differences among the Slavic peoples.

There is no question that Putin's decision to attack a neighbor and inflict terrible suffering on its citizens was deeply immoral. The citizens of Ukraine had freely chosen independence and their government. Putin had no right to override that choice, regardless of his interpretation of history. Although immoral and risky, Putin's decision to go to war was not irrational. He is not a stupid man. Although he made multiple assumptions about the invasion based on solid prewar data that ultimately proved wrong. The independent polling and demographics before the invasion showed that Ukrainian society was deeply divided. About a quarter of the country were Russian speakers who were Greek Orthodox and attuned to Russian culture. Two-thirds of the country were Ukrainian speakers, Catholic, and more attuned to the West. The total population had declined by 16% since peaking in 1991. Ukraine was the second poorest country in Europe. The majority of Ukrainians (67% vs. 22%) believed that the country was headed in the wrong direction. The government was regarded as highly corrupt and unresponsive. A large minority (40%) said they would not defend the country if attacked.

After a career as a comedian and an actor, Volodymyr Zelensky was elected president of Ukraine in 2019 as a protest against governing elites and corruption. Before the war, President Zelensky's approval rating was barely above 30%. Expecting that Zelensky would, like Winston Churchill, rally the country behind him, vow to never surrender, and physically face danger when under attack would have been a huge stretch. Another assumption was that Russian armed forces were highly effective. They weren't. I guess one could say the Russian Army was a "Paper Bear." The Ukrainian military performed poorly in 2014 when Russia supported the separatists in the Donbas region. Their equipment was obsolescent, dating almost entirely from the Soviet era. In virtually every category, Russia had more modernized and capable equipment than Ukraine. Still another incorrect assumption, a costly one made by the Russians, was that the United States and NATO would be slow and limited in supplying weapons to Ukraine. I can understand this thought process. European nations normally have a difficult time agreeing on anything and then actually following through after reaching an agreement. Unfortunately for the Russians, Europe responded expeditiously and significantly. Also, the invasion of Ukraine was less than six months after the United States ignoble departure from Afghanistan. That debacle possibly factored into the decision made by Putin to go to war.

I am not a supporter of the imposition of draconian economic sanctions, and those imposed on Russia by the U.S. and the West are no exception. I question the effectiveness of these measures in curing the actual problem. The burden will fall on the shoulders of the Russian populace. The ordinary citizen in Russia will be subjected to a deluge of state propaganda. They will conclude that Russia is a fortress, under siege from the West. If anything, the hardships experienced by the Russian people due to the sanctions will strengthen Putin. Russia's typical response to external threats, from Napolean to Hitler, has been to unite in defense of the Motherland. In Russia, a shift of public opinion against the Western-led world is the most likely scenario.

In my opinion, there are numerous risks to the United States due to our proxy involvement in the Russia-Ukraine conflict. Those risks should not be ignored and should be part of any national discussion dealing with a policy on our continued participation. It might come as a shock to Kyiv's strongest supporters, but Ukraine is not the center of the universe. Ukraine isn't important geopolitically and is largely irrelevant to American security. Kyiv's future matters more to Europe. Let's face it, Russia matters more than Ukraine to America. Treating Russia as an enemy risks turning it into one. Pushing Russia into a closer relationship with China is simply not smart foreign policy.

The 1994 Budapest Memorandum on Security Assurances is often brought up by pro-Ukrainian advocates. This agreement dealt with Ukraine relinquishing the nuclear weapons left by the dissolution of the Soviet Union. The three signatories, U.S., Britain, and Russia – made a series of commitments regarding Ukraine. But none of them involved going to war. If the Clinton administration had intended to defend Ukraine, the former would have presented a treaty for Senate approval or forced through Kyiv's accession to NATO.

Vladimir Putin is not Hitler and Russia is not Nazi Germany, or Stalin's Soviet Union for that matter. Even if Putin harbored a plan for widespread territorial conquest, he is without the economic resources and power to pull that off. Putin's ambitions may outrage the West, but they appear bounded. Indeed, if Putin hopes to reconstitute the Soviet Union, as charged by some, he's not doing very well. In power for over 20 years, he only has gained Crimea,

20% of Georgia, and 18% of Ukraine outside of Crimea. Perhaps my concerns are not justified, but I also believe the imposition of severe economic sanctions and the massive amount of financial aid to Ukraine from the U.S. carry with it possible negative repercussions to the U.S. The dollar is still the world's leading reserve currency. For now. The demise of the dollar would be catastrophic to the U.S. economy. A few years ago, Obama's treasury secretary, Jacob Lew, warned, "The more we condition the use of the dollar and our financial system on adherence to U.S. foreign policy, the more risk of migration to other currencies and other financial systems grows. Such outcomes would not be in the best interest of the United States." In absolute terms, the largest supporter of the Ukraine – by a very large margin – was the United States. The total exceeds $50 billion, all of it borrowed from America's creditors. That's a lot of money for a country already in debt of more than $31 trillion.

Henry Kissinger has seen a thing or two in his time as concerns global geopolitics. In 2015 shortly after Russia gobbled up Crimea, the former secretary of state admitted: "If the West is honest with itself, it has to admit that there were mistakes on its side." While Moscow was not justified in forcibly changing boundaries, he argued, "Ukraine has always had a special significance for Russia. It was a mistake not to realize that." Mr. Kissinger urged forbearance in attempts to defeat or marginalize Russia. He called on Ukraine to accept the territorial losses of 2014 to possibly reach a settlement to end this war. I consider his counsel wise and hope it is taken seriously by our leaders. It is in the best interest of the United States to pressure and push for a settlement of this conflict before somebody does something unbelievably stupid.

VANISHING WORKFORCE

Something has changed. The Covid-19 pandemic received most of the blame and no doubt accelerated and exacerbated the problem. But the transformation started a decade before the virus from Wuhan hit our shores. Men have been steadily clocking out of the American workforce since pre-pandemic times – even now despite there being millions of job openings and an uncertain economic climate. An estimated 7 million "prime age" men between the ages of 25 and 54 are reportedly sitting on the sidelines and not participating in the production side of our economy. They are not even looking for work. They've punched out. And sadly, this may not be a temporary situation. They may be throwing in the towel and simply declaring they're done with providing their labor.

With all of this free time, how do the majority of these prime-age men that have exited the labor force spend their day? Are they helping out and doing all of the housework? No. Are they volunteering with local charities and service organizations that assist community members in need? No. Reportedly, they spend around 2,000 hours a year looking at screens. That comes to about 40 hours per week of screen time or an average of just under six hours every day. Needless to say, that represents a staggering amount of time looking at televisions, tablets, smartphones, and computer monitors.

The labor participation rate has been in decline since it peaked at 67.3% in early 2000. Between 2013 and 2020 the labor participation rate hovered around 63%. As of late 2022, the rate stood at 62.1%. The reduced labor force participation rate has especially taken a toll on the leisure, hospitality, and retail sectors. One outcome is there is more pressure on the remaining employees, who often are dealing with longer hours, tougher responsibilities, and burnout. The Minneapolis Federal Reserve Bank found that 25% of prime-age Americans (men and women) aren't working. The primary reasons given for being out of the labor force were caregiving for an elderly parent or child, health-related concerns, and retiring early. Of Americans who lost their jobs during the pandemic – 25% said federal aid incentivized them to not look for work and 50% aren't willing to take jobs that don't offer the option of remote work.

Views and attitudes about work have changed in the first quarter of the 21st century. People have an overall lower willingness to work. Rarely have we seen so much unrealized opportunity combined with so little enthusiasm to seize the opportunity. Many young people want work that has purpose and that they find rewarding instead of a job that pays the bills and offers upward economic advancement. If not dead, ambition is on life support. Many employees do the bare minimum to retain their job. Coming in early, staying late at the office, volunteering to help on extra projects, taking pride in, and "owning" a job, are all on the endangered species list.

A strong economy cannot exist without workers returning to their job. Basic economics and human nature were conveniently ignored during the pandemic. For an extended period, the government paid more unemployment benefits to millions of workers than they were previously receiving in compensation for working. This was well-meaning, but at the same time, it was bone stupid to destroy the incentive to work. Another problem I see is that Americans are increasingly reluctant to move to another geographic location to pursue work and economic opportunities. This is a far cry from the behavior of the country's citizens for the first 200 years of American existence.

Still another disturbing trend is there is no longer a social stigma attached to being on the dole and sucking at the teat of U.S. taxpayers. If anything, people who don't want to work naturally fall into victimhood status and are thus held in higher regard than the people who still make products and provide services in our national economy. It's not difficult to see where this is headed. Due to declining fertility rates and a general lack of enthusiasm for a growing segment of the population to work – the response will be more immigrants and increased automation.

VICTIMHOOD

In terms of dealing with actual or perceived insults, there has been a cultural evolution since America's founding in 1776. At the time of the American Revolution and up until the Civil War, an "honor culture" existed in the nation. An honor culture is described as an environment where people strive to avoid intentionally offending others and maintain a reputation for not accepting improper conduct by others. A classic example of this in our country's history would be the 1804 duel fought between U.S. Vice-President, Aaron Burr, and former U.S. Treasury Secretary, Alexander Hamilton. The two men had long been political rivals, but the immediate cause of the duel was disparaging remarks Hamilton had allegedly made about Burr at a dinner. Strange as it may seem today, duels were fairly common in 19th-century America when it came to settling disputes. Men saw them as a way of restoring honor in the face of a personal insult. And that Burr-Hamilton duel in 1804 – let's just say it ended badly, very badly, for Alexander Hamilton.

The honor culture was eventually supplanted by what became known as the "dignity culture." In a dignity culture, a person's worth is wholly internal and stable, isolated from public opinion and social norms. There is a sense of strength and integrity independent of what others may think or say. When intolerable conflicts do arise, dignity cultures prescribe non-violent actions. Instead of challenging the offender to a duel, an aggrieved party might exercise covert avoidance or treat the problem as a minor disruption and seek only to restore harmony without holding a grudge. People in a dignity culture first attempt resolution through restraint and tolerance. Legal action or going to the authorities is the last resort, not the first. A dignity culture has moral values and behavioral norms that promote the value of every human life, encouraging achievement in its children while teaching them to look inward to solve problems. I believe it is also beneficial to tell children that life is often far from fair. There will be huge hurdles, some seemingly insurmountable, and resilience and mental toughness are a prerequisite for living a rewarding and positive life.

After a century and a half of dominance, the dignity culture has seemingly been bumped aside by the "victimhood culture." Now, for many young Americans, the notion of quietly bearing one's trials has become passe. Sociologists Bradley Campbell and Jason Manning describe the victimhood culture as follows: "A culture of victimhood is one characterized by concern with status and sensitivity to slight combined with a heavy reliance on third parties.

People are intolerant of insults, even if unintentional, and react by bringing them to the attention of authorities or the public at large. Domination is the main form of deviance, and victimization is a way of attracting sympathy, so rather than emphasize their strength or inner worth, the aggrieved emphasize their oppression and social marginalization." Many subscribe to the theory that America's inner spirit has embraced victimhood. This does not bode well for the future of our nation.

The obvious question is how did we get to the point where victimhood is so prevalent? One reason can be attributed to America's previous success, affluence, and prosperity. National achievement breeds national entitlement. National success sows the seeds in which victimhood takes root. American prosperity breeds laziness through the abundant flow of easy money. That laziness in turn breeds victimhood as the idle proclaim they deserve to receive money without working for it. Government policies have created a culture of laziness. Victimhood fits laziness like a glove. A good victimhood narrative dresses up naked self-interest until it looks like nobility. Arguing that you're more oppressed than someone else is a powerful way to claim you deserve government largesse more than they do.

A school of thought exists that believes the victimhood culture is at the heart of America's malaise and national decline. Life is difficult, often tragically so, rife with suffering and betrayal. Thus, the temptations of victimhood eternally beckon. People increasingly demand help from others and advertise their oppression as evidence they deserve respect and assistance. At some point in the not-too-distant past, America's focus shifted from producing wealth to arguing over how to distribute wealth. Laser-like, victimhood focuses on how to allocate the economic pie, rather than how to make the pie bigger. In doing so, it makes the pie smaller. Like many issues in current times, the classification of "victim" has become a moral absolute – no one can argue in favor of its fallibility. Even more disturbing is that victimhood has become the ultimate status symbol.

It is not surprising that the victimhood culture has risen to prominence at elite colleges. Only under such pampered and comfortable conditions could this kind of silliness prosper. Although any worldview that prizes victimhood struggles outside the environment of a college campus. The real world – with its job markets, mortgage payments, and adult responsibilities -has a way of encouraging us to prize dignity over victimhood. Capitalism insists on results and is relatively unconcerned with our subjective emotional evaluations of the world.

It is not a coincidence that victimhood and the social justice movement are simultaneously in vogue. Some hope to make the case that the small slight that they'd seized upon and leveraged was evidence of a larger, significant injustice to a whole class of people. The culture of victimhood sees moral worth as largely defined by skin color and membership in a fixed identity group such as LGBTQ. All in all, it's rather a ridiculous concept. Social media platforms enhance the prevalence of victimhood. Insulted, offended, and injured parties who might once have thrown a punch or filed a lawsuit now appeal for support on social media. It is not uncommon for the aggrieved to attempt to cancel or reputationally destroy people via social media if the aggrieved are on the receiving end of deeds or words known as micro-aggressions. The purpose of calling attention to micro-aggressions is to elevate the status of the offended victim. They call attention to what they see as the deviant behavior of the offenders. The goal is to lower the offender's moral status and raise the moral status of the victim. Advancing victimhood as a meritorious state while simultaneously expanding the criteria by which it is established means that those seeking social status are in constant competition with each other. The byproduct of a culture that engenders "competitive victimhood" is quite obvious to those who don't consider themselves perennial victims. Eventually, it reaches the point where it turns into an endless, self-devouring loop. The victims feed on their own.

CHAPTER ELEVEN

PUBLISHED
LETTERS-TO-THE-EDITOR

"Madison Doesn't Need More Regulation"
– *Wisconsin State Journal* – January 12, 2019

The pending proposal in Madison to levy fines on local businesses that leave doors or windows open too long while running air conditioning is ludicrous. The concept is almost inane as having an ordinance that limits the time vehicles can remain idling. Punitive, knee-jerk reactions to an enormously complex global issue that will take a century to fix are counterproductive. The gentleman from the Chamber of Commerce was diplomatic in his response to the proposal, not wanting to offend zealots who worship at the high altar of mitigating carbon dioxide emissions. He was also insightful by indirectly mentioning the law of unintended consequences. Less regulation and more common sense would be refreshing.

—Mark Dunavan, McFarland, Wi.

"NYC Progressive Politicians Missed Math Class"
– *Wisconsin State Journal* – March 3, 2019

Our educational system has apparently dropped the ball when it comes to certain NYC "progressive" politicians and community activists' math skills. It is my understanding that Amazon will no longer be bringing 25,000 prime jobs to the Big Apple. The reason is attributable to certain grandstanding pols vigorously objecting to a mix of $3 billion in current expenditures and future tax concessions negotiated in good faith by other New York Democrats, namely the mayor and governor. Projections were that Amazon's major expansion in NYC would result in increased tax revenues to New York in the amount of $25 billion over a span of 30 years. In other words, for every $1 of infrastructure improvements and "missed" future tax revenues, $8 would be coming back to the city and state's coffers. Sounds like a good deal to me, and probably most other people as well, with the exception of those grossly deficient in the discipline of mathematics.

—Mark Dunavan, McFarland, Wi.

"Scapegoating Ignored Personal Responsibility"
– Wisconsin State Journal – September 24, 2019

It appears that baseball has been displaced as our national pastime. The unworthy successor is the pathetic art of scapegoating. To support this contention, I offer the following examples: - Slightly over a decade ago the financial system was in meltdown mode. Blame was universally assigned to Wall Street, rogue mortgage lenders and bond ratings agencies. Was the role played by deadbeat borrowers even mentioned?

- People die every day from gunshot wounds. The majority of these deaths are self-inflicted. Yet somehow the losers in this blame game are gun manufacturers, gun sellers and responsible gun owners. Did they pull the trigger?

- We have an opiate overdose epidemic. In this case, blame is assigned to pharmaceutical companies and physicians. Where are the users in this equation? Anybody with half a brain knows that these drugs can be severely addictive for certain people and thus should be handled with care or totally avoided.

Much of the time when I read or hear journalists and politicians ranting about various problems, I wonder whatever happened to personal responsibility and accountability?

— Mark Dunavan, McFarland, Wi.

"National Pastime Is Diversion We Need"
– Wisconsin State Journal – April 24, 2020

Whatever happened to American ingenuity, common sense and courage? If some of those qualities can be located, maybe the Major League Baseball season can be started May 15. The season would start exclusively in the Phoenix, Arizona, metro area. Players would play without fans in various spring training facilities. Managers could manage from either the clubhouse or off-site. All umpires would be under the age of 40. The time has arrived for players to give and fully earn their seven-figure and eight-figure annual salaries. The country is in desperate need of a diversion. What better source than the national pastime? The "Great Bambino" Babe Ruth beat the 1918 flu. Twice. Play ball.

—Mark Dunavan, McFarland, Wi.

"Grading Floor Won't Help Achievement"
– Wisconsin State Journal – August 30, 2020

I recently read with interest the Aug. 21 article, "District adopts grading change," about the Madison School District's proposal to reduce the traditional 100-point grading scale by 50%. As noted in the article, a student who answers 20% of questions correctly on a test would receive the same score as a student who answers 50% of the questions correctly. Apparently, systemic grade inflation has been deemed insufficient in elevating and coddling marginal students. Playing games with statistics and data will only obfuscate the measurements of learning and educational achievement. If this new grading system is implemented, it could initiate a statistical revolution that spreads to other segments of our culture. Just imagine, a Major League Baseball player with a batting average of .210 would magically be hitting at a .710 average. In that same light, Ted Williams' lifetime batting average would suddenly be .844 in this new world.

—Mark Dunavan, McFarland, Wi.

"Trump Made Us Review Constitution"
– Wisconsin State Journal – January 23, 2021

For both pragmatic and ideological reasons, I have traditionally voted Republican at the presidential and congressional levels during elections. This past November was no exception. Though half of the country would no doubt disagree with this assessment, I opine that besides some glaring failures, the outgoing chief executive was responsible for a few accomplishments during his tenure in office. Without going into multiple, mundane economic details and some foreign policy improvements, I would like to point out an ancillary benefit accrued over the past four years. Without offering any objective data to support this contention, I would venture to guess that no other four-year period in the past century witnessed more Americans researching and reviewing the provisions and language incorporated within the United States Constitution.

—Mark Dunavan, McFarland, Wi.

"Fearmongering On Climate Must Stop"
– Wisconsin State Journal – February 8, 2021

To date, I have failed to embrace many of the various sacraments pontificated by the high temple of climate change. The fearmongering perpetuated by numerous politicians, journalists and climate activists is continuous and exhaustive. Undeservedly, fossil fuels have been demonized and deemed an existential threat to mankind and the planet we inhabit. Does it ever occur to anybody that fossil fuels have been a major, if not the major, contributor to the dramatic increase in the world's standard of living as well as a significant reason for the virtual eradication of organized mass human muscle power (slavery)? I accept the fact the Earth is warming and that the long-term goal should be less carbon spewed into the atmosphere. But instead of an emphasis on solar panels and wind turbines, my preference would be resources and efforts focused on green innovation, geoengineering and adaptation to a warmer climate. Furthermore, the gradual introduction of a carbon tax would unleash the incredibly beneficial power of capitalism. Lastly, until so-called climate activists incorporate nuclear energy in their list of solutions to the problem, I am unable to take them seriously.

—Mark Dunavan, McFarland, Wi.

"Bird-Safe Glass Won't Stop Cats"
– Wisconsin State Journal – March 12, 2021

The article in the March 4 State Journal about litigation over Madison's "bird-safe" glass ordinance raises some questions and concerns. Are our flying feathered friends smart enough to avoid crashing into buildings of less than 10,000 square feet? I also wondered why the Madison City Council seems to consistently go out of their way to hamstring developers and development projects in Madison. Also, are the lives of a few birds more important than human beings enjoying a transparent, aesthetically pleasing view of the Capitol Square and the surrounding lakes? If the powers that be are serious about saving the lives of local feathered fauna, maybe they should consider implementing feline genocide. Cats, especially feral cats, are far and away the leading cause of violent bird deaths.

—Mark Dunavan, McFarland, Wi.

"CEOs Should Stay Out of Politics"
– Wisconsin State Journal – May 1, 2021

It appears we are living in an era increasingly dominated by the "lemming effect." This psychological phenomenon enables entire segments of a society to lose their sense of judgment. The most recent segment of the population to be "lemmingized" would be corporate CEOs. I struggle with the concept of corporate business leaders publicly opining on controversial political and social issues. The argument can be made that these actions are nothing more than glorified public relations stunts. These opinionated CEOs are unnecessarily rolling the dice. What is the purpose and logic of taking risks that potentially antagonize 50% of the company's customers and shareholders? Even the ongoing trend away from shareholder capitalism and to stakeholder capitalism is latent with pitfalls. Good luck appeasing the various and often conflicting interests of employees, customers, suppliers,   local communities, and shareholders. My preference would be for corporate management to focus on building their businesses and legally and ethically making money for their shareholders.

—Mark Dunavan, McFarland, Wi.

"Head Coach Isn't Your Best Buddy"
– Wisconsin State Journal – July 1, 2021

I read with interest the June 23 front-page State Journal article "Seniors confronted Gard," about Wisconsin Badgers basketball players questioning coach Greg Gard's leadership. Apparently, the duties and responsibilities of the head coach at a major college basketball program have expanded in recent years. Besides the traditional requirements of recruitment, conditioning, skill development, and game management, the head coach now is being called on to extend to his players the loving,

233

compassionate embrace normally provided by a parent, best buddy, or emotional support animal. Brother. Furthermore, it's despicable that this private meeting was made public. I guess leaking sensitive information to harm somebody in a prominent leadership position is not confined to Washington, D.C.

—Mark Dunavan, McFarland, Wi.

"Capitalism Is Essential For Political Freedom"
– Wisconsin State Journal – August 2, 2021

A disturbing number of people, particularly those who are young, appear to want to obliterate our economic system of capitalism due to erroneously perceived pass excesses and so-called social injustices. These same individuals harbor fantasies that capitalism is standing in the way of an egalitarian utopia in which everybody eagerly subordinates their unique thoughts, aspirations and efforts for the collectivist benefit of all. Karl Marx has been dead and rotting for 138 years, but his ideas and principles are certainly enjoying a resurgence. This would especially be the case among faculty members at various institutions of higher education. People ignore history and past social and economic experiments at their own risk. Look no further than the previous century to see how Joseph Stalin and Mao Zedong "transformed" their respective nations. Between manmade famines and political executions, they cumulatively exterminated tens of millions of their countrymen. And check out the current status of North Korea, Cuba, and Venezuela – police states that have embraced the Marxist doctrine. As evidenced by China, it is possible to have economic arrangements that are fundamentally capitalist and political arrangements that are not free. But capitalism is an absolute prerequisite condition for political freedom. Lastly of note, American capitalism has created a standard of living for the vast majority of citizens unparalleled in any other society.

—Mark Dunavan, McFarland, Wi.

"National Service May Aid Tolerance"
– Wisconsin State Journal – October 9, 2021

I have an observation on the evolution of race relations in my lifetime and an idea for possible improvements in the future. First, the observation:

Real and sustainable cultural change and acceptance are incremental over time. My parents were more tolerant than my grandparents. I am more tolerant than my parents. My children are more tolerant than I am. And I expect my grandchildren will be more tolerant than my children. I would argue this type of positive change over five generations is more the rule than the exception. My idea for accelerating improvements is actually a recycled idea that should be given serious consideration at this time. One year of mandatory national service for young citizens would be beneficial to both our country and the individual participants. The year of service would immediately follow departure from high school and precede entry into either college or the labor force. When people from varied backgrounds, races, economic conditions, and genders share an experience together, such as required national service, it will erode some of the polarization that currently dominates our national landscape.

—Mark Dunavan, McFarland, Wi.

"We Have Created A Culture Of Victims"
– Wisconsin State Journal – November 6, 2021

A perfect storm has conspired to create a culture of victimhood in America. The definition of social hardship, trauma, and victimization has greatly expanded in recent years. As a result, more individuals than ever now eagerly identify as victims. Today, progressives have concluded that it is socially acceptable and rewarding in many cases to denigrate others – often even themselves – for simply belonging to a certain ethnic or socioeconomic group. This is commonly done while simultaneously elevating those so-called victim categories to higher social, moral, and even spiritual status. Some people have come to learn that playing the role of the social victim gets them favors. Virtuous victims – those who broadcast their morality alongside their victimization – have discovered they are more likely to gain resources from others. This is risky business for perceived victims and society in general. The more you play the victim, the more of a victim you'll become.

—Mark Dunavan, McFarland, Wi.

"Left Doesn't Want To Waste Crisis"
– *Wisconsin State Journal* – January 15, 2022

In the words of former Chicago Mayor Rahm Emmanuel, "Never allow a good crisis (to) go to waste. It's an opportunity to do the things you once thought were impossible." Progressives, in particular dwellers on the radical left, have embraced the pandemic with vigor to realize their causes and advance their political wish list. Though the unemployment rate among bachelor's degree recipients has fallen to 2.3%, the Biden administration recently extended its payment moratorium on student loans until May 2022. This is beyond questionable. Come April, there will no doubt be still another excuse to defer repayment on these legal financial obligations. The real goal for progressives is to have student loan debt disappear with the wave of the government wand. Senate Majority Leader Chuck Schumer, D-N.Y., and U.S. Sen. Elizabeth Warren, D-Mass., want the Biden administration to discharge $50,000 of student debt per borrower. This could cost taxpayers $1 trillion. Most reasonable people would consider that a boatload of money. But for those on the left who believe the proverbial money tree grows in every backyard, it is a mere pittance.

—Mark Dunavan, McFarland, Wi.

"Cryptocurrency Has No Real Value"
– *Wisconsin State Journal* – January 16, 2022

I have a book recommendation for these investors – make that speculators – who did not sell their Bitcoin or other cryptocurrencies in 2021. The name of the book is "Extraordinary Popular Delusions and the Madness of Crowds" by Charles Mackay. Of particular interest would be the section on the infamous Dutch tulip bulb market bubble of 1634 – 1637. The primary problem with cryptocurrency is that it is totally void of intrinsic value. Those who opine that crypto replicates the financial attributes of gold are mistaken. Besides a 6,000-year history of stored value, gold has myriad uses. Applications in jewelry, electronics, aerospace, dentistry, and mobile phones would rank high in the commercial uses of gold. Central banks across the world are becoming increasingly fearful of cryptocurrencies destabilizing their financial systems. They will act accordingly to defend their turf. Defenders of Bitcoin (about 60% of the market) proclaim the supply is limited to just 21 million bitcoins. While that is true, other competing digital currencies (more than 30% of the market) have no such limits. Owners of cryptocurrencies have only one way to make money with this so-called "asset": Find a willing buyer – make that sucker – to pay more than they did. When the music stops, good luck scrambling for a chair.

—Mark Dunavan, McFarland, Wi.

"Nothing There"
– *The Cap Times* – March 2, 2022

Congress is making noise about banning its members from trading individual stocks. This is another case of our lawmakers resorting to moralistic, populist grandstanding to solve a problem that doesn't exist. Insider trading laws and disclosure rules effected a decade ago sufficiently address the financial ethics of representatives and senators as concerns equity purchases. In addition, the electorate is readily able to discharge politicians from office even for legal trading activity that demonstrates poor judgment. There is no real evidence that Congress is both receiving and acting upon "insider information." I would venture to guess that congressional stock pickers fare worse than the average investor who favors index funds instead of a portfolio of individual companies. A ban on stock trading would be counterproductive if it precluded exceptionally talented and intelligent individuals from running for office. The actual corruption is the use of the tools of taxation, spending, and regulation to stay in power – and expand the size and power of the federal government in the process.

—Mark Dunavan, McFarland, Wi.

"Thoughts On Trump"
– *The Wall Street Journal* – April 9, 2022

Without hesitation, I cast a ballot for President Trump in the 2020 presidential election. For reasons that Ms. Noonan states eloquently, however, Mr. Trump has irrevocably forfeited my support in the future. I can tolerate a personality that is bombastic, prone to narcissism and needlessly contentious. I cannot abide a presidential candidate who lost a close election refusing to accept the outcome to the detriment of the country. The graceful transfer of executive power is a tradition over 230 years old. Nixon narrowly lost in 1960 and then ascended to the presidency in 1969. Mr. Trump's postelection behavior and antics will preclude a similar result in 2024.

—Mark Dunavan, McFarland, Wi.

"U.S. Headed Toward Fiscal Cliff"
– *The Cap Times* – April 23, 2022

The "dismal science" is a derogatory alternative name for the discipline of economics. The United States economy is very likely to soon be described as "dismal," or as something far worse. The Federal Reserve Bank and Congress have managed to dig a deep hole from which there is no escape without inflicting much pain on American citizens. Forty years ago, in the epic battle to quell inflation running at an annual rate of 14%, the fed funds rate was 19%. In other words, "real" interest rates were positive 5%. Fast forward to April 2022. With an inflation rate of 8.5% and fed funds rate currently at 0.5%, "real" interest rates are negative 8%. Inflation will not be cured until "real" interest rates are positive. The capital markets are anticipating higher interest rates, but can they handle a 7% or 8% increase in the next year or two? I think not. If interest rates do skyrocket by that level, the interest payments alone on $30 trillion of debt will gobble up about 50% of the annual federal budget. The Fed has publicly claimed it is pivoting from quantitative easing to quantitative tightening in order to reduce its $9 trillion balance sheet. Who exactly is going to buy our debt as the largest buyer (Federal Reserve Bank) becomes a net seller of treasury securities? Don't hold out any hope for foreign central banks, sovereign wealth funds and other entities to fill the void. Unless interest rates are high enough to justify the investor's risk, looks to me like the party, financed with huge fiscal and trade deficits and enabled by cheap and loose money, is about to end.

—Mark Dunavan, McFarland, Wi.

"Musk's Twitter Buy A Welcome Change"
— *The Cap Times* — April 27, 2022

Although the odds were once thought to be prohibitive, it now appears that Elon Musk will be taking Twitter private. Assuming the deal is consummated this summer, the risk to Musk's personal fortune will be considerable. That said, thus far in multiple business ventures he has demonstrated more of a Midas Touch than a Sidam Touch. As a staunch conservative, I welcome with open arms Musk's proposal to expand the digital public square and provide more diversity, equity and inclusion of thoughts on political issues. And I must confess, I am thoroughly entertained by the mindless blather, whining and Chicken Little antics erupting on the progressive left.

—Mark Dunavan, McFarland, Wi.

"Backdoor Wealth Tax Is A Bad Idea"
— *Wisconsin State Journal* — May 12, 2022

Though the United States already has one of the least regressive income tax systems in the developed world, the Biden administration fiscal 2023 budget re-proposes an idea that is, well, bad. They propose a new tax on Americans with $100 million or more assets whose effective tax rate is less than 20% of their income. Here's the trick, the gimmick: The 20% minimum tax rate would apply both to ordinary income and the increase in the value of assets in a given year. In other words, this is a backdoor "wealth tax" on unrealized capital gains. This is both unprecedented and ludicrous. Besides enormously complicating the tax code and creating huge investment distortions, this type of tax could be ruled unconstitutional. Progressives claim the new tax would unlock capital by discouraging the wealthy from holding stock over time. If liberals want to encourage capital to flow more frequently, they should make the capital gains rate zero.

—Mark Dunavan, McFarland, Wi.

"Heed Henry Kissinger On Peace In Ukraine"
– Wisconsin State Journal -June 2, 2022

Henry Kissinger celebrated his 99th birthday on May 27. Needless to say, Kissinger has seen a thing or two in his time concerning global geopolitics. A few days before this birthday, Kissinger, via a virtual appearance, addressed the World Economic Forum gathered in Davos, Switzerland. The former secretary of state urged forbearance in attempts to defeat or marginalize Russia. He called on Ukraine to accept the territorial losses of 2014 to possibly reach a settlement to end the war. For myriad practical reasons, I consider his counsel wise and hope it is taken seriously by our leaders. There is a great economic risk to the West, particularly the United States, from a long, drawn-out military conflict in Ukraine. Layered on top of the financial risk to America resulting from the imposition of economic sanctions on Russia, this may well be an unacceptable level of risk.

—Mark Dunavan, McFarland, Wi.

"Biden's Economic Policies Don't Work"
– Wisconsin State Journal – July 7, 2022

Are progressives born without any commonsensical economics in their DNA, or does persistent anti-capitalist propaganda take a toll on their developing brains? A case in point would be the Biden administration's disastrous energy policies. From day one, through both words and deeds, Biden and his minions have conducted a full-scale assault on the American fossil fuel industry. Besides canceling the Keystone XL Pipeline on his first day in office, he paused new oil and gas leases on federal lands and waters a week later. The Environmental Protection Agency has been weaponized to achieve progressive political goals at the expense of all Americans. A specific target for the EPA has been the small U.S. refineries, which produce much of America's gasoline and diesel fuel. The Securities and Exchange Commission has introduced measures to make it more difficult for the oil and gas industry to access funds in the capital markets. After doing everything in his power to constrict fossil fuels, Biden is now threatening a windfall profits tax on oil and gas production. In what world does increasing

240

taxes on profits derived from a specific product lead to an increase in the supply of that product? Unbelievable.

—Mark Dunavan, McFarland, Wi.

(236.)

"Good Job, Supreme Court"
– The Cap Times – July 13, 2022

I applaud the Supreme Court for the recent flurry of rulings prior to their three-month summer recess. It is refreshing to see a judicial body that is actually following the language, directives and parameters of the United States Constitution. The court's decision to rein in the EPA's climate authority is as significant, and maybe even more so, than reversing Roe v. Wade. For far too long, lawmakers have deferred to unelected bureaucrats' supposed expertise. The message to Congress is loud and clear. Get off your butt and legislate. Relying on bureaucratic and judicial decisions to impose policies that Congress won't take responsibility for passing is no longer an option. It's about time.

—Mark Dunavan, McFarland, Wi.

"Climate Change Fears Are Overblown"
– Wisconsin State Journal – August 9, 2022

Based on the shockingly abysmal track record of "experts" in climate-related predictions over the past 50 years, it is amazing anybody would give their dire prophecies the time of day. Apparently, the "if it bleeds, it leads" strategy still dominates the world of political progressives, climate activists and the mainstream corporate media. How else does one explain the overwhelming focus on the negative side effects of fossil fuels, while the unprecedented and massive benefits that cost-effective fossil fuel provides to billions of people are systemically ignored? How come one rarely reads or hears that climate-related disasters kill 99% fewer people than 100 years ago, according to Bjorn Lomborg, president of the Copenhagen Consensus? How come there is so much hostility toward a big piece of the puzzle – nuclear energy? Until the doomsayers address these questions and others, I will remain cynical of their prophecies.

—Mark Dunavan, McFarland, Wi.

"Quit Whining About Democracy"
– The Cap Times – September 8, 2022

The progressive left incessantly whines and complains about our democracy being under attack and Republicans being "a threat to our democracy." Frankly, it is getting old. As evidenced by the following historical quotes, our founding fathers expressed a distaste and distrust for a pure democracy. "One of the worst forms of government is a pure democracy, one in which the citizens enact and administer the laws directly," said James Madison. "Such a government is helpless against the mischief of faction." John Adams said: "Remember democracy never last long. It soon wastes, exhausts, and murders itself. There never was a democracy yet that did not commit suicide." The solution to mitigate abuse by the majority and to protect the minority was to design a form of government known as a constitutional republic. Those that currently advocate packing the Supreme Court along with deep-sixing the Electoral College and Senate filibuster should be grateful the founders had the foresight to bypass a pure democracy in favor of a republic.

—Mark Dunavan, McFarland, Wi.

"We Can't Let Debt Get Out Of Control"
– Wisconsin State Journal – October 21, 2022

To combat inflation, the Federal Reserve Board has been aggressively raising interest rates. Due to significantly higher interest rates accruing on $31 trillion of debt, servicing costs on the federal debt could soon reach $1 trillion a year. Interest payments will thus become the largest expenditure in the federal budget, exceeding both entitlements and defense spending. Has anybody wondered what would happen if and when America's creditors finally say, "No more!" The game, as they say, will be over. The fat lady will sing. Don't look for spineless politicians to suddenly develop a case of fiscal responsibility. They will do as they always do and default to doing what is politically expedient. In other words, blame everything and everybody but themselves.

—Mark Dunavan, McFarland, Wi.

"GOP Should Kick Trump To The Curb"
— *Wisconsin State Journal* - November 18, 2022

I don't anticipate being contacted by the Republican National Committee and asked for my opinion on how to start winning more elections. But if asked, I would advise the RNC to do the following:

- *Kick Donald Trump to the curb. The "Big Orange Albatross" is unelectable in general elections and his anointment of specific candidates is too often the kiss of political death for those anointees in a general election.*

- *Cease and desist the 2020 election denial nonsense. Without concrete evidence to support the contention, constant bellyaching and whining are counterproductive to winning future elections. Move on.*

- *After articulating the benefits of federalism, go on record and say it would be acceptable for women to exercise their rights to an abortion during the first 15 weeks of pregnancy.*

- *Attempt to convince MAGA Republicans that it is in their best interest to make peace with moderate Republicans and Independents if they hope to win future elections.*

Again, I doubt the RNC is interested in my "redprint" detailed above.

— Mark Dunavan, McFarland, Wi.

"Adopting Culture is Really Flattery"
— *Wisconsin State Journal* – January 24, 2023

Of all the various thoughts, comments and complaints issued by the "woke" warriors over the past few years, at or near the top of the heap in terms of nonsensicalness and silliness would have to be criticism of "cultural appropriation." A specific identity group or ethnic group does not "own" the various elements of their perceived culture. They do not hold a copyright or patent on certain types of food, music, dress attire, hairstyle or language, just to name a few. Anybody is free to extract any parts they so desire from any and all cultures. America has typically prided itself on the ability to assimilate peoples and cultures from various parts of the world into a "melting pot." I end with a question: Whatever happened to the idea? 'Imitation is the sincerest form of flattery?"

— Mark Dunavan, McFarland, Wi.

"Obsessions With Pronouns Is Silly"
– *Wisconsin State Journal* – March 7, 2023

I can't say that I am confronted with this situation often, or even ever for that matter. But I have decided not to participate in the pronoun declaration movement as it currently exists. The entire concept is ridiculous, nothing more than publicly preening about one's chosen identity and declaration of self-importance. Pronoun-centric individuals place a premium on this practice of narcissistic validation. The pro-pronoun argument is based on the premise that addressing a person the way they have requested is a sign of respect. The operative word in that last sentence is "respect." In the real world, respect cannot be bought or given for free – it must be earned. Starting a personal interaction with self-centric demands and conditions would at a minimum elicit laughter from me, and possibly even a microaggression.

—Mark Dunavan, McFarland, Wi.

"Banning guns is wrong strategy"
– *Wisconsin State Journal* – April 23, 2023

I hereby tender some unsolicited advice to those politicians, activists and mainstream media acolytes who are bent on depriving law-abiding Americans of the legal and responsible use of guns. The majority of gun owners do not have significant reservations concerning multiple gun control laws. But the proverbial line is crossed in the sand when the word "ban" is uttered in any context involving the ownership and use of firearms. Besides this fundamental error in strategy, the most vocal gun control advocates have historically displayed a consistent ability to get the basic facts surrounding this issue wrong. I suggest they go back to the drawing board and come up with an alternative approach that relies more on reality, logic and compromise – and less on knee-jerk emotions and antics.

—Mark Dunavan, McFarland, Wi.

"Debt, not ceiling, is real problem"
– *Wisconsin State Journal* – May 12, 2023

Don't be misled by the blather emanating from the White House and Treasury Secretary Janet Yellen about the ramifications if the debt ceiling is not raised in the next few weeks. The problem is not the debt ceiling, the problem is the debt level and the mindset that perennial massive deficit spending will not eventually adversely affect all Americans. For once, Congress should act in a fiscally responsible manner instead of a politically expedient manner. In addition, don't accept the debt default myth. The United States has previously defaulted on its debt obligations: in 1862, 1933, 1968, and most recently, in 1971. The most egregious default was in 1933 when Franklin Delano Roosevelt took the U.S. off the gold standard. This action effectively wiped out around 40% of U.S. private and public debt. In August 1971, the government reneged on its debt commitments when President Richard Nixon closed the U.S. gold window to foreign central banks. Until I see serious and competent leadership in Washington, I will continue to short the dollar and buy gold.

—Mark Dunavan, McFarland

CHAPTER TWELVE

DEATH

NEAR THE END OF THIS BOOK, which is only apropos, we look at the opposite of life: death. Death is defined as a state of the total disappearance of life, the irreversible cessation of the functions of organs that are necessary for life. There is a traditional view maintained that philosophizing is the thinking and meditation on death because death is a reference point for discussion of the most important questions about the meaning of life. The great Greek philosopher, Socrates, saw no point in fear of death since the death of the body is not important when there is a soul, and it will be released at the time of the death of the body. Death exists in life and gives meaning to life. If there were no death, then there would be no life.

Awareness of the finiteness of life gives meaning to life as a challenge and task. Mortality is that condition with which everyone must be reconciled because it is inevitable and the natural state of affairs. With a terminal illness, there are multiple stages of dying. Upon reaching acceptance, the terminally ill person does not demonstrate jealousy toward the living and healthy any longer and accepts their fate. They wonder about impending death with quiet anticipation. Awareness of what is coming influences everybody with a permanent concern, anguish, or terror. It is so intense that it affects the psychological processes and social behavior of the individual. In the case of older people, social contact is of particular importance. Relationships with loved ones can be a vital mechanism for protection against existential anxiety.

Sigmund Freud first introduced the concept of the "death drive" (Thanatos) in his essay, "Beyond the Pleasure Principle." He theorized that humans are driven toward destruction and death, famously declaring that "the aim of all life is death." Freud believed that people typically channel this death drive outward, which manifests as aggression toward others. People also can direct this drive inward, however, which can result in self-harm or suicide.

Freud based this theory on clinical observations, noting that people who experience a traumatic event often recreate or revisit it. For example, he noted that soldiers returning from World War I tended to revisit their traumatic experiences in dreams that repeatedly took them back to combat. From these observations, he concluded that people hold an unconscious desire to die but that life instincts largely temper this wish. In Freud's view, the compulsion to repeat was "something that would seem more primitive, more elementary, more instinctual than the pleasure principle which it overrides." Thus, Thanatos stands in stark contrast to the drive to survive, procreate, and satisfy desires (Eros).

There are a couple of fascinating opinions on death from the 17th Century. Donne wrote his *"Devotions Upon Emergent Occasions"* in 1624. This work of literature contains the greatest of all exhortations to commiserate with the dead: "Any man's death diminishes me, because I am involved in Mankinde. And therefore never send to know for whom the bell tolls; It tolls for thee." In 1655 the Neapolitan artist, Salvator Rosa, described the human condition stripped down to its bleak essentials: "Conception is sin, birth is pain, life is foil, death is inevitable." Needless to say, life was a bit more challenging in the middle of the 17th Century compared to the first quarter of the 21st Century.

Although life is treated as sacred by the majority of people, some folks reach a point where their preference is to die. This is the case for those who battle extreme physical pain and exhaustion on a daily basis. After a while, for the elderly, it is simply not worthwhile to keep on living. Loved ones and friends have passed on, the kids and grandkids have come and departed to separate lives, and there are fewer people to live for. The truth is, at 80 or 90 you've simply been through it all.

There has been much debate in recent years over issues concerning the end of life. Assisted suicide is when a doctor helps a patient to kill themselves by prescribing a lethal drug for the patient to take. This becomes euthanasia when the doctor administers the drug directly. Supporters of assisted suicide believe that allowing people to "die with dignity" is kinder than forcing them to continue their lives with suffering. They believe that every patient has a right to choose when to die. Proponents believe that assisted suicide can be safely regulated by government legislation. Eighty-four percent of the public support the choice of assisted dying for terminally ill adults. The actor, Patrick Stewart, states, "We have no control over how we arrive in the world but at the end of life we should have control over how we leave it."

On the other side of the coin, the late French philosopher, Rene Girard, opined: "The experience of death is going to get more and more painful, contrary to what many people believe. The forthcoming euthanasia will make it more rather than less painful because it will impact the emphasis on personal decision in a way which was blissfully alien for the whole problem of dying in former times. It will make death even more subjectively intolerable, for people will feel responsible for their own deaths and morally obligated to rid their relatives of their unwanted presence. Euthanasia will further intensify all the problems its advocates think it will solve."

Suicide has been compared to what you see when a pebble is dropped into a calm pond. It's something small that makes a big impact. The first waves, close by, are big, and as they move outward, they get smaller and smaller. The reach of the pebble's wave is much greater than the size of the pebble itself. When someone dies by suicide, the people impacted most dramatically are those closest to the person who died: family, friends, co-workers, classmates. As a result, the people who interacted regularly with the individual who ended their life will miss the physical presence of that person and typically feel the loss more intimately. But those people represent only the first wave or the initial level of impact. Those people who are members of an individual's community, such as members of a faith community, teachers, staff, and other students in a school, or service providers, may also be affected by a suicide. Ultimately, in the way that a pond is changed because of the pebble, an entire community can be changed by suicide. According to a 2016 study, it is estimated that 115 people are exposed to a single suicide, with one in five reporting that this experience had a devastating impact or caused a major-life disruption.

For those struggling with suicidal thoughts, access to mental health treatment can be key to saving a life. That said, if somebody is hell-bent on killing themselves, rarely can anything be done to preclude that from happening. According to the CDC, the number of people taking their own lives rose by 30% in some regions of the country between 1999 and 2016. Spouses are sometimes blamed for suicide by their partner's family. This blame can cause a partner to feel they weren't good enough. The effects of suicide on parents and children alike are immense. When a child takes their own life, parents are at a higher risk for anxiety and divorce. Comparatively, when a child's parent has taken their life, children are at a higher risk of suicide (up to twice as likely, particularly in boys).

Siblings can feel forgotten and left out of the healing process as their parents try to protect them from grief. Grandparents often experience hidden grief, where they feel they must keep their composure to protect the rest of the family. Friends often start to question the relationship they had with victims of suicide. They can experience feelings of guilt, abandonment, and even anger toward the person. Teachers, who are responsible for managing several students, can feel they have not done enough to prevent suicide. A survey of Australian teachers showed that 76% of them felt the suicide of a student affected their personal life, while 85% said it had affected their professional life.

There is a concept embraced by all cultures that I will call the "natural order of death." The concept stipulates that parents' deaths should precede their children's deaths. The death and loss of a child is frequently called the ultimate tragedy. Nothing can be more devastating. Many parents who have lost their son or daughter report feeling they can only exist, and every motion or need beyond that seems nearly impossible for an extended period. Coping with the death and loss of a child requires an inordinate amount of challenging work. Parents commonly feel an overwhelming sense of failure for no longer being able to care for and protect their children.

It feels unnatural and wrong to outlive a child and it doesn't make a difference whether your child is 8 or 80 when your son or daughter dies. The emotion is the same. Losing a child feels like the ultimate violation of the rules of life. Studies have shown that the death of a child will not necessarily strengthen a marriage. Grief can sometimes lead to its demise. Parents that suffer the loss of a child must be mindful of surviving children. The whole extended family needs to step up and help to the extent possible. It's a well-worn cliche, but it does take time to heal and recover.

Research on the subject shows that people tend to grow a lot when they are faced with their mortality. Almost every terminal patient finds peace before they depart the Earth. There is also no shortage of regrets expressed by the dying. The most common regret is, "I wish I'd had the courage to live a life true to myself, not the life others expected of me." When people realize that their life is almost over and look back clearly on it, it is easy to see how many dreams have gone unfulfilled. From the moment that you lose your health, it is too late. Health brings a freedom very few realize until they no longer have it. Another regret, mostly from men, is "I wish I didn't work so long and hard." They missed their children's youth and their partner's companionship.

Then there was the regret, "I wish I'd had the courage to express my feelings." Many people suppressed their feelings to keep peace with others. As a result, they settled for a mediocre existence and never became who they were truly capable of becoming. Next up in the major regrets, "I wish I had stayed in touch with my friends." Many had become so caught up in their own lives that they had let golden friendships slip by over the years. Everyone misses their friends when they are dying. It all comes down to love and relationships in the end.

Lastly, there is the regret, "I wish that I had let myself be happier." Many did not realize until the end that happiness is a choice. They had remained stuck in old patterns and habits. Fear of change had them pretending to others, and to themselves, that they were content.

I've known a few people that would opt for immortality if extended the opportunity. They would consider that state a blessing, while many people would say it was a curse. I come down on the curse side. We've limited time on Earth and though it can be tiresome and challenging at times, it is the momentariness of life which makes it valuable and gives us purpose. Gold is valuable because there's not a lot of it. If there was an infinite amount of gold, it would be worth nothing. The same concept applies to immortality. Being mortal is a fundamental part of being human.

There are myriad other reasons why immortality would be a curse. Frankly, after a while, there is nothing new that you haven't experienced. Many people and things you have loved die, fade away, or change beyond recognition. Many things that you have disliked, been pained by, or disappointed by persist. The sheer repetitive boredom of it all would be smothering. If the Earth no longer exists, you could be alone floating in space. Another issue with humans being immortal is their brains are probably not capable of remaining sane for eternity. Death is a well-deserved prize at the end of a long journey, where nothingness is vital for eternal peace. Lastly, I am fundamentally not a greedy person in any respect, even in the longevity of life. Although it would be nice to spend a healthy century above the dirt.

It is totally within the realm of human nature for anybody and everybody to contemplate their eventual demise well before they draw their last breath. We like to think we can predict our mindset and behavior following the receipt of a terminal prognosis, but we really won't know our thoughts and actions until reality inserts itself without a proper invitation. I have two friends that have had to face that type of reality. The first gentleman died in 2010 after dealing with ALS (Lou Gehrig's Disease) for a couple of years. There is no cure for this insidious disease. It is always fatal. My friend dealt with this terrible situation with an amazing amount of resilience and dignity that was void of self-pity. My other buddy was dealt a bad hand when he was diagnosed with pancreatic cancer in 2019. He too has displayed an abundance of courage and strength in his ongoing battle. My respect and admiration for each of these fellows' comportment under duress and adversity is immense.

Knowing myself, I highly doubt that I would handle a terminal, or highly probable terminal, diagnosis with the grace and fortitude displayed by my two friends. A part of me thinks there is a possibility that I would turn to mush at a fairly rapid pace. I do know that I would definitely experiment with psilocybin mushrooms. Heck, I might someday try psychedelics regardless of my health status. When I was younger and discussing the subject of death with peers, I told them my preference was a violent, fiery death instead of a lingering, drawn-out affair. As I enter "winter" in the four seasons of my life, I'm slowly but surely shifting toward the long, non-sudden type of death preference (not that I have any control whatsoever).

Research and previous studies suggest that when considering our own death, we are most concerned about potential pain, helplessness, dependency, and the well-being of our loved ones. There is only so much you can do in anticipation of pending death, but you can prepare yourself by trying to review relationships and tie up loose ends. Also, one can take the opportunity to put things into words that you have never had a chance to say. Value the time you have left. Although obviously a sad time, it also can be a time to underscore all the good times you have had together with family and friends. Coming to terms with the inevitability of death can help teach us to live more fully in the here and now. The consciousness of our mortality can enable us to cherish every moment of the life we have.

FINAL COMMENTS

THIS CONCLUDES MY THOUGHTS on many of the issues of the day. Whether I waxed eloquently or not over the previous pages of this book will ultimately be determined by readers. Of more importance to me is posting information in a historical context that serves as a basis for the establishment of opinions accrued over a lifetime. I can't say for certain whether the aforesaid opinions are accurate or not when faced with the ultimate test of objective reality, but it is my good faith perception they align with reality.

The book was not about me making intellectual arguments to convince people my viewpoint is right. In today's hyper-polarized environment, it is practically impossible to change anyone's mind once a narrative is established. The sheer volume and complexity of news emanating from mass and social media preclude the average citizen from taking the time to study and analyze an issue. The tendency is to rush to judgment based on a handful of select assumptions and then close the door to any alternative viewpoints. Appeals to rationality, logic, and empirical evidence apparently no longer carry much weight.

I detest the practice of "canceling" people for ideological reasons. Freedom of thought and diverse opinions are essential to the functioning of our society. Instead of embracing identity politics that are defined by race and sexual orientation, it would be nice if the concept of diversity, equity, and inclusion were extended to different mindsets, beliefs, and viewpoints within our organizations and institutions.

It may be a pipe dream, but I hope that the principle of compromise returns to our public forum. It would be refreshing if the certainty of our convictions were tempered. The acceptance of standards that are lower than optimum or desirable is the only healthy way to avoid wasting time, resources, and goodwill in a prolonged conflict facilitated by stubbornness, arrogance, and hubris.

Readers are invited to direct any comments, questions, and concerns my way at markdunavan55@gmail.com as relates to the book. I welcome feedback. Although individuals can harbor dramatically different views on the same issue, instead of trading insults and slurs, a healthier approach involves a civil exchange of ideas and thoughts when each party could conceivably learn something new.

This book may represent the conclusion of my book-writing career. If I tackle book project number three, it just might be a work of fiction. Of course, some people will consider *"Everybody Has One"* a work of fiction.

ACKNOWLEDGMENTS

A QUALIFIED TRIO of editors contributed to the finished product of my previous book, "*Almost An Eagle*." One of those editors convinced me that a wiser course was to incorporate a single editor for "*Everybody Has One*." Although it involved a lot of work for one person, the consistency and writing style limited to one editor offered a superior approach.

I nominated my good friend and fellow scribe, Max Hall, for that unrewarding endeavor. Fortunately, Max accepted the role of editing and did an outstanding job. Max – I can never thank you enough. I would also like to extend a huge thank you to Julie (Kubicek) for her contributions to the artwork that graces the book's cover. Julie is a talented artist and special young lady. Lastly, I would like to express my gratitude and appreciation for Joe and Jan McDaniel, the owners of BookCrafters. Joe and Jan provided exceptional service and I would recommend them to any aspiring writer pursuing the self-publishing route.

www.ingramcontent.com/pod-product-compliance
Lightning Source LLC
Chambersburg PA
CBHW032052020426

42335CB00011B/305